Police Suicide

This text makes a primary and informed contribution to a subject that is under-researched in the UK – the suicide of those who work in the UK police service – by offering an analysis of UK case-studies of officers and staff who have either completed suicide or experienced suicide ideation, and referring to the likely prime suicide precipitators in these situations. This analysis is followed by an examination of literature that discusses general and police-specific suicide. The text then examines intervention measures and support mechanisms that are currently offered to those working in the police service, as well as other measures that might be introduced in the future. Designed for criminal justice professionals and affected laypeople, including the families of those in the police service, *Police Suicide* is a crucial text for any who have an interest in the holistic and psychological welfare of police officers and staff.

Richard Armitage, PhD, attended King's College London from 1969 to 1972, after which he was awarded the academic qualification Associate of King's College. In 1974 he was ordained priest in the Church of England. He served as a voluntary police chaplain with West Mercia Police for many years, and was Senior Chaplain to Wiltshire Police (UK) from 2005 until 2016. He gained a PhD from Birmingham University in 2007 and has been awarded a research grant by the Home Office Police Research Group Award Scheme. His works include *Police Chaplaincy: Servant to the Service* and the published thesis *Issues of Religious Diversity Affecting Ethnic Minority Personnel in the Workplace*. Armitage has been invited to speak at various conferences and to advise on the development of chaplaincy to the police at national, regional and local levels.

Police Suicide

Risk Factors and Intervention Measures

Richard Armitage

Routledge
Taylor & Francis Group

NEW YORK AND LONDON

First published 2017
by Routledge
711 Third Avenue, New York, NY 10017

and by Routledge
2 Park Square, Milton Park, Abingdon, Oxon, OX14 4RN

Routledge is an imprint of the Taylor & Francis Group, an informa business

© 2017 Taylor & Francis

Library of Congress Cataloging in Publication Data
    Names: Armitage, Richard Norris, author.
    Title: Police suicide : risk factors and intervention measures /
    Richard Armitage.
    Description: New York, NY : Routledge, 2017.
    Identifiers: LCCN 2016058666 | ISBN 9781138221376 (hardback) |
    ISBN 9781138050822 (paperback)
    Subjects: LCSH: Police--Suicidal behavior--Great Britain.
    Classification: LCC HV7936.S77 A76 2017 | DDC
    362.28088/36320941--dc23LC record available at https://lccn.loc.
    gov/2016058666

ISBN: 978-1-138-22137-6 (hbk)
ISBN: 978-1-138-05082-2 (pbk)
ISBN: 978-1-315-41061-6 (ebk)

Typeset in Goudy
by Sunrise Setting Ltd, Brixham, UK

Contents

Preface

This book focuses on the suicidal ideation of police officers and staff. My attention was drawn to the importance of this issue following a series of suicides of officers and others who had recently retired from officer roles. The pain and distress of those who had taken their own lives must have been acute. As a consequence of their deaths, this pain will have been reflected in the distress of families and in the deep concern of close friends and colleagues. For my part, a greater appreciation of the contextual causes of the suicides was required.

Having embarked on measures to acquire a greater appreciation of relevant factors, it became apparent that no previous UK research of any substance had addressed the issue of suicides of those who work in the police environment. The focus of the proposed research was determined: it would examine suicide among those who work in the police service, offering an analysis of risk factors and an identification of appropriate intervention measures, with the intention of reducing the number of completed suicides and parasuicide incidents.

To fulfil this intention, the book first examines the difficulty of undertaking relevant research, including acquiring pertinent data. Having determined these difficulties, it analyses a number of case-studies and identifies key precipitators. The analysis of these precipitators is considered alongside a survey of literature on police-specific suicide. This literature is primarily from the US, where a great deal of research has been undertaken into this subject.

The book then examines intervention measures which may assist in reducing the number of suicides among those who work in the police service. The implementation of preventative measures is the responsibility of many, including police forces, family, close friends and individuals within the police service.

As the analysis of these issues concludes with recommendations for the implementation of intervention measures, the book is useful to those responsible for the creation of policies that relate to the employment of officers and staff. Equally, it is a valuable resource for officers, staff, their families and any who have a concern for the well-being of those who work within the police service.

Acknowledgements

I express my deep gratitude to Dr Tim Meaklim, an independent learning consultant and academic, previously a senior officer in law enforcement. I thank him for his supportive and affirming supervision of my research.

I express my gratitude to the families, friends and colleagues of those officers and staff who have supported my research in many different ways. They have given freely of their time and shared their innermost thoughts, which at times has been painful for them.

I express my gratitude to those officers, staff and others who work with the police service and have supported and believed in the aims of this research. Their commitment to the purpose of this study has given me the energy to pursue the objective to its conclusion.

Finally, I express my gratitude to those who currently work within the police service for their commitment to all they strive to achieve. Their dedication, often under great stress, has been the absolute motivation to undertake this research.

Glossary of Abbreviations

Acas	Advisory, Conciliation and Arbitration Service
ACPO	Association of Chief Police Officers
ACT	Australian Capital Territory
AFP	Australian Federal Police
BBC	British Broadcasting Corporation
BMJ	*British Medical Journal*
DCC	Deputy Chief Constable
DPS	Department of Professional Standards
DSH	deliberate self-harm
FLO	family liaison officer
HMIC	Her Majesty's Inspectorate of the Constabulary
IACP	International Association of Chiefs of Police
IPCC	Independent Police Complaints Commission
MPS	Metropolitan Police Service
n.d.	no date
n.p.	no publisher
NARPO	National Association of Retired Police Officers
NCALT	National Centre for Applied Learning Technologies
NNG	National Negotiators Group
NPCC	National Police Chiefs' Council
NPIA	National Police Improvement Agency
NYPD	New York Police Department

OHU	Occupational Health Unit
ONS	Office for National Statistics
PCC	Police Crime Commissioner
PMR	proportional mortality ratio
PTG	post-traumatic growth
PTSD	post-traumatic stress disorder
QPR	question, persuade and refer
TRiM	trauma risk management

1   A Way Forward

Prologue

In 2013, *Police Oracle* reported:

> A Devon and Cornwall Police officer has been found dead, the force has confirmed. The 46-year-old woman, whose rank and name have not yet been disclosed, was found in a car in the Hornick Hill area of St Austell, Cornwall on June 15. Police were called at around 9.15am after concerns were expressed for the woman's welfare. A force spokesman said there were no suspicious circumstances. Next of kin have been informed and a file will now be prepared for the coroner.[1]

Media reports such as the one above appear with regrettable frequency. Having read in the media of similar deaths some time ago, it was with unease that I realised that, within less than two years, four people who were employed by the force in which I worked as chaplain and one who had recently retired from it had completed suicide. Of these five people, four were male and one was female; all five had been officers, although one had retired as an officer and was working as a staff member at the time of his death.

Working within this force, I had also become increasingly aware of a number of officers and staff who had been involved in parasuicidal incidents. (The term *parasuicide*, as opposed to *attempted suicide*, is used within this book to embrace those whose self-harm was such that it was life-threatening. Further comment on the term parasuicide is made in Chapter 3.) In addition to these incidents, I had a growing awareness of other officers and staff who had spoken confidentially to me of their suicidal ideation. As a police chaplain, my initial response to these human dilemmas was, not surprisingly, one of deep concern.

Following the deaths of those who had completed suicide within the force in which I worked, when talking with many force members, genuine concern was evident. Awareness of officer and staff vulnerability to suicidal ideation was noticeably evident among chief officers, human resource managers, the Occupational Health Unit (OHU) and line-managers generally. The speed with which line-managers referred personnel who indicated signs of stress to the OHU appeared to accelerate markedly. This quickening pace in referrals appeared to arise out of a concern for personnel but also, it appeared, because line-managers felt they needed *to be seen* to have given all possible support when officers and staff were displaying signs of stress.

My personal challenge was to determine what actions I might undertake that could lessen officers' and staff members' vulnerability to suicide. Suicide was not unheard of in the world in which I had worked as a priest; yet there was a sense of caution on my part. My hesitancy to enter this arena lay in an awareness that others would have greater knowledge of the stress under which police personnel work, and still others, such as psychologists and psychiatrists, would have a more detailed understanding of suicides and suicidal ideation.

However, as a police chaplain who had worked within the service since 1990, I felt increasingly confident that my knowledge of both the police service and the stress under which police personnel work was sufficient to develop my own understanding.

Over the past three decades the number of chaplains appointed to the police service has grown at a quickening pace, and they have come to have an acknowledged role within many forces. In these forces, chaplaincy has a privileged position working alongside officers, staff and management. Therefore, as a chaplain contracted by the police service, I decided that I would be well placed to embark upon research into the suicide of officers and staff. Any knowledge I could glean which might lessen the number of suicidal or parasuicidal incidents could only be for the good of those working in the service.

I was encouraged by the knowledge that chaplaincy, offering confidentiality and sensitivity, has the trust of many police forces, as demonstrated by the increase in chaplaincy posts. These qualities of confidentiality, sensitivity and trust would be essential in the examination of issues relevant to suicide. Furthermore, it seemed that chaplaincy also offers the means by which, through 'reflective friendship', research conclusions might be articulated and fed back to those in positions of authority and responsibility within the service. Chaplaincy can speak with an independence that might at times be denied to other roles, and the sharing of any conclusions would need to be as sensitive as the research itself.

Consequently, because of my role within the police service and because of my concern for the vulnerability to suicide of those working in the police service, I concluded that I could make an informed contribution to a dilemma that causes deep distress to many.

An Initial Hypothesis

The suicide of police officers is an issue that is reported in the media with some frequency and because of these reports, I gained the initial impression that officers could be at greater risk of suicide than others in the general community. This was the hypothesis to be explored. In examining this hypothesis, there were a number of accompanying issues of related concern. As the examination of the hypothesis commenced, it was important to me that:

i. My own understanding and development should be enhanced to enable me to offer greater support to members of the force who were experiencing suicidal ideation.

ii. The support I might offer could be developed if I were more aware of the potential precipitators leading to suicide ideation.

iii. My support would equally be enhanced if I had greater knowledge of the effectiveness of current intervention measures.

iv. I should extend my knowledge and understanding of police suicides so that my support could be extended to the family members and colleagues of those who had completed suicide.

My concern originated at a time of great change for the police service nationally. Because of the changes to the police service brought about by the well-publicised national economic constraints on local policing budgets, there were new pressures and stresses within the workforce. Redundancies, questions of job security and greater expectations of a limited workforce could only have a detrimental effect on the psychological stamina of the workforce. Clear objectives needed to be set if research were to be undertaken that would potentially enable me to offer informed, relevant comment and enhance my further understanding of an under-researched issue.

Aims and Objectives

There were two initial aims in exploring the initial hypothesis:

i. to make an informed contribution to a subject that appeared to be currently under-researched in the UK;

ii. to determine whether there are specific groups within the police service that may be particularly vulnerable to suicide, for example officers or staff, males or females.

To meet these aims, the following objectives were set:

i. to examine available statistics of those in the police service who had taken their own lives and thereby determine whether officers and staff might be more vulnerable to suicide than those in the general community;

ii. to determine the specific vulnerability of those employed in the police service – that is, which factors and issues, if any, might significantly contribute to suicidal ideation;

iii. having researched the vulnerabilities, to examine the available intervention techniques and suggested coping mechanisms;

iv. to do the above in order to ascertain whether current measures might be enhanced or others introduced to further minimise the risk factors for suicide;

v. if it was established that these measures fell short of the ideal, to consequently make recommendations and seek to influence policy makers, leaders and implementers of policy to improve intervention techniques.

After consideration of all these factors, a working title was adopted for the research: *The suicide of police personnel in the UK: an analysis of risk factors and an identification of appropriate intervention measures to reduce the number of completed suicides and parasuicide incidents.* This working title served me well throughout the research.

When deciding upon this working title, I was aware that because of my personal interest in the research issues, I would need to ensure that I retained a level of objectivity as I undertook the research and examined its findings. As I was a part of and belonged to the system that I wished to research, objectivity would be essential. This requirement was demonstrated, even as I formulated a potential research scheme, by the difficulties and successes I was experiencing in the preliminary discussions. Even though, as Jennifer Platt suggests, 'a single case can undoubtedly demonstrate that its features are possible and, hence, may also exist in other cases and, even if they do not, must be taken into account in the formulation of general propositions' (Platt 1988: 11), the research had to be objective, and if it were to be unbiased, then it would need to adhere to a strict methodology.

Initial Difficulties and Successes

The initial difficulties and successes in the work were important in the development of my research and the choice of a research methodology. In the first place, I felt it was important to have the support of my chief officers, which I gained after a lengthy exchange of correspondence. Their concerns related to issues such as the need for the research, my intended aims, sensitivity and confidentiality. Their support was given once the aims of and the need for such research were explained and an assurance was offered concerning the sensitivity and confidentiality of my intended approach to the research, as explained in Chapter 3.

Having gained this support, particularly the support of the Chief Constable, I was confident to approach potential contacts – people whom I had identified both internally and externally to the force in which I worked. I assumed that the heightened level of concern within the force in which the five police personnel had completed suicide might be equally shared by managers within the force and others within the police service generally who might be aware of and concerned about similar situations.

Within my force, I spoke with the lead personnel of a number of departments, including the Occupational Health, Communications, Human Resources and Professional Standards departments and the Force Disclosure Manager. A number of individuals within the force were most supportive. However, when I sought to obtain families' contact details, departmental heads explained that they would be unable to assist me in identifying details of the families of those who had completed suicide, and offered a number of reasons. These included:

- the breaking of data protection regulations;
- the fact that some of those who had completed suicide had been under investigation by the Professional Standards Department, and therefore contact would be inappropriate from the force's perspective;
- principles of client confidentiality in terms of releasing family contact details;
- the fact that family contact details held by the departments would probably be incorrect because of the time that had lapsed since the death.

At the early stage in the research, with the hope of engaging a force-wide audience and thereby identifying potential respondents, I had hoped to write an article for publication in the force magazine. Initial approval was received but, on submitting the article, I was informed that the article would not be included for publication as it:

- could upset readers;
- would be untimely;
- might raise issues which force members and families had 'laid to rest';
- could encourage others to follow the example of those who had completed suicide;
- might bring inappropriate attention to the force.[2]

The general negative response to these early endeavours indicated to me that for some, my research subject would be an unwelcome intrusion, even though certain individuals were encouraging. I felt that the negative responses reflected:

- a fear of suicide;
- an ignorance about suicide;
- a departmental fear of making a decision that could have negative professional repercussions for managers;
- a fear of professional challenge.

For me, the main consequence of these responses was a realisation that obtaining overall support would be difficult to achieve, and obtaining the contact details of families I might interview would be virtually impossible. While I found the unhelpfulness of these responses discouraging, the negative responses acted as a stimulus to explore situations which some others, possibly, wished to avoid.

In September 2011, a further opportunity to gain support for my research work arose. Following the suicide of the force's Deputy Chief Constable (DCC), Her Majesty's Inspectorate of Constabulary (HMIC) undertook a review of the context of his death. Along with many others in the force, I was invited to attend an interview with the HMIC investigators. According to a paper made available by the investigators, the brief of the interview was as follows:

> Although we will not be looking at the specific circumstances of [the DCC's] death since these are a matter for the coroner, we do hope to better

understand how the events surrounding his death were managed and what impact this had on people so that we can learn any lessons for the future.

Both before and at the beginning of the interview, I made it clear that I did not wish to discuss the context of the DCC's death, but wished to offer a résumé of my intended research work. Possibly, I was aware that some initial underlying causes of the suicide of officers generally may have been relevant to the context of the death of the DCC. Possibly, I had also hoped that, through the HMIC investigation, I might identify some within the Association of Chief Police Officers (ACPO)[3] who would be interested in my research and be prepared to offer their active support to my enquiries. The interest of the interviewers was generally mild and polite, but it was made clear that any hopes I might have had of finding allies would not be realised.

Similar overall difficulties to the ones which I experienced were encountered by two officers in the USA, both of whom were eventually successful in publishing their research papers. I was privileged to meet and discuss these difficulties with one of these two officers,[4] and reference is made to the problems encountered by the second officer, Louis Martinez, in Chapter 2. As these officers found, the frustration arising from the difficulties acted as a stimulus to achieve what others were suggesting would not be possible.

In spite of the practical difficulties at the commencement of my research, there were also many encouraging early developments. In discussion with others, anecdotal comment suggested that the suicide of officers was of deep concern to at least one, recently retired, leading member of the HMIC. In discussion and through an exchange of correspondence, he commented on his own lack of success in following through such research and described how he had approached others at a national level to find that there was 'little or no interest' in the subject matter. Nevertheless, the retired HMIC inspector was most helpful in sharing with me an exchange of correspondence in which he had expressed his interest in this subject shortly before his retirement. The correspondence indicated that I might find support for my research project from a named DCC.

A meeting was subsequently arranged with the DCC, who fully supported my proposed research but felt, based on his own initial inquiries into undertaking similar research, that the project would be problematic and fraught with difficulty in identifying people who would offer proactive support. He was therefore unable to recommend possible ways in which I might proceed. Indeed, with a degree of humorous cynicism, he suggested that I would have more success if I were to choose to write a dissertation on the reasons *why it is not possible to undertake research on the subject of the suicide of officers and staff*.

The meeting with the DCC was nevertheless helpful and he suggested that I should meet the Chief Constable of another force. In this subsequent meeting, the Chief Constable offered me the support of his force as far as the force was able, specifically offering the possibility of relevant family contacts.

Other early successes were the identification of a number of people employed within the police service who indicated their willingness to support my research in whatever way they could. They included a senior officer who retired from the UK police service during the period in which my research was being undertaken, and who was prepared to support my research as guide and mentor. Other individuals were supportive in drawing my attention to papers and media reports which they felt would be helpful.

All of these initial encounters – both those that were positive and those that were less so – increased my confidence that the research aims and objectives were viable and an examination of them would make a valuable contribution to a greater understanding of the suicide of those who work in the police service.

Whether stimulated by potential problems and difficulties or fortified by encouragement and support, there were many rewarding experiences throughout the research. The opportunities for discovery were productive, challenging early assumptions and enabling me to embark upon a study which I felt could be of some value to:

- officers and staff generally;
- chief police officers and staff at force level;
- those with national strategy and policy responsibilities within, for example, the ACPO and HMIC;
- those with line-management responsibility;
- staff associations;
- those who work in OHU and welfare departments;
- the families of officers and staff;
- chaplains to the police;
- those in the community who have responsibility for the psychological support and primary care of police personnel (for example, general practitioners and counsellors).

The Chapters Ahead

To fulfil the research aims and objectives, the narrative that follows first offers, in Chapter 2, an initial literature review with regard to contextual issues relating to the suicide of those who work within the police service. This review of relevant literature includes reference to the practical difficulties experienced by others in undertaking their research. The intention in this introductory literature review is to investigate the broad context of the research subject matter. Following this introduction to relevant literature, an account of the methodological approach by which the research was undertaken is offered in Chapter 3.

After these early chapters, an analysis of specific case-studies is presented in Chapter 4. By researching actual examples, the analysis seeks to determine those who may be at the greatest risk of suicidal ideation and identify key suicide precipitators.

However, as noted in Chapter 4, the extent to which suicide is prevalent within the police service needs to be established. This is an issue to which reference is made in this chapter (sections entitled 'An Initial Hypothesis' and 'Objectives') and in Chapter 2 (section entitled 'Research Difficulties'). Chapter 5 therefore examines the availability of statistical data and its reliability.

Chapter 6 returns to the research of others and offers an in-depth examination of suicide precipitators; that is, the precipitators that relate to society in general and those that relate to officers and staff. Continuing with this theme, Chapter 7 offers a comparative examination of the precipitators identified by the primary research (in Chapter 4) and the research of others (in Chapter 6).

Having identified the key precipitators, in Chapters 8–10, the book examines suicide-preventative measures. This examination includes measures that may be currently in place within the police service and also offers examples of additional measures to be considered where safeguards may be lacking or fall short of what is required (Chapter 8). In addition to these preventative measures, the two chapters that follow Chapter 8 examine personal initiatives that officers might embrace to safeguard their own emotional well-being (Chapter 9) and measures that families and friends of officers might adopt to support those for whom they are concerned (Chapter 10).

Before some brief concluding comments in Chapter 12, Chapter 11 recommends intervention procedures and safeguarding measures that might be introduced or enhanced.

In following this approach to what is an issue of deep concern, the intention is to offer informed insight into a subject that, certainly within the UK, is under-researched, and which some would seemingly prefer not to focus on or draw attention to.

Notes

1 Somers, Jack, *Police Oracle*, 'Officer found dead in car', June 19, 2013, available from www.policeoracle.com/news/Officer-found-dead-in-car_66931.html; accessed June 30, 2013.
2 I wrote a similar article which was later published in the national publication *Police Professional* (January 12, 2012). Valuable contacts were made as a result of this.
3 During the research period, ACPO evolved into the National Police Chiefs' Council (NPCC).
4 Orlando Ramos. Important references to his *A Leadership Perspective for Understanding Police Suicide: An Analysis Based on the Suicide Attitude Questionnaire* (Boca Raton: Dissertation.com) are made throughout this book.

Bibliography

Burgess, Robert G. (Ed.) (1988) *Studies in Qualitative Methodology: A Research Annual* (vol. 1). London: JAI Press.
Platt, Jennifer (1988) What Can Case Studies Do? In Burgess, Robert G. (Ed.) *Studies in Qualitative Methodology: A Research Annual* (vol. 1). London: JAI Press, pp. 1–23.
Ramos, Orlando (2008) *A Leadership Perspective for Understanding Police Suicide: An Analysis Based on the Suicide Attitude Questionnaire*. Boca Raton: Dissertation.com.

2   Initial Literature Survey

Introduction

As stated in Chapter 1, a research title was formulated: *The suicide of police person-nel in the UK: an analysis of risk factors and an identification of appropriate intervention measures to reduce the number of completed suicides and parasuicide incidents*. Having determined this working title and the general parameters of the proposed research, a preliminary survey of relevant literature was undertaken. This was to identify the major considerations that the intended research would need to examine. The Bramshill library was the prime source of identified relevant literature.[1] However, it was soon established that much of the relevant material in this library consisted of American literature published before the year 2000 and written by American psychologists, psychiatrists and officers. Literature concerning officer suicides in the UK was not evident, and this remained the case throughout the research.

Several of the American psychologists and psychiatrists had considerable police experience, but it was possible that their insight could have failed to keep pace with an ever-changing police service. The research would need to take this into consideration. For example, an American psychologist writing before the year 2000 primarily for an American audience may be helpful in setting some research parameters, but their research findings might not necessarily relate to a UK police context and speak in a relevant way to a UK audience more than a decade later.

A further difficulty raised by the predominantly American literature was that many of the writers' observations focused on the availability of firearms to US officers. The majority of UK officers would not have the same access. Other ques-tions concerning the relevance of American literature were also raised. Ameri-can Ellen Kirschman, for example, comments that 'cops may try to cover up a suicide out of pride and a desire to protect the surviving family from losing their insurance benefits' (Kirschman 1997: 169); throughout this research there was no evidence that this could occur in the UK.

As the initial research proceeded, it remained evident that much of the police-specific literature relevant to the research was material published in the USA and written by American writers.[2] The lack of UK literature on the subject of research was to be regretted, as this would have been a valuable resource to contribute to a contextual appreciation of issues specifically relevant to the UK police service, its officers and its staff. Nevertheless, the available literature in the Bramshill library offered an informed introduction to the subject matter. Previous American analysis of police suicides assisted the research greatly in a number of different ways; for example, by challenging initial impressions, bringing focal points to the fore and offering a greater appreciation of the potential difficulties in the research. These were issues that were relevant to the research, that were likely to relate to the experiences of UK officers and that could be tested against the case-studies to be examined in Chapter 4.

To give an overview of some of the prime topics in the research, a résumé of some of these issues is now offered and reference is made in this initial literature review to:

- the benefits of future research;
- the difficulties of researching suicide of those who work within the police service;
- general causes of suicide;
- the potential suicide of police personnel;
- officers' stress and family implications.

Subsequent references to those who have undertaken previous research on these subjects are relatively brief within this chapter, but are offered to illustrate contextual issues of research which suggested that further in-depth investigation or consideration would be required within this research study. Further reference to literature relevant to this research is made throughout the chapters that follow.

The Need for Further Research and Its Potential Benefits

In spite of the copious amount of American literature available, many of those who have contributed to the research suggest the need for further studies. John Violanti, a retired New York officer and later an academic, who has undertaken significant research studies on officer suicides, comments: 'It is considerably difficult to disentangle the complex causal web of police work and suicide, however, one point remains clear: far more research into every aspect of police suicide is necessary' (Violanti 2007: 28). He also states: 'We may be better informed if we know the inherent risk of police suicide in a quantitative, qualitative, and contextual sense' (Violanti 2007: 50).

Psychologists Terry Beehr, Leanor Johnson and Ronie Nieva, whose analysis of police suicides would appear to be aimed at clinicians working within a police environment and context, also refer to a lack of research, specifically with regard to the connection between suicide, alcohol and divorce: 'These three have been named as emotional effects of stress that are especially common in the police profession, but empirical research on these three potential outcomes of job stress, whether in police or other work, has been minimal' (Beehr et al. 1995: 10).

Violanti regards continuing research to be essential in securing the welfare of officers. Appropriate research will offer the means by which officers can be stimulated by their work and at the same time remain emotionally strong. As will be further discussed later, there is a clear requirement for continual research that takes into account the multi-faceted factors that can lead to the suicide of those who work in the police service.

Research Difficulties

Even though researchers suggest further research is desirable, attention was drawn in Chapter 1 to the practical difficulty of embarking on such study. In his book *The Secret Deaths*, Louis Martinez, a Chicago police officer, reflects on some of the difficulties he experienced in commencing his research. He explains how, after lengthy correspondence, initial meetings and writing a research proposal, he was required to meet 'several months later' with 'the head of the Crisis Intervention Department, two psychologists and the assistant director of the Research and Development Section' (Martinez 2010: 84).

He describes how, after arguing with zeal in support of his research request and resubmitting his research methodology, his request for the support of his police department was rejected. He comments that consequentially he had to embark on his research without this support. The reason for the lack of support, he suggests, was that:

> It was obvious that those involved in the process felt threatened and insecure about allowing this kind of research to take place. They'd rather keep suicide hidden and hope for the best, than confront it and save the lives of men and women in uniform who put their lives on the line every day. It was a great disappointment and a rude awakening to me that police departments continue to shun suicidal individuals and their families at a time when they need them the most.
>
> (Martinez 2010: 86)

The experience that Martinez describes, of failing to acquire departmental support after submitting research proposals and intended methodologies, is only one of the difficulties reported by identified researchers. A further difficulty commented upon by other researchers, including Violanti and Martinez, is the lack of research data available. For example, Martin Reiser, a psychologist working within the Los Angeles Police Department, describes the difficulty of determining reliable statistics of officer suicides in the USA: he suggests that there is a 'dearth of hard data on police suicide' and that where statistics are available, 'glaring differences' can be seen. He refers by way of example to the apparently low number of suicides in New York compared with the high number of suicides in the state of Wyoming (Reiser 1982: 172). He reaffirms this scepticism regarding available statistics when he adds: 'in discussions about the problem, several administrators have claimed no suicides over a 15-year period while others report fairly high numbers' (Reiser 1982: 172). With regard to the lack of reliable statistics, he suggests that the statistical discrepancy calls for greater reporting and more detailed recording of police suicides – 'otherwise, the tendencies to stereo-type and generalize continue' (Reiser 1982: 172).

As dated as Reiser's comments may be, they are helpful to this research for two specific reasons. In the first place, his comments highlight the difficulty presented by a lack of reliable statistical data. It would appear that this data was, and remains, unavailable in the USA, but initial investigation suggests that such data is equally unavailable in the UK. Reference is made to the data that is available in Chapter 5.

Research may uncover a genuine lack of statistics, but it may also reveal a reluctance to release statistics regarded as sensitive. Some researchers have referred to this general reluctance to respond to research enquiries as 'chilling' (Lee 1993: 35).[3] This is an apt term to describe the general difficulties experienced in undertaking certain aspects of this research when the answers provided by some respondents appeared unhelpful, as described in Chapter 1 in the section entitled 'Initial Difficulties and Successes'.

Second, Reiser's comments are helpful to this book in their warning of the dangers of stereotyping and generalisation. He reaffirms this point in stating that 'the variables related to police suicides are multiplex' (Reiser 1982: 172). A study must reflect contextual reality, and this research endeavours to analyse what this reality may be in a UK context, as discussed in Chapter 3.

Understanding Suicidal Ideation in the Wider Community

According to the Department of Health report *Preventing Suicide in England*, even though the suicide rate in England has reduced in recent years, suicide continues to be 'a major issue for society … over 4,200 people took their own life in 2010' (2012: 9).

Unlike literature regarding police-specific suicide, a great deal of UK literature is readily available on suicide generally, and an understanding of the general context of suicidal ideation in the wider community offers a broad introduction to police-specific suicides. Psychologists, for example, refer to the risk factors for suicide; to assist medical students, Dalton and Noble suggest that these may be recalled by using the mnemonic SAD PERSON:[4]

- **S**ex: male or female [higher risk in male]
- **A**ge: more likely in older people
- **D**ivorced or separated
- **P**hysical illness, especially long-term poor health
- **E**mployment: higher risk in unemployed
- **R**ecurrent attempts
- **S**ocially isolated, living alone
- **O**ther mental illnesses, i.e. depression, alcoholism, schizophrenia
- **N**ote left, to explain the reasons for suicide.

(Dalton and Noble 2006: 172)

Among those who refer to the suicide-risk factors of those in the wider community, there is wide agreement on the general precipitators suggested by Dalton and Noble. These factors and precipitators are highlighted by the Department of Health publication *Preventing Suicide in England*, which states that the factors which can affect suicidal ideation are:

- gender – males are three times as likely to take their own lives as females;
- age – people aged 35–49 have the highest suicide rate;
- mental illness;
- the treatment and care they receive after making a suicide attempt;
- physically disabling or painful illnesses including chronic pain; and alcohol and drug abuse.

(Department of Health 2012: 9)

As will be demonstrated in later chapters, some of these risk factors are relevant to officers who take their own lives.

A further issue, which is also examined later for its relevance to officers, is the way in which suicide can be 'contagious' (see Chapter 6, section entitled 'Community Contagion'). Malcolm Gladwell comments that suicidal ideation 'has fed upon itself … so that the unthinkable has somehow been rendered thinkable' (Gladwell 2001: 218). Community contagion is also known as 'copy-cat suicide', inferring that one suicide may lead to others. The implication is that the suicide of one person gives others 'permission' to do likewise. Gladwell offers examples of this contagion with reference to suicides in Micronesia and the USA. The suicides in Bridgend, South Wales in the first decade of this millennium offer further examples.[5]

Also of interest to this research is that those who take their own lives may not be totally aware of the consequences of their decision. Harry Olin, a psychiatric hospital director, puts forward a hypothesis which he refers to as 'the third wish'. He explains that 'the nonpsychotic patient in the immediate presuicidal state may suffer from impaired reality testing in which the consequences of the planned suicide are distorted and minimized. Suicide then becomes a means of dying without terminal death' (Olin 1998: 78).

As the suicidal person may not fully appreciate the significance of their choice of action, so too may the actions of those experiencing suicidal ideation and engaging in parasuicide be misunderstood. At length, William Fremouw, Maria de Perczel and Thomas Ellis list misconceptions about suicide commonly held by both professionals and those in the general community. They suggest professionals can erroneously consider that:

- Improvement following a suicidal crisis means the suicide risk is over.
- If a person survives a suicide attempt, he or she must have been doing it as a manipulation.
- If a person is talking to a therapist about suicide, he or she probably is not going to do it.
- A person truly intent on suicide is likely to hide it from people who might stop him or her.

(Fremouw et al. 1990: 13–19)

The authors suggest that those in the general community can mistakenly consider that:

- People who threaten suicide don't do it.
- People who really want to die will find a way; it won't help to try to stop them.
- The tendency towards suicide is inherited and passed from generation to generation.

(Fremouw et al. 1990: 13–19)

Offering further comment on possible underlying intentions for parasuicide, Fremouw et al. suggest: 'while manipulative motives sometimes play a role, it stands to reason that any expression such as "nonserious suicide attempt" is a self-contradiction' (1990: 23). With regard to 'nonserious suicide attempts', Fremouw et al. comment that 'parasuicide is a major public health problem, occurring at least 10 times as often as suicide', but 'as many as 15% of these individuals eventually do kill themselves' (ibid.).

These misconceptions relating to suicide are important, and further reference will be made to them, specifically in Chapter 10. Successful implementation of essential intervention measures will depend on how suicide is understood by peers, line-managers, family members and professionals.

Police-Specific Causes of Suicidal Ideation

Many of the factors given above are relevant to an understanding of police suicides but, importantly, there are risk factors which are specific to police personnel. A brief introduction to some of these issues is now offered, with further in-depth analysis in the chapters that follow.

Beehr et al., referring to issues of pressure of work experienced by officers, report that 'Police questionnaires measured nine potential stress outcome or strain variables: assignment satisfaction, experienced stress, suicide thoughts, drinking, divorce potential, somatic complaints, emotional exhaustion, and depersonalization' (Beehr et al. 1995: 10). Noting these stressors, Violanti suggests that officers are not encouraged to recognise these possible signs and do not necessarily have, nor are they given, the coping mechanisms required to relieve the effects of stress. He explains that from the day on which officers join the police and begin their training, they are encouraged to regard themselves, with their many forms of protection (such as body armour, self-defence training and the ability 'to talk people down'), as 'far different from the average citizen and certainly beyond self harm' (Violanti 2007: 14).

He further suggests that the training provided 'attempts to instill a sense of superhuman emotional strength in officers' (Violanti 2007: 15). The point emphasised by Violanti is that officers mistakenly have higher expectations of their natural ability to respond to trauma and stress. He suggests that these false self-expectations, alongside other contributory factors which are analysed in this research, make them more vulnerable to suicide.

As police careers progress, so can associated stress factors accumulate. Orlando Ramos, a New Jersey state trooper, notes: 'Literature shows that the previous method of suppressing or compressing the emotional feelings associated with exposure to critical incidents is detrimental to officers over extended periods of time' (Ramos 2007: 25).

There are other key suicide precipitators. Brief reference has already been made in this chapter to the combined effects of alcohol, divorce and suicide. Ellen Kirschman, a police and public safety psychologist, comments on the association of alcohol and suicide and further states: 'some studies predict that fifteen percent of all alcoholics will commit active suicide during their lifetimes' (Kirschman 1997: 172).

As later analysis demonstrates, other precipitators remain to be examined within this book. The analysis of the case-studies in Chapter 4, for example, identifies many different precipitators, ranging from disciplinary issues to alleged bullying and harassment; additional analysis of these and other precipitators is offered in Chapter 6 when reference is made to factors which include dichotomised decision-making and peer pressure.

Identifying and Responding to the Potential Suicide of Police Personnel

Earlier in this chapter, reference was made to the lack of statistical data regarding police suicide. However, statistics are equally absent for those situations whereby suicide has been successfully averted because intervention has occurred. Referring to the success of intervention measures, George Murphy comments: 'It is important to realize that *the absence of a suicide generates no data.* Thus, we can never prove what has been accomplished. Yet we can hardly doubt that it occurs' (Murphy 1998: 55). Intervention can effectively prevent suicide from occurring. As Ellen Kirschman comments: 'Intervention is the key to preventing suicide. The consequences of getting help to someone are never as permanent as the consequences of suicide' (Kirschman 1997: 176).

When potential suicides can be identified, the greater the opportunity will be for the successful implementation of intervention measures. However, Violanti (2007) comments on the difficulty of implementing intervention measures, due, in part, to the difficulty of defining the risk precipitators. He comments that due to the historical lack of research, it is difficult to be clear as to the prevention measures that might be successfully implemented.

Kirschman suggests that indicators may be simply missed by those close to the suicidal, and states:

> Most suicidal people are undecided about living or dying. It is rare that someone commits suicide without letting others know in advance how he or she is feeling. Unfortunately, their 'cry for help' is often indirect and hard to decipher.
>
> (Kirschman 1997: 173)

While it is difficult to define risk factors, Violanti suggests that they may be deter-mined by a range of measures which include psychological autopsies, the use of statistical data and reference to 'knowledgeable professionals' who can offer advice based on their experience (Violanti 2007: 43–4). Ramos also makes reference to 'knowledgeable professionals', suggesting that 'officers may need to see a counselor for prolonged lifesaving efforts, exposure to a scene of death, sexual assault cases, disaster scenes, and other highly stressful situations' (Ramos 2007: 25).

In addition to Violanti's suggestions set out above, he suggests that there might be three levels of intervention. These measures would be implemented at 'peer, supervisory and administrative levels' and he recommends that 'each of these lev-els should be evaluated separately as well as together to determine effectiveness' (Violanti 2007: 158).

Peer, supervisory and administrative support intervention mechanisms are all examined in detail in Chapter 8, along with other intervention support pro-cesses. Psychological counselling, training and the availability of a crisis tele-phone hotline are further examples of successful intervention measures that may be offered and are examined in Chapter 8.

As well as intervention measures, Violanti and others refer to 'coping mecha-nisms' to which officers may be introduced, and which may thereafter be employed by the officers themselves. It is Violanti's view that officers can be provided with an understanding of suicide and of the preventative measures that can be imple-mented. So resourced, the measures, he suggests, will reduce the risk of suicide and the officer's vulnerability to that risk.

Coping mechanisms can be employed, for example, to respond to what Beehr et al. refer to as the 'rugged individualism' of police officers (Beehr et al. 1995: 19). Martinez uses the phrase 'macho man syndrome' (Martinez 2010: 68) to describe the same behaviour. It is suggested that at the most simple level, one coping mechanism can be to instil in officers the confidence to know that asking for support is not a sign of weakness but an indication of strength.

A further coping mechanism to which Beehr et al. refer is religion. Noting the results of previous research undertaken by others, they suggest that for some offi-cers, religion may offer 'a stable personality dimension rather than … a response to specific stressful situations'. However, they conclude:

> Religiosity seemed to have no effect, one way or the other, on the police offi-cers' strains, although it might be useful for spouses. Thus, while turning to religion was clearly a coping technique reported by some officers, it appears unlikely to be either particularly helpful or harmful in coping with police stress.
>
> (Beehr et al. 1995: 19)

The identification of suicide precipitators and how to implement preventative measures are the essence of this research, and the later chapters of the book focus on detailed analysis of these issues. Chapters 4, 6 and 7 examine the precipitators, while Chapters 8–11 focus on the preventative measures.

The Consequential Impact of Police-Related Work Stress within the Context of the Family

Beehr et al.'s mention of 'spouses' in the quote above raises the importance of an employee's family. The context of officers' families cannot be ignored within any research on the suicidal ideation of officers. A great deal of literature is available on the impact of police-related work stress within the family. Violanti, for example, notes that stressed officers may take their stress into the home environment. However, distressed officers may feel unable to turn to their partners for emotional support. Partners may be the ultimate and perfect choice for this support, but the officer nevertheless may remain unable to be open with them and share their distress.

As the officer's stress goes unexpressed, an already strained relationship may become even more tense. Divorce may ensue, but domestic violence may also arise as a consequence of the officer's stress. As Jean Larned comments, an officer's depression can lead to 'negative coping techniques like violence' (Larned 2010: 69) – violence that may be directed at the officer's partner. Chapter 4 offers examples of occasions on which officers' violence has become so extreme that they have murdered their partners before completing suicide. The relationship between domestic violence and suicide is a further issue examined later in this book.

Concluding Comments

Even though a great deal has been written in relation to officer suicides in the USA, researchers such as Violanti nevertheless suggest there remains a need for further study and research. However, as stated earlier in this chapter, there appears to be a dearth of any substantial research into police suicides published in the UK. A great deal of UK literature on suicide generally is readily available – for example, there is published data referring to those in the general community who may be at a greater risk of suicide, such as males within a given age range and those who are isolated – but no parallel information is offered with reference to those who work in the UK police service.

In seeking to evaluate the problem of suicides of those who work in the UK police service, more information resulting from detailed research is required. This information would refer, for example, to contextual causes and statistical data. This information and data would enable an in-depth analysis and further a greater understanding of the subject matter. As referenced in this chapter, and as Reiser comments in the quote provided earlier in this chapter, the accuracy of any statistical data is essential. Data and information that are both correct and contextually relevant to the UK are required.

Reference has also been made in this chapter to the need for suicidal ideation to be correctly identified so that an appropriate response may be made. Once again, whereas literature on suicide-intervention processes for those in the general community is readily available, there is a dearth of information regarding intervention mechanisms in a police context. Literature that suggests intervention mechanisms for those in the general community will apply to officers, but should also be reinforced with resource material that is specifically orientated to those working as police officers, in a police context, with certain specific precipitators. As Murphy states in the quote set out above, intervention measures prevent many suicides. Consequently, intervention measures and coping mechanisms, which are often suggested by psychologists to the suicidal as a means of self-intervention, are identified as issues worthy of further examination in this research.

Earlier in this chapter, comment was made that any research into suicides within the police service should avoid generalisations and stereotyping. One cannot generalise and assume that the principal factors of one suicide relate to the principal factors of another. Before Ernest Hemingway[6] completed suicide, for example, it is claimed that he told A.E. Hotchner, his friend and biographer: 'Hotch, if I cannot exist on my own terms, then existence is impossible. Do you understand? That is how I lived and that is how I must live.'[7]

A comment such as this raises several questions relating to the police suicides examined in this book. With this comment, was Hemingway seeking to manipulate others or to take control over his given situation? Is Hemingway asking for Hotch's intervention or offering a final declaration? As Hemingway's brother, sister and father, and one of his granddaughters, also took their own lives, does this mean that suicide is contagious or genetic? There are no simple answers to these questions; neither can there be any generalisations or stereotyping, as is demonstrated by analysis of the case-studies used in this research.

It is a premise of this research that the suicide of police personnel is a matter of deep regret to those who hold officers and staff in high regard. It is a further premise of this research that supporting the welfare of all officers and staff, and particularly those who are vulnerable to suicidal ideation, is to the benefit of all police personnel, their families and the police service generally.

Kirschman states, citing Sgt Michael Tighe of the New York Police Department (NYPD), that 'Suicide among police officers is a dramatic example of what happens when those entrusted with the protection of others fail to protect and care for themselves' (Kirschman 1997: 169). The welfare of those who work in the police service consequently becomes, as Kirschman intimates, the challenging responsibility of others. As the initial literature survey presented in this chapter suggests, in seeking to respond to this challenge within this research, there is much to be examined. This includes further detailed reference to literature, case-studies and policies. However, before this material is examined, Chapter 3 explains the research process, including an account of how the interviews and case-studies were selected and how the analysis of the issues raised is carried out.

Notes

1 At the time of the initial literature survey, the Bramshill library was the main library of the National Police Improvement Agency. This library was and would remain the prime source of identified relevant literature.

2 For example, serving officers: Orlando Ramos, Louis Martinez and John Violanti (who on retirement became an academic researcher); psychologists: Terry A. Beehr, Leanor

B. Johnson, Ronie Nieva, Martin Reiser, Harry Olin, William J. Fremouw, Maria de Perczel, Thomas E. Ellis, Ellen Kirschman (some of whom had specifically worked with the police).

3 Lee writes: 'Although for critics the existence of such sanctions [of chilling] and their effects are self evident, claims of this kind are notoriously difficult to evaluate. The deterrent effect of chilling has, by definition, no visible outcome. Its extent is therefore difficult to measure. Neither can one take the fact that research studies are absent from a particular area as evidence of chilling' (1993: 35).

4 The same mnemonic is offered by MedicineNet.com with a slightly different use of each letter (see Chapter 6, section entitled 'General Factors and Mnemonics').

5 *Telegraph*, 'Bridgend hanging is 23rd suicide in same area in 20 months', August 11, 2008, available from www.telegraph.co.uk/news/uknews/2540984/Bridgend-hanging-is-23rd-suicide-in-area-in-20-months.html; accessed September 19, 2015.

6 Ernest Miller Hemingway (July 21, 1899–July 2, 1961), American author and journalist.

7 Quote accessed at www.goodreads.com/book/show/17159022-papa-hemingway?from_search= true&search_version=service; accessed April 10, 2015. It is similar to the comment offered by an interviewee in one of the case-studies: 'if there is no hope that I can retain who I am, I have no further desire to live.'

Bibliography

Beehr, Terry A., Johnson, Leanor B. and Nieva, Ronie (1995) Occupational Stress: Coping of Police and their Spouses, *Journal of Organizational Behaviour*, Vol. 16, No. 1, 3–25.

Dalton, H.R. and Noble, S.I.R. (2006) *Communication Skills for Final MB*. London: Elsevier.

Department of Health (2012) *Preventing Suicide in England*. London: HM Government.

Fremouw, William J., de Perczel, Maria and Ellis, Thomas E. (1990) *Suicide Risk: Assessment and Response Guidelines*. New York: Pergamon Press.

Gladwell, Malcolm (2001) *The Tipping Point: How Little Things Can Make a Big Difference*. London: Abacus.

Kirschman, Ellen (1997) *I Love a Cop*. New York: Guilford Press.

Larned, Jean G. (2010) Understanding Police Suicide, *Forensic Examiner*, Vol. 19, No. 3, 64–71.

Lee, Raymond M. (1993) *Doing Research on Sensitive Topics*. London: Sage.

Lesse, Stanley (Ed.) (1998) *What We Know about Suicidal Behavior and How to Treat It*. Northvale: Jason Aronson.

Martinez, Louis Enrique (2010) *The Secret Deaths: Police Officer's Testimonial Views on Police Suicides and Why Suicides Continue to be Hidden in Police Departments*. Denver: Outskirts Press.

Murphy, George (1998) The Prediction of Suicide. In Lesse, Stanley (Ed.) *What We Know about Suicidal Behavior and How to Treat It*. Northvale: Jason Aronson, pp. 47–58.

Olin, Harry (1998) The Third Wish. In Lesse, Stanley (Ed.) *What We Know about Suicidal Behavior and How to Treat It*. Northvale: Jason Aronson, pp. 77–84.

Ramos, Orlando (2007) *A Leadership Perspective for Understanding Police Suicide: An Analysis Based on the Suicide Attitude Questionnaire*. Boca Raton: Dissertation.com.

Reiser, Martin (1982) *Police Psychology: Collected Papers*. Los Angeles: LEHI.

Violanti, John M. (2007) *Police Suicide: Epidemic in Blue* (2nd edition). Springfield: Charles C. Thomas.

3 Methodology

Introduction

Having identified the aims and objectives of the research and encountered some initial difficulties and successes (as detailed in Chapter 1), an initial survey of relevant literature was undertaken to offer a focus on some of the issues that would require further consideration (Chapter 2). Following this initial literature survey, at an early stage in the research, it was apparent that relevant literature would be useful as only one resource among others, since this literature could well be limited to the situation in which it was written. Paul Leedy and Jeanne Omrod recommend: 'do not use literature to provide concepts or theories for your study, but do use it to provide a rationale and context for your study' (Leedy and Ormrod 2005: 141). Although its use might be limited, the research carried out by others would offer helpful contextual pointers.

Theories might assist, but for the research to offer validity, it would need to be grounded in the day-to-day context of the working UK police environment and provide analysis of identified examples. As Denscombe comments, 'theories should be useful at a practical level and meaningful to those on the ground' (Denscombe 1998: 91).

By necessity, determining the resources would be strongly influenced by the experiences and available opportunities explained in Chapter 1 (section entitled 'Initial Difficulties and Successes'). In responding to the difficulties involved in identifying possible resources, two of Denscombe's comments remained upper-most in the selection of an appropriate methodology.

In the first place, when embarking upon research, he asks: 'Given what I already know about the research topic and about the range of people or events being studied, who or what is likely to provide the best information' (Denscombe 1998: 17). To gain an understanding of suicide in the UK police service, it would be essential to be informed by those as close to the situation as possible. Second, Denscombe comments that the researcher must be sufficiently flexible so as 'to pursue areas of investigation that might not have been foreseen or planned' (Denscombe 1998: 97). The research would need to be sufficiently open to explore unforeseen possibilities.

A comment by Violanti was also helpful in determining the methodology: 'we may be better informed if we know the inherent risk of police suicide in a quantitative, qualitative, and contextual sense' (Violanti 2007: 50).

With all these points in mind, acknowledging that the research demanded a wide range of investigative approaches, it was essential that the methodology used in the research should have the capacity to gain and process information in the most productive and objective way possible.

Definitions of the Terminology Relating to the Research

The term *completed suicide* is used throughout this book to denote that a person has taken her or his own life. Whereas the popular term 'commit suicide' may still be in common usage, it is more appropriate to refer to 'completing suicide'. The term 'commit suicide' invokes connotations of committing a crime and was therefore seen as appropriate until 1961, when suicide was decriminalised. Equally, the term was used historically with reference to those who were 'committed to an asylum'. Whereas people may now be legally sectioned for their own safety, no longer are they 'committed to asylums'.

As noted in Chapter 1, the term *parasuicide* is used within this book, as opposed to the term *attempted suicide*, to embrace those whose self-harm was such that it was life-threatening. 'Attempted suicide' pre-judges motivation and the possible consequences. Furthermore, to use the term 'attempted suicide' implies failure: as Fremouw et al. state, '"suicide attempt" suggests that an individual sought to end his or her life and somehow failed' (Fremouw et al. 1990: 23). Implications of failure are not appropriate, especially when those concerned may feel that they have failed generally.

Coroners' *narrative verdicts* were first introduced in England and Wales in 2004. Narrative verdicts allow the coroner to explain the circumstances of a death rather than attributing the cause of the death to a named individual.

An *open verdict* is offered by coroners when other available verdicts cannot be given because of lack of information. According to Wikipedia, 'Mortality studies consider it likely that the majority of open verdicts are recorded in cases of suicide where the intent of the deceased could not be proved'.[1]

The Resource Material to be Analysed

The problems identified in the initial literature survey (see Chapter 2) demonstrated the need for this research to focus on UK data. Furthermore, it became apparent that analysis of individual case-studies would be essential, especially as UK statistical data of a quantitative nature might be unavailable (Chapter 2, section entitled 'Research Difficulties'). These case-studies would involve those who had taken their own lives and others whose self-harming activities had been life-threatening, and would offer valuable qualitative research resources. Uwe Flick explains the value of qualitative research when she comments that 'exceptional persons or situations [may] be found, but not necessarily in sufficient numbers to justify a sample for a quantifying study and generalizable findings' (Flick 1998: 5). Analysis of the case-studies would respond to the difficulty to which Flick refers.

Explaining the importance of the case-study, Denscombe explains that it 'can deal with the case as a whole, in its entirety, and thus have some chance of being able to discover how many parts affect one another' (Denscombe 1998: 36). Jennifer Platt highlights the significance of such qualitative research in her comment that 'case study material gives aesthetic appeal by providing "human interest", good stories and a more humanistic mode of presentation than that of the "scientific"/quantitative style' (Platt 1998: 11).

After consideration of the importance that researchers such as Denscombe and Platt place on case-studies, it was concluded that the data selected for qualitative analysis should relate to UK police officers/staff and embrace the following:

- deaths with a following inquest at which the coroner had given a verdict of suicide;
- deaths with a following inquest at which the coroner had given a narrative or open verdict;
- media reports of deaths which, for example, stated 'there are no suspicious circumstances surrounding the death' or 'the police are not looking for any other person involved in connection with this death';[2]
- incidents when it was possible that death would have occurred if there had been no social/medical intervention;
- those who had engaged in parasuicide;
- those who had spoken of suicidal ideation.

Notwithstanding the research commitment to qualitative analysis of case-studies, Platt counsels caution, commenting:

> This may be bought at an unacceptable price of sacrifice of systematic presentation of evidence, but it does not have to be. How great the tension is between the aesthetic and scientific criteria probably varies with the character of the case study and its role in the research as a whole.
>
> (Platt 1988: 7)

The case-study analysis would need to be placed alongside contextual issues identified by others' studies and presented in their research analysis. This would be undertaken by reference to their works as part of an overall literature review (Chapters 6 and 7).

Identifying Case-Studies

In response to the comments of research analysts considered above, much time was spent and preparation undertaken in seeking to identify families of those who had completed suicide who would be prepared to be interviewed. A letter of introduction and explanation of the intended research was written and signed by a Chief Constable, who made it available for use as an introduction to families who might be willing to be interviewed for research purposes. However, because of the practical difficulties described in Chapter 1 (section entitled 'Initial Difficulties and Successes'), this letter of introduction was never used.

Certain families were, however, identified and interviewed through personal contacts. On the occasions when this was possible, a letter of introduction was sent which also explained the purpose of the research interview. Without exception the families responded positively, and before the interview date was arranged, a second letter was sent outlining the format of the interview. This process resulted in six interviews with relatives of officers who had completed suicide. The interviews were semi-structured with relatively simple questions to allow for as full a response as the respondent wished to offer (see Appendix 3.1). Each of these families talked willingly and openly. The interviews related to deaths that had occurred between 2005 and 2009, with the exception of one earlier death, which is included in the analysis at the request of both the force concerned and the family of the deceased. These six deaths are included in the number of deaths given in Table 3.1, as accounts of these deaths were each also accessed through the media.

Interviews were also held with officers and staff who had experienced a strong sense of suicidal ideation. In all, ten interviews were undertaken. These interviews were held after 2010. They were arranged without any difficulty and were less structured than the six interviews discussed in the previous paragraph. As with the families of the officers who had completed suicide, respondents were open and willing to explain their situation. For some respondents, this was because they had felt under-supported by their particular force and wished to improve the working conditions of and the support mechanisms provided for others in the future. Although information gathered in these interviews is not included in Chapter 4, which presents analysis of the primary research, reference to issues raised in these interviews is made when recommendations for appropriate suicide-intervention measures are given in Chapters 8, 9 and 10. They are not considered in Chapter 4 because, even though these ten people had experienced a strong sense of suicidal ideation, they had not engaged in activity which had threatened their lives.

As has been stated, because the number of interviews with the families of those who had died was lower than had been originally anticipated, there was a need to identify a greater number of case-studies. Identification of potential case-studies was undertaken through searching media reports in publications such as *Police Oracle* and *Federation News*. Extensive information was also accessed through the use of internet search engines to find links to national, regional and local news articles. The deaths identified by this process occurred between 2000 and 2012.

The media accounts that were particularly helpful included:

- reports made immediately following a death;
- reports following coronial inquests;
- reports relating to parasuicidal behaviour and suicidal ideation.

Certain geographical areas provided a relatively high number of case-studies – for example, the North East – while other areas provided either none or a minimal

Table 3.1 Media accounts of suicidal ideation

Suicide	44
Open verdicts	3
Narrative verdicts	2
Parasuicides	7

number. As there was no identifiable reason to suggest that the number of police suicides depends on geographical factors, it is possible that some media publications are more reluctant than others to report on and publish the details of police officer/staff suicides. There is therefore no reason to suggest that the regional variation in reports should invalidate the research findings.

The numbers of case-studies identified in and through the media are given in Table 3.1.

After initial identification of the above case-studies, internet searches were carried out periodically to determine whether further information had subsequently become available. When available, the research findings were updated.

Following identification of five of the case-studies in which suicide had occurred, the initial details (gained solely through media accounts) were supplemented with further information from other non-media sources. Where such information was received, an assurance was given that this information would be regarded as confidential and that no person to whom the information related would be identifiable.

The Methodology of the Analytical Process

At the root of all the research lies, as previously stated, a commitment to a qualitative approach to collect the required data. This approach allows 'procedures which produce descriptive data: people's own written or spoken words and observable behaviour' (Bogdan and Taylor 1975: 4). Furthermore, as Robert Bogdan and Stephen Taylor comment, this methodology permits the research to direct itself

> at settings and the individuals within those settings holistically: that is, the subject of the study, be it an organization or an individual, is not reduced to an isolated variable or to an hypothesis, but is viewed instead as part of a whole.
>
> (Bogdan and Taylor 1975: 4)

Similarly, Flick explains how this application allows the research 'to take contextual conditions into account in [a] complex quantitative research design' (Flick 1998: 5).

As previously stated, information was gleaned through interview whenever this was possible. These interviews offered the opportunity to question 'the motivation behind a subject's remarks' (Bogdan and Taylor 1975: 116) and allowed the research to 'do justice to the complexity of the object under study' (Flick 1998: 5).

All interviews were carried out by asking a sequence of questions, but at all times the interview questions were flexible to allow the respondents the opportunity to offer as many details as possible. Denscombe describes this approach:

> The point is to generate theories, not to test them, and so there is a preference for unstructured interviews ... for the use of open-ended questions ... and the use of field notes. ... The preference ... is for the use of methods that produce qualitative data that are relatively unstructured.
>
> (Denscombe 1998: 93)

This approach to the interviews produced valuable information which was in many ways unique to each different case-study, yet contributed to the research as a whole. Platt describes the importance of the individual case-study when she writes: 'A single case can undoubtedly demonstrate that its features are possible and, hence, may also exist in other cases and, even if they do not, must be taken into account in the formulation of general propositions' (Platt 1988: 11).

To examine and analyse the individual case-studies, the research adopted grounded-theory principles to assimilate the gathered details and to identify any common trends. Denscombe describes the principles of analysing the data as:

- coding and categorizing the raw data,
- constantly comparing the emerging codes and categories with the data and
- checking them out against the new data specifically collected for the purpose, with a view to
- generating concepts and theories that are thoroughly grounded in the data and that
- have relevance to the practical world from which they were derived.

(Denscombe 1998: 99)

Applying these principles, a detailed examination was undertaken of all available information relating to those who had completed suicide. A similar examination of the details of the parasuicidal was also processed.

First, memos, 'short documents that one writes to oneself as one proceeds through the analysis of a corpus of data' (Borgatti 1996: 4), were taken. The memos used 'the natural language of people in the social context being studied rather than ... "sociologically constructed codes"' (Bryman 2008: 547). These memos served as 'shorthand devices to label, separate, compile and organise data' (Bryman 2008: 542).

From these memos, codes were created. As Earl Babbie explains, 'systematic coding is important for achieving validity and reliability in the data analysis' (Babbie 2001: 284). Rather than requiring data to fit into preconceived standardised codes, this ensured that – as Bryman, citing Charmaz (1983), states – 'the researcher's interpretations of data' allowed the research findings to 'shape his or her emergent codes in grounded theory' (Bryman 2008: 542). Examples of these initial codes created as the analysis proceeded were depression, partner relationships and disciplinary action.

Core categories were next created. These were categories, as Bryman explains, 'around which all other categories are integrated. It is what Strauss and Corbin call the storyline that frames your account' (Bryman 2008: 543). Examples of these core categories created as the analysis proceeded were emotional context, difficulties within the home and workplace issues.

From these codes and categories it was possible, as Leedy and Ormrod explain, to go 'back and forth among data collection, open coding and axial coding, continually refining the categories and their interconnections as additional data are collected' (Leedy and Ormrod 2005: 141). Strauss and Corbin describe this process as 'the procedure of selecting the core category, systematically relating it to other categories, validating those relationships, and filling in categories that need further refinement and development' (Strauss and Corbin 1990: 116).

This process of using the theory of grounded research meant all information that had been captured was relevant and it became possible to examine and analyse what Leedy and Ormrod describe as the conditions, the context, the strategies and the consequences of the research data (Leedy and Ormrod 2005: 141). A full analysis of these characteristics is offered in Chapter 4. Following this analysis, a further examination of available literature that relates to the case-studies is undertaken in the subsequent chapters.

Appendix 3.1: Questions Posed at Interview

Male/female
Age
Employment status: officer/staff/rank

Employment prior to joining the police service

The length of service within the police

Relationships within the family and the home

> Parents
> Siblings
> Partners
> Children
> Generally

Medical history

Previous identification as being at risk of suicide

Had there been any history of suicide within their family

Was there any disciplinary hearing, charges for professional misconduct or legal prosecutions pending?

Relationships within the place of work

> With senior management
> Line managers
> Colleagues

The means by which death occurred

Whether those who died left any indication as to their reasons for taking their own life

What reasons do you feel led to the suicide?

What other issues do you feel may be relevant?

Notes

1 http://en.wikipedia.org/wiki/Open_verdict; accessed February 22, 2014.
2 The term 'media reports' refers to incidents reported in news articles which were accessed through the internet.

Bibliography

Babbie, Earl (2001) *The Practice of Social Research* (9th edition). Belmont: Wadsworth/Thomson Learning.

Bogdan, R. and Taylor, S.J. (1975) *Introduction to Qualitative Research Methods: A Phenomenological Approach to the Social Sciences*. New York: Wiley Interscience.

Borgatti, Steve (1996) *Introduction to Grounded Theory*, available from www.analytictech.com/mb870/introtoGT.htm; accessed February 7, 2017, p. 4.

Bryman, Alan (2008) *Social Research Methods*. Oxford: Oxford University Press.

Burgess, Robert G. (Ed.) (1988) *Studies in Qualitative Methodology: A Research Annual* (vol. 1). London: JAI Press.

Charmaz, K. (1983) The Grounded Theory Method: An Explication and Interpretation. In Emerson, R.M. (Ed.) *Contemporary Field Research*. Prospect Heights: Waveland Press, pp. 109–26.

Denscombe, Martyn (1998) *The Good Research Guide for Small-Scale Social Research Projects*. Maidenhead: Open University Press.

Flick, U. (1998) An *Introduction to Qualitative Research*. London: Sage.

Fremouw, William J., de Perczel, Maria and Ellis, Thomas E. (1990) *Suicide Risk: Assessment and Response Guidelines*. New York: Pergamon Press.

Leedy, Paul D. and Ormrod, Jeanne Ellis (2005) *Practical Research*. New Jersey: Pearson Education International.

Platt, Jennifer (1988) What Can Case Studies Do? In Burgess, Robert G. (Ed.) *Studies in Qualitative Methodology: A Research Annual* (vol. 1). London: JAI Press, pp. 1–23.

Strauss, A. and Corbin, J.M. (1990) *Basics of Qualitative Research: Grounded Theory Procedures and Techniques*. Newbury Park: Sage.

Violanti, John M. (2007) *Police Suicide: Epidemic in Blue* (2nd edition). Springfield: Charles C. Thomas.

4   Analysis of and Initial Comment Relating to the Primary Research

Introduction

As explained in Chapter 3, the primary research was undertaken through a qualitative investigation of case-studies and the data was scrutinised by adopting the grounded-theory approach to analysis of the acquired data. This method was productive, confirming Lee's comment that 'field research, based on qualitative methods such as participant observation or in-depth interviewing, has often seemed like the method of choice in studying sensitive topics' (Lee 1993: 119). This chapter now offers a detailed analysis of the qualitative primary research data. This is an analysis of the details of the case-studies acquired from media accounts, supplemented with further information when this was available (see Chapter 3, section entitled 'Identifying Case-Studies'). This analysis does not include information gained through the ten interviews with the officers and staff who had experienced a strong sense of suicidal ideation (as explained in the same section in Chapter 3).

The analysis is presented as follows:

- contextual similarities in the case-studies
  - officer and staff ratio
  - data relating to the different sexes
  - age at which suicidal ideation occurred
  - length of service
  - occupational rank or position
  - the acknowledged calibre of officers
  - premeditated or impulsive suicide
- identified possible causes
- possible links to key components leading to suicidal ideation
- concluding comments.

Every effort has been made to avoid possible identification of those involved in any of the case-studies within this analysis. The numbers given to each case-study (e.g. case-study 1, case-study 2, etc.) refer to the case-studies within that section only. This is to avoid the possible identification of any individuals.

Unless the examination states the derivation of the case-studies, the following analysis does not differentiate between deaths or parasuicidal actions. This designation is not given as it is the shared motivation that is central to the contextual examination within the particular situation.

Contextual Similarities of the Case-Studies

Officer and Staff Ratio

Individuals in the four primary research categories (suicides, open verdicts, narrative verdicts and parasuicides) to which reference is made in the following analysis include:

- serving officers;
- retired officers working as police staff;
- officers who had retired as a consequence of ill health;
- officers who had left the police service under difficult circumstances, for example because of disciplinary issues;
- one serving staff member.

A possible reason for the wholly disproportionate number of officers compared with the single staff member may be that the media fails to report the suicides of those who are not either officers or past officers; it may consider the suicide of officers more sensational and therefore more newsworthy. However, the research suggested that the media reported suicides regardless of occupation. Therefore, even though this research was initially concerned with the suicides of officers *and* staff, as the overwhelming majority of 'police suicides' appear to be officers rather than staff, the prime focus of the analysis relates to officer suicide.

Data Relating to the Different Sexes

Within the general population, according to national statistics, 'British men are three times as likely as British women to die by suicide'.[1] The Samaritans offer a comparative figure, stating that in 2011, 'male suicide rates [were] on average 3–5 times higher than female rates'.[2] However, analysis of the research data, as shown in Table 4.1, reveals that when considering suicide and parasuicidal activity, the number of police-service males involved far outweighs that of females. As Table 4.1 shows, males accounted for 86 per cent of activity across all categories, and of those who took their own lives, 88 per cent were male.

Even given that the national average of male suicides is acknowledged to be far higher than that of female suicides, the numerical difference between the sexes of officers within this analysis appears disproportionate. The figures given above may not, however, suggest that male officers are more vulnerable. Two factors could account for the difference in the proportionate ratio.

First, there are more male officers than female. In March 2010, 25.7 per cent of all officers within the police service were female. This percentage had increased

Table 4.1 Data relating to the different sexes

Suicide		Open verdicts		Narrative verdicts		Parasuicidal activity	
Male	Female	Male	Female	Male	Female	Male	Female
39	5	2	1	1	1	6	1
	44		3		2		7

slightly to 26.2 per cent by March 2011.[3] It is possible that as the number of recruited female officers rises, the ratio of male/female suicides will become more proportionately equal. Furthermore, as David Aldridge comments in reference to suicide generally, the ratio of female suicides compared to their male counterparts may change with the development of a greater appreciation of gender-role expectations (Aldridge 1998: 107). Within the police service, there is already an equal role expectation with regard to male and female officers.

A second reason for the disproportionate number of male/female suicides may be that, as David Aldridge also suggests, coroners are more willing to record a suicide verdict for males than they are for females. However, the research found no evidence of this. Further reference to Aldridge's suggestion can be found in Chapter 5.

Age at which Suicidal Ideation Occurred

The age at which officers died, or were involved in parasuicidal incidents, is of further significance to this research. Analysis of the research data reveals that the ages of those concerned range from 27 to 62. This is a broad spectrum. However, as Table 4.2 shows, there are two significant concentrations of deaths: at the ages of 37 and 38, and between the ages of 45 and 49.

Furthermore, there is a significant difference with regard to the ages of the two sexes. With the exception of one female at the age of 44, the suicidal ideation of females occurred at the age of 38 or before. This contrasts with male suicidal ideation, which took place at the age of 34 or after, with the one exception of a male suicide at the age of 27.

This analysis offers a clear indication that younger female officers are more vulnerable to suicide in their late twenties and early thirties, whereas their male counterparts are more vulnerable in their late thirties or mid- to late forties. The ages at which the officers experienced suicidal ideation reveal a disparity when compared with the ages of those in the general community who complete suicide.

In 2011, the Samaritans reported that nationally, 'men aged 30–44 are the group with the highest rate' of suicides.[4] More precisely, another report by the same organisation stated that 'in the UK, the age group with the highest suicide rate per 100,000 for all persons and males is 40–44 years; for females the age group with the highest rate is 50–54 years'.[5]

Table 4.2 Age at which suicidal activity occurred

Age

6
5
4
3
2
1

27 28 29 30 31 32 33 34 35 36 37 38 39 40 41 42 43 44 45 46 47 48 49 50 51 52 53 54 55 56 57 58 59 60 61 62

O   P   P   N   O   P   P   N   P   O   P   P   N   O   P

NB coroners' narrative verdicts were first allowed in 2004

56 case-studies

Male suicide
Female suicide
N Male narrative verdict
N Female narrative verdict
O Male open verdict
O Female open verdict
P Male parasuicide
P Female parasuicide

It is not clear from the undertaken analysis that the ages at which suicidal ideation occurred can be linked to specific precipitators. However, it is possible to state that, within the primary research, there was a trend which revealed that the older officers were suffering from long-term depression and the younger officers were experiencing difficulties within partner relationships. There were exceptions to this trend, though. For further comment concerning long-term depression and partner relationships, see later in this chapter, section entitled 'Identified Causes of Suicidal Ideation'.

Length of Service

Comment and analysis within this section refer only to those whose deaths received a coronial verdict of suicide. The media reports in other research categories did not offer sufficient detail for inclusion in this analysis. Equally, not all the media reports of suicides provided the number of years served by officers. However, the details that were given in the media reports tend to show that the length of service after which suicide occurred generally correlated with the ages of the officers concerned; for example, the youngest officer to take his own life was 27 years of age and had completed four years' service, while another officer, aged 48, had completed 29 years' service.

From the information that was available, it was found that:

- Two officers had served less than five years. Both these officers were under the age of 30 at the time of their deaths.
- Four officers had served between five and ten years. All these officers were aged between 30 and 40 at the time of their deaths.
- Seven officers had served between 11 and 20 years. Four of these officers were under 40 years of age and two were between 40 and 45 years of age.
- Fourteen officers had served between 20 and 30 years. All of these officers were over 40 years of age.

These details suggest that the older a male officer is and the greater that officer's length of service, the more that male officer is at risk of suicidal ideation. However, as noted in the previous section, it would appear that female officers may be more vulnerable at an earlier age and after less service than their male counterparts.

Occupational Rank and Position

The members of the police service whose suicidal ideation is analysed in this research had the following occupational rank or position:

- 30 constables
- 6 sergeants
- 6 inspectors (2 retired)
- 2 chief inspectors (1 retired)

- 1 chief superintendent
- 4 of ACPO (Association of Chief Police Officers) rank
- 1 staff member
- 6 not given (4 retired).

As previously stated, except for one staff member, all had been or were serving officers at the time of their deaths. It would seem that officers of all ranks are vulnerable to suicide, whether constable or senior officer.

The number of those at ACPO rank appears to be proportionately higher than that of those at constable or sergeant level. This possible disproportion may be because the death of those at ACPO rank is more newsworthy and more likely to be widely reported than the deaths of others. It cannot therefore be concluded that chief officers are more vulnerable to suicidal ideation.

Having considered the employed status, sex, age, length of service and rank of those whose cases fall within the remit of this analysis, before an analysis of the possible causes of suicidal ideation is presented, there are two issues that offer further contextual insight. The first is an appreciation of the acknowledged calibre of some of the officers who took their own lives. The second is an understanding of the extent to which the suicides were premeditated or completed on an act of impulse. These two issues are now examined.

The Acknowledged Calibre of Officers

Following any tragic death, it is usual for media accounts to include personal tributes from families, friends and colleagues. Tributes are not exceptional. However, this research revealed that a high percentage of those officers whose suicides were reported were described as being in particularly good standing within the police service, the local community or both.

A high number of officers received – either immediately following their deaths or subsequently at the coronial inquests – specific tributes from senior officers or colleagues. These tributes reveal that many of those officers who took their own lives were highly successful in their careers and well respected by colleagues and members of the communities they served; examples of these comments, which are in the public domain, are now offered. The comments were made by either the coroner or senior colleagues of the officer:

Case-study 1

[The officer] was a well-respected and hardworking officer working within a difficult and demanding role ... he committed himself greatly to the job and showed professionalism and dedication throughout his service ... he received two commendations for good police work and two for bravery.

Case-study 2

We put him forward as his commitment is commendable ... he is so keen and enthusiastic and has the view he is never off duty.

Case-study 3

The officer had a [great number of years] in the police service, with an exemplary record and had several commendations from the Chief Constable – the last one being awarded posthumously for the work done with the team who brought [named offenders] ... to justice.

Case-study 4

His superiors say his personal file illustrated his commitment to community policing. It includes several letters of appreciation from members of the public and commendations from senior officers for his efforts in the community and in carrying out operational duties.

Case-study 5

A popular policeman twice named the [force's] community constable ... he was totally dedicated to his life as a community officer and I know from many community functions that I attended just how loved and respected he was within the community. To describe him as unique would not be far from the truth. A highly intelligent individual, extremely well read ... always able to relate to the common man. I am sure he will be sorely missed within the community and by his countless friends.

Case-study 6

He was very proud of what he had achieved.

Case-study 7

He has an awful lot of friends out there. He had a great deal of support from serving officers in the force.

Case-study 8

[The] Divisional Commander said the officer was highly respected by his colleagues with 'undoubted potential' for advancement within the force ... I know the community also shared that sense of loss from the number of telephone calls we've had since his death and some members of the public have sent flowers as well as messages of condolence.

Case-study 9

The officer was highly respected 'for his intellect, and had been held in high regard, particularly for his ability to discard red tape and bring the best out of his officers'.

Case-study 10

He spent all his life involved in officer safety and what happened was a result of him being worried about the welfare of officers.

Case-study 11

[He] had a great passion for the job he did; he was dedicated, hardworking and respected by everyone who knew him and who worked with him … he was an extremely valued member of [the force] and we shall all miss him greatly.

The examples offered reveal the officers' high level of commitment to their colleagues and to the communities they served. Consequently, consideration should be given to whether the pride these officers took in their work increased their vulnerability to suicide. Violanti refers to the shame that some police officers feel when their actions fall short of perceived expectations and suggests that 'some police suicides may be therefore based on shame or inability to fulfill role expectations of the organization, police peers, the public, or oneself' (Violanti 2007: 22). As an example, he offers a vignette of a newly trained officer who shot himself. The officer had caused a road-traffic collision in which two people had been injured. Following the collision, the officer lied. As a consequence of his deceit, the officer took his own life and, in a letter, confessed the shame he felt at letting his parents and colleagues down.

Violanti further describes how the perception that one has brought shame on the police service can contribute to suicidal ideation. Referring to Durkheim's theory of 'altruistic suicide', Violanti comments on the effects of actions that inflict ignominy on one's colleagues. He explains how certain suicide letters reveal the depth of shameful culpability that officers can feel at failing to fulfil the expectations of officer colleagues.

In support of Violanti's comments, it is the suggestion of this research that the officers' sense of personal achievement, as in the examples described above, has the potential to exacerbate feelings of personal failure. This suggestion was corroborated by some of the families with whom interviews were held. It was also reinforced by officers who were interviewed as part of this research.

To the successful officer, of whatever rank, failure comes heavy and is unexpected. The officers who, for example, are 'keen and enthusiastic' or hold 'the view they are never off duty' clearly have high and possibly unrealistic expectations of their ability to deliver. The self-esteem of officers who have exemplary records can be severely damaged by perceived failure, whether in the workplace or within their personal lives. This damage, as Violanti suggests, can be one of the precipitators of suicidal ideation.

These feelings of failure will affect officers of all ranks. Following the death of, for example, a community beat manager, expressions of grief and thanks are expressed freely, signifying the esteem in which that beat manager has been held within the community. For those officers who are considering suicide, this awareness of the deep respect in which they are held may be an additional significant factor in their decision to take their own lives.

Equally, senior officers who have gained the respect of their forces, for example by bringing 'the best out of their officers', may be devastated by personal actions which fail to live up to the standard they expect of others. Showing professionalism in their careers but being seen to exhibit a lack of judgement in their personal lives or in an aspect of their day-to-day work may be devastating.

Following perceived failure or misdemeanour, officers not only face the judgement of colleagues within the service, but also know that details of their private lives, for example, might be published by the news media. Such information in the public domain may be accessed by friends, neighbours and colleagues outside the police service, from whom information may have been withheld. Such publication will certainly tarnish the officers' standing in the community, may destroy highly successful careers and potentially threatens the security of the officers' family lives and homes. (Reference is made to officers who displayed negative self-perceptions later in this chapter.)

Premeditated or Impulsive

Ronald Mintz refers to suicidal impulses and appears to suggest that suicides are impulsive acts: 'there is no one single motivation of all or most suicidal impulses' (Mintz 1998: 243). To explain the impulsive nature (and also the irrationality and ambivalence) of suicidal ideation, Mintz offers the following fictional account of a man who sought to take his own life by jumping from a bridge into the San Francisco Bay:

> Quite miraculously, he rose to the surface of the water alive and unharmed. A policeman on a patrol boat ordered him to climb aboard. The young man refused. The policeman drew his revolver, pointed it at the young man, and warned, 'If you don't climb aboard this minute, I'll shoot.' The young man promptly climbed aboard.
>
> (Mintz 1998: 242)

Some others researchers appear to take a broader view and refer to suicide being carefully planned and premeditated; for example, Violanti (2007) comments on parasuicidal actions and suggests that, given the means, each thought of suicide, each plan and each 'attempt' increases the likelihood of suicide being successfully completed.

Whether a suicide is an act of impulse or carefully planned will generally be difficult to determine with any accuracy. It is possible that the officer with suicidal ideation has been contemplating suicide for a long time and has previously sought to take his own life; yet it is also possible that he has successfully controlled these suicidal thoughts but then completes suicide on impulse. As perplexing as it may be to try to determine the extent to which the suicide may be premeditated, it will be helpful to this analysis to examine the resolve behind the suicidal ideation. An understanding of the decision to complete suicide will offer a greater understanding of the context of the suicide and of possible intervention processes by which suicide might have been averted.

In determining the suicidal resolve, one might examine the means by which lives were ended. Many of the analysed suicides were by hanging or firearms. Hanging requires preparation; firearms are almost invariably not available. One might therefore assume that these suicides were planned and carefully premeditated, but the possibility must still remain that death was sought on impulse.

Another factor that might be considered in determining this question of the premeditated or impulsive nature of the suicide is whether a letter was written prior to death. This may be a helpful indicator, but the possibility remains that a letter, carefully written over a period of time, may have been withheld from authorised enquiry by someone close to the person who has died or someone who has worked closely with that person.

Determining whether the suicide was an act of impulse or premeditated does not necessarily assist in determining the causes that led to the suicide but, as previously mentioned, an appreciation of *impulsivity verses premeditation* will assist in understanding the context behind the suicide and whether or not the suicide followed a period of planning. Understanding this context will also be helpful when considering possible intervention measures. Examples are therefore now offered that seek to show which of the suicides in the case-studies may have been premeditated and which others may have been an act of impulse.

Premeditated

Many of the case-studies examined suggest that the deaths were premeditated:

Case-study 1

A previous attempt had been made. The inquest was informed that 'The idea was to do it in his car using a hose pipe so he didn't ruin the car and it could be sold so the money would go to his daughter ... [he] had tried it before in the car but it hadn't worked.' On the occasion when he completed suicide, by driving over a cliff, he had twice made local enquiries as to the feasibility of his plan. At the inquest into his death, the coroner commented: 'Having looked at the letters left by [him], a copy of which was on his body when he was found – fairly typical of an ex-police officer – he left all his affairs in order.'

Case-study 2

A family member commented in an interview: 'He had spoken about suicide during his illness. He planned his death meticulously.'

Case-study 3

The online report commented, 'In a four page suicide note … [the officer] accused members of the … team … of bullying. [The officer] had struggled with depression in the past and had attempted suicide by overdose on three previous occasions'.

Case-study 4

The coroner commented: 'it would appear that he could not face the predicament he had left himself in and that was exhibited in the notes to his children.' The press report on the inquest made no reference to previous parasuicidal behaviour.

Case-study 5

The media report on this inquest commented that 'A note was also found loaded on to the family computer'. The press report made no reference to previous parasuicidal behaviour.

Case-study 6

The coroner said: 'He had recently suffered domestic difficulties and left a note to indicate his intentions.' The inquest was told that 'he was very strong minded and once he had made his mind up about something, nothing anyone could say could stop him'.

Case-study 7

The media report on the inquest stated: 'An exercise book with a six-page note was found in [his] house on the day given as the date of his death. The last lines read: "This is a nightmare for me. I know I did nothing wrong, however, I can't face the next few months"'. The media article also reported that the officer had taken an overdose a few weeks prior to his death.

Case-study 8

The inquest was told that the officer 'had a history of depression and had twice tried to kill himself', the last occasion being two weeks before he died. The inquest was also told that on the day of his death, the officer's partner had phoned him to 'see how he was' and 'he seemed "at peace" and very calm'.

Case-study 9

The officer had previously sought suicide, although this was some years prior to his death and by a means which allowed for intervention. This death was by an action in which intervention would not have been possible.

Case-study 10

He had attempted to take his own life just four months earlier but on that occasion was stopped after colleagues intervened.

Case-study 11

The officer had previously sought suicide a few months prior to the death by a means which allowed for intervention. Following this event, the officer continued to talk about suicide, before following a course of action in which no one could intervene.

Case-study 12

According to the media account, the officer sent text messages 'expressing a wish to kill himself just days before he died, an Inquest heard'. The inquest was also told that he had visited suicide websites and had 'aborted one attempt at suicide shortly before he died', and that colleagues 'became concerned about the welfare of [the officer] after taking a series of increasingly desperate telephone calls from him'.

Case-study 13

Speaking at the inquest, the officer's line-manager reported that the officer 'said to me during a visit to the office that … he had found himself near the railway line that day. I wasn't sure what he had meant at that point; he said that he felt it wasn't worth going on'. The officer's psychologist also reported at the inquest that the officer 'had told her that he had thought up four ways for killing himself, including jumping off a motorway bridge and driving onto a level crossing'.

Case-study 14

The inquest was informed that the officer had discussed suicide and had spoken clearly about the manner in which he would seek to take his own life.

Other inquests merely reveal that officers had spoken about suicide. For example:

Case-study 15

He had told [two members of his family] of suicidal thoughts.

Case-study 16

'He had spoken of suicide "some months" before he took his own life.'

In some cases, inquests were informed that officers had spoken about suicide but the deaths nevertheless took some by surprise. For example:

Case-study 17

The inquest was told that the officer 'had hinted at suicide months before his death but not in the immediate days or weeks before he was found hanged … he had seemed normal on the day he died'.

Case-study 18

The officer's psychologist informed the inquest that while the officer 'admitted looking up sections on suicide on the internet … she believed he "wasn't going to carry it out"'.

Case-study 19

It was claimed at the inquest that the officer's partner had told those informing her of the death that he had 'promised he wouldn't do it'.

Case-study 20

The officer had spoken of suicide to colleagues, who said that he had later changed his mind. The officer's partner said he had spoken to her once about suicide, but added he was 'only joking'.

Case-study 21

At the inquest the officer's partner, answering questions about whether the officer had previously talked about taking his own life, said that 'during one particular argument he had talked about suicide but had indicated that he didn't have the guts to take his own life'. The psychologist reported 'surprise' when he killed himself.

Case-study 22

The officer had previously engaged in parasuicide and had a history of depression.

Impulsive

Other suicides appear to be more spontaneous. In the following examples, no letters were found; possibly the suicides were an act of impulse, and little, if any, planning had been done.

Case-study 19

This example highlights the difficulty in determining the extent to which a suicide was an impulsive act, as reference was also made to it in the previous section. One might consider from the media account of the death that the death was premeditated, and the suggestion that the officer had previously discussed suicide was raised at the inquest. However, at the inquest the coroner also stated: 'You might think people who take their own lives leave notes ... but by no means does everybody make it abundantly clear what they're about to do. Sometimes it can be a spur of the moment decision.'

Case-study 23

'At the inquest, the Occupational health officer ... gave evidence that [the officer] went to see her because he had been suicidal in the past and feared he was on the brink of becoming seriously depressed again ... [The officer] told her he was not considering suicide because he had a very happy relationship with his [family].'

Case-study 24

Evidence was offered at the inquest that 'toxicology reports showed no drugs or alcohol in [the officer's] body and he left no suicide note and gave nobody any indication of what he intended to do'.

Case-study 25

The coroner stated that '[the female officer's] suicide seems to have been an impulsive act, described to me as more like a male suicide, spontaneous and unplanned'.

Case-study 26

The coroner was informed that, on the day of his death, the officer had telephoned a relation; he was in tears and stated: 'I've done it'. During the brief and truncated phone call, he said 'I love you', and hung up. Recording a suicide verdict, the coroner commented that 'something must have acted as a catalyst that day' for the officer to have acted as he had done.

The above situations raise a number of questions which are worthy of further comment. Such exploration might consider the following points:

- The partner of the officer in case-study 8 referred to the officer's calmness on the day of his death. Similarly, it was reported that the officer in case-study 17 seemed '"normal" on the day he died'. This is not necessarily surprising as it is well accepted that many people, before taking their own lives, experience a sense of calmness resulting from their purposeful choice.
- It was reported that the psychologist in case-study 18 didn't think suicide would take place. The psychologist in case-study 21 made similar comments. One might ask: would a psychologist make such comments because they wish to refute any possible blame for the death, or are they genuinely surprised?
- The reports of officers speaking about suicide in case-studies 17 to 21 suggest that these comments should be taken more seriously than perhaps was the case. Here is a demonstrable need that those who hint at suicide should be encouraged to discuss their feelings openly.
- The coroner's comments with regard to case-study 25 raise interesting questions: 'her suicide seems to have been an impulsive act, described to me as more like a male suicide, spontaneous and unplanned.' In the research on which this analysis is based, the majority of suicides by male officers have not been spontaneous, as suggested by the coroner; there is every indication that they have been planned.

Comment on the Above Analysis concerning Premeditated and Impulsive Suicidal Ideation

From analysis of all the case-studies, and as demonstrated by the examples above, it would appear that more than 80 per cent of the suicides to which reference has been made above were premeditated. In support of this proposition, it would appear that each of the premeditated deaths revealed at least one of the following factors:

- Previous attempt(s) had been made.
- Those who took their own lives had spoken about completing suicide before their deaths.
- The death was carefully planned and implemented.
- A situation was contrived whereby it would be virtually impossible for immediate intervention measures to be implemented to prevent the death occurring.
- Messages had been sent before the death, or letters written to be found after the death.
- Business affairs/issues had been placed in good order before the suicide occurred.

Therefore a further suggestion of this research is that, even if the suicides had not taken place at the time they occurred, it is likely that many of the deaths could have taken place at a later date. This research therefore suggests that for many suicides to be avoided, the root causes of the suicide should be resolved and not just the recognisable symptoms.

Identified Causes of Suicidal Ideation

Introductory Comments

The case-study analysis that follows refers to information relating to those case-studies shown in Table 4.1. As Table 4.1 indicates, the case-studies are predominantly those in which suicide has been determined. As explained in Chapter 3, much information regarding these suicides was taken from the media accounts following the coronial inquests. These inquests offered crucial data for research purposes. However, as previously stated, media accounts of the inquests were not always available, and therefore analysis of the data relies solely on media coverage of the death itself.

The analysis that follows is also possibly further restricted by the lack of information offered at the coronial inquests. For example, in some cases the media report has suggested that information was withheld from the coroner or that the coroner was not satisfied with the information offered. There are also instances in which family members of the deceased, for example, were dissatisfied with the course the inquest took. These situations are illustrated by the following case-study examples:

Case-study 1

At the inquest of Officer 1, it was concluded that 'stress alone could not be blamed' for the suicide. There was a notable inference that details of the actual precipitators were not determined. At a later date, a psychologist who was not part of the inquest proceedings but had examined the potential causes of the suicide also appeared to doubt the fullness of the evidence as presented.

Case-study 2

A close relative of the officer commented after the inquest that 'the circumstances leading up to [the officer's] death were not properly explored'.

Case-study 3

The coroner seeking to determine the reasons behind the suicide of the officer cross-examined the officer's partner, suggesting that important information had not been presented.

Case-study 4

Following the conclusion of the inquest into this officer's death, the family felt that they were still no wiser as to the circumstances of the death. They commented: 'we don't want a witch-hunt – we just want answers.'

The different examples offered above illustrate the potential difficulties involved in attempts to identify all the possible causes of suicidal ideation. Nevertheless, the valuable information gleaned at the coronial inquests offers a reliable resource for gathering information relevant to this research.

The information which was consequently assembled – along with information relating to the other case-studies, as shown in Table 4.1 – enabled examination of the motivations/causes under the following headings:

- emotional context
- criminal investigation issues
- internal investigations for professional misconduct
- difficulties within the home and family context
- workplace issues
- alcohol abuse
- bereavement
- history of suicide within the family
- financial concerns
- health concerns of a physical nature
- unwillingness to accept help.

Emotional Context

This section examines depression, anger and the negative self-perceptions of those who completed suicide.

Depression

Media accounts of the deaths of 39 of the officers referred to the officers' preceding depression. Some of those described in the case-studies were said to have experienced long-term depression over many years, whereas other officers suffered from short-term depression following a specific incident in their lives.[6]

The examination that follows does not attempt to diagnose or comment on the different types of depression, but rather to show the contextual depressed state of officers and whether they had suffered from depression for any time of length before they completed suicide. There was only one case in which a definition of 'depression' was given; the psychologist concerned suggested that the officer was not suffering from depression, but rather from an adjustment disorder.

Initially, this analysis attempts to differentiate between those who had suffered from long-term and those who had suffered from short-term depression, but it should also be noted that there are case-studies in this examination in which officers were working successfully with long-term depression until a specific incident caused their depression to worsen significantly, which resulted in suicide.

Within the following sections, brief reference is made to various factors that would appear to have particularly contributed to the depression. It should be noted that more than one factor may have been linked to the long-term depression, e.g. bereavement and partner difficulties. Further analysis of possible links between the given contributory factors is offered in the section of this chapter entitled 'Possible Links between Key Precipitators Leading to Suicidal Ideation'.

LONG-TERM DEPRESSION

Of the case-studies, 23 were suffering, or had been suffering, with long-term depression at the time of their suicidal ideation. Most of these were males aged 40 years or older. The related associated factors are as follows:

Partner Relationships/Family Difficulties   Of those featured in the case-studies, eight were experiencing difficulties in their long-term partner and/or family relationships. These are case-studies 1, 3, 4, 5, 15, 16, 20 and 21.

Bereavement   Of those featured in the case-studies, six were struggling with bereavement issues and depression. These are case-studies 1, 2 (two bereavements, including a suicide), 10, 11, 16 and 21. Further comment concerning bereavement issues is offered in the section of this chapter entitled 'Bereavement'.

Work-Related Issues   Of those featured in the case-studies, eight experienced depression thought to be related to workplace issues. These are case-studies 4 and 20 (caused by bullying), 6 and 18 (caused by the amount of work), 12 (post-traumatic stress disorder, or PTSD) and case-studies 8, 9 and 17 (unable to respond to designated tasks).

Financial Concerns   Of those featured in the case-studies, three referred to depression related to financial concerns. These are case-studies 5, 7 and 8. Further analysis concerning financial issues is offered in the section of this chapter entitled 'Financial Concerns'. References within that particular section include situations which are relevant to the suicidal ideation but not necessarily linked to the initial cause of depression.

Non-Work Incident Causing PTSD   Only one of those featured in the case-studies (case-study 19) appeared to link depression and PTSD from a non-work-related cause.

Long-Term Depression Under Control but Exacerbated by a Further Incident   Of those featured in the case-studies, two were suffering from long-term depression which had been satisfactorily managed until incidents occurred which resulted in potential/actual criminal investigations. These are case-studies 19 and 20.

No Specific Indicators Offered at the Inquest or Presented in the Media   Of those featured in the case-studies, three were reported to have been suffering from depression, but the media reports offered no specific reasons linked to this depression. These are case-studies 10, 13 and 14.

SHORT-TERM DEPRESSION

Partner Relationships and Family Issues   It was suggested by the media reports that five of those featured in the case-studies (case-studies 22, 23, 24, 27 and 30) were suffering from short-term depression. It would appear that this depression was closely linked to partner relationships and family issues.

Financial Concerns   The report on one case-study (case-study 24) appeared to link short-term depression with financial concerns.

Professional and/or Criminal Investigation (Potential or Actual)   The reports on case-studies 25, 26, 27, 28 and 31 appeared to link short-term depression and investigations into either criminal or professional misconduct.

Health Concerns and Issues   The report on one case-study (case-study 27) appeared to link short-term depression with health concerns.

Work-Related Issues   The reports on two case-studies (case-studies 28 and 29) appeared to link short-term depression with work-related concerns. Reports of being bullied were alleged.

Anger

Some of those for whom depression was a contributory factor within suicidal ideation also displayed and expressed anger. Anger was identified within the following case-studies:

ANGER AND LONG-TERM DEPRESSION

Three officers who had experienced depression over a long period of time also displayed anger. These are those featured in case-studies 3, 5 and 30. One officer featured in the case-studies was described as 'hot-tempered and volatile'.

ANGER AND SHORT-TERM DEPRESSION

Two officers who experienced depression over a short period of time also displayed anger. These are the officers featured in case-studies 24 and 27. An associate described the officer in one of these case-studies as 'frustrated and angry inside'.

ANGER WITHOUT SIGNS OF DEPRESSION

In four case-studies the officers showed no evident signs of depression, but displayed anger. These are case-studies 32, 33, 34 and 35. Typical media comments included: 'The officer would "smash things up in the house and get angry over trivial matters" … he was "a volatile man".' The media report of the coroner's comments at the inquest of another officer stated that following a particular incident 'the police officer flew into a rage' and that 'something must have acted as a catalyst that day to make the "well respected officer" behave so aggressively … What is clear is that the behaviour of [the officer] was entirely out of character'. The coroner added that many had described the officer as 'not a very aggressive man'.

Negative Self-Perceptions

The officers featured in case-studies 3, 15, 36, 37, 38 and 39 were reported to have had a specific negative view of themselves prior to suicide.

The media reported that the officers, some of whom were said to have had enjoyed *earning* self-respect, spoke of the sense of shame they felt before taking their own lives. Media comments suggested that those who had completed suicide 'didn't feel good about themselves' and had particularly low self-esteem. Typical media comments included:

He was a proud man and he felt ashamed at recent developments.

A colleague said that the officer felt 'left behind … at the bottom of the pile and … worthless'.

Such sentiments were confirmed in interviews with some of the family members and colleagues of those who had completed suicide.

Criminal Investigation Issues

Of those featured in the case-studies, 21 had been, were, or potentially would have been under criminal investigation at the time of their deaths, had death not intervened. Reference to these people and the case-studies in which they feature does not imply that they had been convicted of any offence. Some had been convicted, others were under investigation, some would have faced criminal investigation had they not completed suicide and some, media reports suggest, would not have been charged with any offence. The reasons for their investigations are as follows:

- Assault: case-studies 1, 2, 3 and 4.
- Fraud: case-studies 5 and 6.
- Inappropriate professional behaviour of a criminal nature: case-studies 7 and 8.
- Murder/manslaughter: case-studies 9, 10, 11 and 12.
- Underage sexual offences, including grooming and child pornography: case-studies 13, 14, 15, 16 and 17.

- undisclosed investigation: case-studies 18, 19, 20 and 21. The offences were not disclosed by the media at the time of the deaths or following the coronial inquests.

Difficulties within the Home and Family Context

It would appear that a contributory factor to suicidal ideation is related to the breakdown of partner relationships and/or the family unit: 24 case-studies revealed such difficulties. At the simplest level, there is the breakdown of the family unit; however, the difficulties involved may be far more complex.

The following case-studies reveal different aspects of difficulties within the home that were reported by the media to have contributed to the suicidal ideation of those featured in the case-studies. Important contextual information may be lacking from the media reports, but the following examples offer pointers, at least, to the difficulties in the personal lives of those involved in the case-studies.

The Breakdown of Marriage/Partnership Relationships

In all, 16 of the officers had separated from their long-term partner/spouse or were experiencing significant difficulties within their partner relationships. These were case-studies 1, 2, 4, 5, 6, 7, 8, 9, 10, 11, 12, 13, 14, 15, 16 and 17.

Officers' Extra-Marital Affairs

The media reported that four of those featured in the above case-studies (case-studies 2, 6, 8 and 9) were having affairs at the same time as acknowledging that difficulties were causing problems in their marriages/partnerships. Five of those featured in the case-studies (case-studies 18, 19, 20, 21 and 22) were having affairs while their marriages were not apparently experiencing significant problems.

Partners' Affairs

Media reports suggested that in two cases, affairs in which the officer's partner was involved contributed to the officer suicides. These are case-studies 23 and 24.

Estrangement from Children

There was further media comment about the difficult relationships which six of those featured in the case-studies had with their children:

- In case-study 1, the officer 'had become depressed … over issues regarding their children'.
- In case-study 2, 'His relationship with his sons had deteriorated and they did not attend his funeral'.
- The officer featured in case-study 3 'had become estranged from his family'.

- The officer featured in case-study 4 'was mourning the loss of his … family'.[7]
- The officer featured in case-study 5 had 'a lot of factors weighing on [his] shoulders at the time: his relationship with his children …'.
- The officer featured in case-study 22 'thought he might never see his children again. Maybe that's why he flipped out'.

Workplace Issues

There were media suggestions that workplace issues contributed to the suicidal ideation of some of those featured in the case-studies. These workplace issues are now considered under the following headings:

- internal investigations for professional misconduct
- alleged bullying, harassment, victimisation
- lack of communication
- lack of welfare and colleague support
- post-traumatic stress disorder (PTSD)
- pressure of work-related stress
- re-assignment of working role
- other work-related issues.

Internal Investigations for Professional Misconduct

Of all those featured in the case-studies, eight were facing internal investigation at the time of their deaths. It is not intended here to make any comment other than to offer the reason, where known, for any of the investigations. The internal investigations were all at different stages. Commenting on the stage the investigation had reached could enable possible identification of the officers, and therefore those who were facing internal investigation for professional misconduct are simply identified again as numbered case-studies. The cause of each investigation is as follows:

- Alleged assault: case-study 1.
- Bullying/sexual harassment: case-studies 2, 3 and 4.
- Lack of professional care: case-study 5.
- Misuse of computer database: case-study 6.
- Undisclosed by the media: case-studies 7 and 8.

With reference to two different case-studies, the respective media reports illustrate how opposing perspectives on investigations may be held by those under investigation and those leading investigations. An individual under investigation wrote in his suicide letter: 'This is a nightmare for me. I know I did nothing wrong, however, I can't face the next few months.' At the inquest into the death of another individual featured in the case-studies, it was reported that the force considered the officer under investigation to have 'over-reacted to being interviewed'. Perceptions are clearly important and can potentially influence suicidal ideation.

Alleged Bullying, Harassment, Victimisation

Allegations of bullying of others were made against the officer featured in case-study 1. Similarly, allegations of harassing others were made against the officers featured in case-studies 8 and 12.

Allegations of being bullied were related to the suicidal ideation of those featured in case-studies 2, 3, 4, 5, 6, 7 and 8. These allegations were made by different sources for each of the different case-studies. These sources include the individuals featured in the case-studies themselves, their partners and their colleagues.

The media reported these allegations with comments that included:

- The officer had been 'bullied by superiors over [the officer's] sexuality'.
- The officer had been 'psychologically and verbally bullied'.
- The officer had 'made a grievance claim for bullying shortly before he died'.
- The officer believed that 'people within the force were "out to get him"'.
- 'The hearing into the death of [the officer] heard he felt he was being "targeted" by his supervisors'. The officer's partner alleged that the officer 'had been bullied and victimised over a period of time'.

The reasons for the alleged bullying were not always given, but those that were included underperformance in the workplace, homophobia and racism.

Lack of Communication

There were two areas of disquiet with regard to a lack of communication from the relevant forces. The officers in case-studies 6 and 9 were concerned about the lack of information concerning their future re-deployment posts, while concerns in case-studies 1, 8, 10 and 11 involved investigations and a lack of communication regarding progress and potential charges. The force to which case-study 11 belonged offered a formal apology following the officer's suicide for the breakdown in communication with the officer.

Lack of Welfare and Colleague Support

The families of three officers (those featured in case-studies 12, 13 and 14) felt that there was a clear lack of welfare support. It should also be noted that many suspended officers under investigation are prevented from contact with departmental colleagues. This particular lack of available support was highlighted by the partner of the individual featured in case-study 1.

Post-Traumatic Stress Disorder (PTSD)

Three of those featured in the case-studies were reported to be suffering from PTSD. These are case-studies 11, 16 and 17. The individual featured in case-study 11 was suffering as a result of a personal incident, the individual featured in case-study 16 as a result of serving in HM Armed Forces and the individual featured in case-study 17 as a result of incidents linked to police duties.

Pressure of Work-Related Stress

Reports of work-related stress were offered at the inquests of those featured in three case-studies.

The partner of the individual featured in case-study 8 told of how he had been 'overworked' and had been doing 'a job which previously two officers had been doing'. The inquest into the death of the individual featured in case-study 9 was told that the officer took his own life at a time when he 'felt under pressure from targets and paperwork' and that he 'felt under pressure after being emailed a personal action plan the month before his death'. The officer had told his partner that he was failing to meet his targets. It was further reported that the officer had said: 'I don't know what my job is anymore. They've taken my job away from me.' One colleague told the inquest that 'a monitoring regime introduced the previous year demanding three arrests per week had left his friend unable to cope'. Another added that 'his friend was one of many officers worried they might be transferred to another station if they failed to perform highly'. The report of the inquest into the death of the officer featured in case-study 18 commented that the officer drank to excess because of the 'stress of the job'.

Re-Assignment of Working Role

As noted earlier in this chapter, before their deaths, the officers featured in case-studies 6 and 9 were anxious about the re-assignment of their working roles and felt they were being treated unfairly. The individual featured in case-study 15 was unable to fulfil the role of a response officer and was, the media reported, 'refused a desk job'.

Other Work-Related Issues

The individual featured in case-study 13 'had been involved in a pay dispute with bosses and had also become disillusioned' in his post. His partner told the inquest that 'something … had happened in regard to how he was being treated at work and his financial situation and his police pay'.

In a written statement, the partner of the officer featured in case-study 17 told how the officer 'felt betrayed by his employers' because 'he had to fight so hard to prove his illness and its origins'.

The partner of the officer featured in case-study 19 reported how the officer had taken a complaint from a member of the community personally and felt 'distressed about some of the treatment he received', despite the fact he had been reassured that his work was of a high quality. However, the partner also reported that the officer 'felt trapped in his job'.

Following the death of the individual featured in case-study 20, a colleague commented that the officer 'would be very worried about damaging the reputation of the force'.

Alcohol Abuse

Of the individuals featured in the case-studies, eight were or had been suffering problems with alcohol abuse; six (1, 2, 3, 6, 7 and 8) were suffering from problems with alcohol abuse at the time of their death, and media reports included the following comments:

- The individual in case-study 1 'had some problems with ... alcohol'.
- The individual in case-study 2 'had a history of alcohol abuse'.
- The individual in case-study 3 'often drank two bottles of wine or more in the evening'.
- The post-mortem examination of the individual in case-study 6 revealed liver failure 'due to alcohol abuse'.

Media reports suggested that two of those featured in the case-studies had a history of alcohol abuse, although it was possibly controlled at the time of death:

- Case-study 4: It was reported that the officer hadn't drunk for seven months before he died, but the inquest was informed by the officer's partner that the officer '[had] an alcohol problem and was taking medication for his depression'.
- Case-study 5: 'He admitted having had serious alcohol problems in the past. He stated that he had been off alcohol for the past eight months while attending Alcoholics Anonymous.'

The media reports commented that in all of the case-studies where alcohol was being abused, the individuals were also suffering with depression. With the exception of case-study 1, which appeared to be short-term, this depression was of a long-term nature.

Many researchers link alcohol abuse to PTSD. There was only one case-study in which this link could be determined.

Bereavement

The term 'family member', in reference to the death of a family member, denotes a partner, parent or child. Media reports offered the following information regarding eight case-studies in which such bereavement appeared to be a contributory factor leading to suicidal ideation:

- The individual in case-study 1 was suffering the results of two family bereavements at the time of death. The officer also spoke of two other family bereavements but these 'turned out to be untrue'.
- The individual in case-study 2 had witnessed the death of a family member, which the officer 'never got over'. The officer 'descended into depression'.
- The individual in case-study 3 'was said to have been trying to come to terms' with the death of a family member when the officer 'apparently took his own life'.

- The individual in case-study 4 was suffering from 'anxiety and depression of a long-term nature' following the death of a family member.
- The individual in case-study 5 experienced the death of a family member, which led to 'increased depression'.
- The individual in case-study 6 was suffering from grief when a further traumatic incident occurred. The coroner commented that these factors had 'a cumulative effect'.
- The individual in case-study 7 had killed his wife in a suicide pact.
- The individual in case-study 8 'jumped to his death from a multi-storey car park on the anniversary' of the death of a family member.

History of Suicide within the Family

The issue of suicides of family members of those featured in the case-studies appears sufficiently significant to warrant its own particular section within this analysis. In four case-studies (case-studies 1, 2, 3 and 4), prior to the suicidal ideation of the individual featured in the case-study, family members had also taken their own lives. The deaths of these family members had occurred some years before the deaths of the individuals featured in the case-studies. In another case-study, the individual had experienced the death of a relative within the extended family circle and suicide was suspected.

Financial Concerns

Media reports on four of the case-studies commented that the individuals involved were worried about their financial situation in the months prior to their deaths.

- The inquest was told that case-study 1 had 'killed himself because of worries over debt'.
- The report of the inquest into the death of case-study 2 stated that the officer had 'financial difficulties'.
- The individual featured in case-study 3 was said to have had 'enough savings for only a "couple of months"' after being dismissed from the police service.
- The inquest into the death of the individual featured in case-study 4 found he was anxious about 'his financial situation and his police pay'.

Health Concerns of a Physical Nature

It would appear that health concerns contributed to the suicidal ideation of those featured in four case-studies. The individual featured in case-study 1 planned his death meticulously as he was suffering from a terminal illness and wished his partner to receive maximum financial benefit. A work-related incident incapacitated the individual featured in case-study 2. The individuals featured in case-studies 3 and 4 were both greatly concerned about their physical health, but according to statements made following their deaths, neither had reason for concern.

Unwillingness to Accept Help

The research revealed that in at least eight case-studies, the individuals either failed to share their problems and concerns with their families or failed to engage with their occupational health department after being advised to do so. This lack of engagement may not be a prime cause of the decision to take one's own life, but it would appear to be a contributing factor to the psychological welfare of those considering suicide. The media reports offer the following comments:

- Case-study 1: 'He was very proud and private about his inner thoughts and feelings and would not want to show weakness to others.'
- Case-study 2: 'I think he didn't want me to worry.'
- The partner of the individual featured in case-study 3 commented: 'I personally did not feel that he was ready to go back to work. ... He did his best to hide it from me, being like he was, but he still was not feeling well.'
- Case-study 4: The partner commented that the officer had failed to mention the disciplinary action that had been taken.
- The officer featured in case-study 5 'was scared and concerned about letting anybody know' about the stress that was being experienced.
- Case-study 6: 'The tragedy is that [the officer] never felt able during his career to seek the help he badly needed.'
- Case-study 7: 'On one occasion an appointment was arranged at Occupational Health but he did not attend. He liked to go his own way. He was not good at seeking help from others.'
- Case-study 8: 'He had been advised to go and see Occupational Health as a matter of course but he saw them as a waste of space and wouldn't ask for help.'

Possible Links between Key Precipitators Leading to Suicidal Ideation

Introductory Comments

Analysis of the suicide precipitators cited in the primary research reveals many similarities between them and precipitators identified by others. Stephen Barron, a forensic psychologist who undertook research into the suicide of police officers in New South Wales, suggests that that 'the important contributors to police suicide are depression, relationship problems, financial problems, substance abuse, alcohol abuse, access to firearms, organisational issues such as corruption and management decisions'.[8]

Mintz suggests that such identified motivations 'clinically often appear in combination' (Mintz 1998: 243). Referring to a possible combination of motivations and precipitators, Violanti comments: 'it is considerably difficult to disentangle the complex causal web of police work and suicide' (Violanti 2007: 28). Violanti's description of the combination as a web is most appropriate, as it would seem that many of the factors contributing to suicidal ideation can be closely interwoven.

The analysis now examines possible links between single precipitators to obtain a fuller understanding of how the precipitators can combine in a way that may lead to suicide. Before this examination is offered, reference is first made to the case-studies in which there would appear to be a single motivating precipitator, rather than two or more precipitators contributing to the suicidal ideation. As in the previous analysis, the numbering of each case-study refers only to the case-studies referenced in that section.

Single Contributory Factor

To suggest that there were single causes underlying the suicidal ideation in certain of the case-studies may be considered simplistic, as a single cause may still be multi-faceted. However, the information given concerning the following case-studies suggests that suicidal ideation was a result of a single primary cause.

- Case-study 1: potential criminal investigation.
- Case-study 2: internal investigation.
- Case-studies 3 and 4: extra-marital affair.
- Case-study 5: health concerns .
- Case-study 6: following an assisted suicide.
- Case-studies 7 and 8: depression/stress.

Emotional Context – Depression

Details of individuals featured in case-studies who were experiencing depression were offered earlier in this chapter. The analysis that follows considers the case-studies in which depression was evident alongside other precipitators.

No clear link could be identified between depression and any other common contributory precipitator. However, there were accompanying factors; for example:

- Case-study 1: criminal investigation, partner difficulties, family dysfunction, alcohol abuse and financial concerns.
- Case-study 2: criminal investigation, partner difficulties and financial concerns.
- Case-study 3: internal investigation, lack of welfare support and health concerns.
- Case-study 4: bullying and lack of welfare support.
- In five of the case-studies, including two of those described in this list, the individuals who were experiencing depression also displayed anger.

All male individuals featured in the case-studies who were experiencing long-term depression were aged 40 or over, whereas 80 per cent (four of five) of the female individuals featured in the case-studies who were experiencing long-term depression were under the age of 40.

Criminal Investigations

Details of those individuals featured in the case-studies who were subject to criminal investigations were offered earlier in this chapter. The following analysis includes references to the criminal investigations which:

- would have been initiated had death not intervened;
- were in progress at the time of the suicidal ideation;
- had been concluded with either innocence or guilt determined.

The criminal nature of these referenced situations related to:

- acts of violence
- child pornography/underage grooming
- fraud
- inappropriate professional behaviour of a criminal nature.

It should be emphasised that each of the different investigations will have brought its own additional stressors leading to suicidal ideation. For example, an officer facing charges of violence towards his partner potentially faces losing his job, and therefore his income also; the consequence of this is that the officer will, in all probability, experience some symptoms of depression. The analysis revealed that in the majority of the case-studies, the individuals were facing criminal investigations which involved violence against their partner. The stressors leading to the suicidal ideation were therefore compounded. However, as compounded as the contributory causes may have been, no common pattern of compounded causation was identified within any of these given case-studies.

As will be seen from the examples below, the identified contributory causes offer a broad spectrum of combined stressors. Only case-studies 1 and 2 had close similarities.

Accompanying criminal investigations, the contributory causes leading to suicidal ideation included:

- Case-study 1: long-term depression, bullying, alcohol abuse and difficulties within family relationships.
- Case-study 2: long-term depression, alcohol abuse, stress due to pressure of work and difficulties within family relationships.
- Case-study 3: long-term depression.
- Case-study 4: bullying and lack of workplace support.
- Case-study 5: bereavement.

Internal Investigations for Professional Misconduct

In 11 case-studies the individuals concerned were subject to internal investigations for professional misconduct. These investigations were not linked to criminal investigations, although in three case-studies (case-studies 5, 8, and 9) the individuals were also facing criminal investigations for incidents relating to different internal investigations. The internal investigations were for harassment, assault, fraud and what the media described as 'off-duty incidents'.

With the exception of one female, all of those featured in the case-studies were male. Of the men, five were aged 36/37, one was aged 43 and the others were in their late forties or early fifties.

Media accounts reported that:

- The individuals featured in case-studies 1, 2, 3, 4, 5, 9, 10 and 11 were depressed.
- The individuals featured in case-studies 6, 7, 8 9 and 11 were experiencing partner difficulties. With one exception, these individuals were within the younger age range.
- The individual featured in case-study 10 complained about bullying and a lack of welfare support.
- The individual featured in case-study 11 also complained about bullying and a lack of welfare support. It was reported that he had also experienced difficulties with family relationships and with alcohol.

There did not appear to be strong correlations between internal investigations and any personal contributory factors, with two possible exceptions:

- Three of those in their thirties were also experiencing difficulties within their partner relationships.
- Eight were stated to be depressed.

Workplace Issues

Of the nine case-studies in which claims of bullying, harassment and victimisation were made, eight individuals (case-studies 1–8) perceived a lack of welfare support from their forces. No other contributory links were identified.

Alcohol Abuse and Depression

All those suffering from alcohol abuse problems were experiencing long-term depression, with one exception, whose 'problems with alcohol' may have been related to short-term depression. As stated in the section of this chapter entitled 'Alcohol Abuse', some researchers link alcohol abuse with PTSD; however, there was only one case-study in which this link was evident.

Bereavement

Bereavement was recorded as a significant contributor to the suicidal ideation of eight of the case-studies. The only common accompanying contributors are as follows:

- Six of those featured in the case-studies were living with long-term depression (case-studies 1 to 6).
- Two of these individuals had previously experienced the suicide of a family member (case-studies 4 and 5).

Financial Concerns

As has been stated already, many of the individuals who were under investigation will have had financial concerns pending the outcome of their investigations. The outcome of such investigations may lead to dismissal and therefore lack of income. However, of the case-studies in which reports of specific financial concerns were reported (four in all), only three featured similar precipitators leading to suicidal ideation. These contributory precipitators were alcohol and depression.

Health Concerns of a Physical Nature

No common pattern was identified between health concerns and any other factors contributing to suicidal ideation.

Unwillingness to Accept Help

There were two links between those who were unwilling to accept support and other contributory precipitators. These precipitators were depression and partner relationships. The analysis of the contributory factors revealed that:

- The individuals featured in case-studies 1–6 were suffering from depression.
- The individuals featured in case-studies 1–4 were also experiencing difficulties in their partner relationships.
- The individuals featured in case-studies 7–8 were not suffering from depression but were experiencing difficulties in their partner relationships.

Other contributory factors leading to suicidal ideation were also seen in case-studies 2, 4, 5, 6 and 7, but there was no common pattern to these other factors.

Concluding Comments

It is clear from analysis of the research that, with the exception of one staff member, the individuals featured in the examined case-studies were serving officers or had been serving officers before their retirement, resignation or dismissal. It is also clear that in the majority of those case-studies analysed, the individuals were male and experienced suicidal ideation either at the ages of 37/38 or between the ages of 45 and 49. These officers' length of service approximately corresponded with their age; that is, the older the officer, the greater the length of service. Within the analysed case-studies, a number of officers had served between 11 and 20 years and a larger group had served between 20 and 30 years.

Attention was also drawn within the preceding analysis to the calibre of the officers concerned. The case-studies show that many of the officers were highly respected by colleagues and the community. It would furthermore appear from examination of the case-studies that the majority of the officers had considered their suicide over a period of time and that suicide was premeditated.

The analysis has further shown that there are specific key precipitators, which relate to a broad range of life contexts, including work, home relationships, health and other personal issues. It would appear from the analysis that only rarely was there a single precipitator for the suicidal ideation – although examples of such have been offered within this chapter.

The majority of the case-studies indicate that there were multiple precipitators leading to suicidal ideation; even though no strong correlation could be identified between any key contributory factors, it was possible to identify certain trends.

In the majority, but not all, of the case-studies, the individuals exhibited clear signs of depression; in some of these case-studies, anger was also an inherent characteristic. A strong link between alcohol abuse and depression was identified – all of those featured in the case-studies who suffered from alcohol-abuse problems were also experiencing some form of depression.

Of the case-studies in which internal investigations were a contributory factor, some of the younger officers were also experiencing difficulties in their partner relationships. With regard to workplace issues, a lack of communication from the respective forces was an important factor for those concerned.

The analysis suggests that in many cases, officers experiencing difficult partner and family relationships are among the most vulnerable to suicidal ideation. Also, in a number of the case-studies, individuals experiencing difficulties in their partner relationships were either unable or unwilling to accept support, including some who had engaged earlier in parasuicidal activity or had spoken of their suicidal ideation.

The analysis aims to indicate which officers might be most susceptible to suicidal ideation. Recognising the most vulnerable officers will assist in identifying appropriate intervention measures. These are examined in Chapters 8, 9 and 10 of this book.

However, before determining the appropriateness of intervention techniques, the overall research objective will be assisted by examination of the extent to which suicide is prevalent within the police service. The following chapter therefore focuses on the obtainability and accuracy of available statistics, an issue that was raised in Chapter 2 of this research study.

Following consideration of the availability of accurate statistical data, Chapters 6 and 7 offer an examination of the extent to which the case-study precipitators identified within this chapter are acknowledged in research relating to suicide within both the general and the police communities.

Notes

1 Mental Health Foundation, 'Mental health statistics: suicide', n.d, available from www.mentalhealth.org.uk/help-information/mental-health-statistics/suicide/; accessed March 13, 2014.
2 Samaritans, 'Suicide: facts and figures', n.d. available from www.samaritans.org/about-us/our-research-0/facts-and-figures-about-suicide; accessed March 13, 2014.
3 Dhani, Amardeep and Kaiza, Peter, 'Police service strength, England and Wales, 31 March 2011', *Home Office Statistical Bulletin* (July 2011), available from www.gov.

uk/government/uploads/system/uploads/attachment_data/file/115757/hosb1311.pdf; accessed March 7, 2014.

4 Samaritans, 'Suicide: facts and figures'.

5 Scowcroft, Elizabeth, 'Suicide statistics report 2013 data for 2009–2011', available from www.samaritans.org/sites/default/files/kcfinder/files/research/Samaritans%20Suicide%20 Statistics%20Report%202013.pdf; accessed March 13, 2014.

6 Having read the accounts of those suffering from long- and short-term depression, the analysis defines short-term depression as lasting a few weeks or months only and long-term depression persisting over a longer period.

7 Mourning as in sad at the separation and not as in bereavement.

8 Barron, Stephen W. (2007) *Police Officer Suicide: A Review and Examination Using a Psychological Autopsy*, October 2007, available from www.barronpsych.com.au/ research/Police%20suicide%20in%20NSW.doc; accessed February 12, 2017 (p. 8).

Bibliography

Aldridge, David (1998) *Suicide: The Tragedy of Hopefulness*. London: Jessica Kingsley.

Lee, Raymond M. (1993) *Doing Research on Sensitive Topics*. London: Sage.

Lesse, Stanley (Ed.) (1998) *What We Know about Suicidal Behavior and How to Treat It*. Northvale: Jason Aronson.

Mintz, Ronald (1998) Psychotherapy of the Depressed Suicidal Patient. In Lesse, Stanley (Ed.) *What We Know about Suicidal Behavior and How to Treat It*. Northvale: Jason Aronson, pp. 241–64.

Violanti, John M. (2007) *Police Suicide: Epidemic in Blue* (2nd edition). Springfield: Charles C. Thomas.

5 Statistics: Availability and Reliability

Introductory Comments

As Chapter 4 clearly illustrates, officer suicide is a reality in the life of the police service. However, the question of the extent to which this reality is prevalent needs to be quantified. Before further analysis of the causes of suicide is undertaken, with reference to available literature and the case-studies of the primary research, this chapter considers the extent to which officer suicide is a dilemma to be confronted.

Comment has previously been made concerning the lack of relevant statistical data (Chapter 1, sections entitled 'An Initial Hypothesis' and 'Aims and Objectives' and Chapter 2, section entitled 'Research Difficulties'). From the initial literature survey, it appears that a number of significant difficulties may exist in the procurement of accurate statistics relating to police suicides. Furthermore, it would appear that the use of the statistics that are available may be questionable. This chapter therefore examines the availability of statistical data and its reliability.

Within the first part of the following analysis, as in Chapter 2, reference is made to literature written in the USA, revealing some of the possible limitations of UK data. Following this analysis, reference is made to the statistics available within the UK. The chapter concludes by focusing on statistical difficulties that can impede research relating to officer suicide.

Statistical Data in the USA

Hidden Suicides and Misclassified Deaths

Martin Reiser draws attention to the importance of available and reliable statistical data. More than 30 years ago, Reiser attempted to identify and use statistical data to comment on the reported high number of suicides in the USA. He states: 'Rumor has been perpetuated to the effect that police officers have the highest suicide rate of any occupational group. This notion has also been extant locally, with regard to the suicide rate among Los Angeles Police Department officers' (Reiser 1982: 169).

He adds that 'several administrators have claimed no suicides over a 15-year period' but, in spite of this claim, notes that 'others report fairly high numbers' (Reiser 1982: 172). Seeking to obtain accurate statistics, he states that enquiries to police bodies, insurance companies and suicide-awareness agencies failed to reveal rates of suicide by occupation (Reiser 1982: 169).

To undertake his research, Reiser concluded he would have to rely on anecdotal comment, combined with figures from six police departments (New York City, Wyoming, Chicago, Denver, Detroit and the Los Angeles Police Department, of which he was a member). He appears to have accessed other statistics from 'five published studies [which] have offered specific data on police suicide' (Reiser 1982: 170).[1] Even though Reiser offers specific figures, these are not tabulated and are not from easily comparable time spans; he relies heavily on a comparison of figures from the New York Police Department during the period 1928–33 and figures during the period 1960–73 (Reiser 1982: 171). The figures which Reiser offers are extremely dated, but his comments bring into sharp focus the difficulty that existed some considerable years ago in obtaining accurate statistics.

It apparently remained difficult to obtain statistics in the USA 25 years after Reiser's work was published. Violanti and Martinez make similar comments to Reiser's concerning the absence of statistical data. Violanti remarks on both the apparent lack of statistics held by police departments and the hesitancy of these departments to release whatever statistics they may have. Martinez suggests:

> Suicides in police departments are kept hidden and the only time it [sic] surfaces and made aware [sic] to others is when the dead officer is known in the district he or she worked. ... The only time stories about police officers taking their own lives are on the news when [sic] it is coupled with sensationalism.
> (Martinez 2010: 2)

Both Violanti and Martinez suggest general reasons for this lack of information. Martinez writes: 'Many police departments still see police suicide as a taboo subject. This view is passed down by department leaders to all members of their agency, and it has been happening for generations. It's part of the police culture' (Martinez 2010: 2–3). Violanti writes that the culture in which officers work tends to regard suicide within the profession as ignominious, and that officers rarely speak about the subject among themselves.

Offering more specific reasons for the lack of verifiable statistics, Ramos suggests that this may be due to the misclassification of incorrectly recorded suicides. He explains that there are 'four acceptable classifications for death in the United States' (Ramos 2007: 24): natural, accidental, suicide and homicide. Suggesting that some suicides are misclassified, he explains: 'There is ... a negative stigma, financial motivations with life insurance, and religious reasons why suicides may be classified as accidents. These factors present a dilemma in researching this sensitive topic' (ibid.: 2).

He goes on to comment: 'Many can be listed as accidents. Misclassification occurs to protect the officer from the stigma of suicide, protect the family, and protect the agency from legal ramifications' (ibid.: 24).

Martinez, Violanti and Ellen Kirschman offer similar observations, commenting specifically on misclassification and financial issues. Martinez writes:

> Many police departments see suicide as a disgrace and attempt to shield victim's [sic] families from embarrassment. … As a result, police suicides can be voluntarily misclassified as either accidents or other types of deaths in order to protect the officers' reputations and the family's [sic] financial benefits.
>
> (Martinez 2010: 14)

Kirschman, meanwhile, notes: 'Many professionals assume that the statistics they have are artificially low, as cops may try to cover up a suicide out of pride and a desire to protect the surviving family from losing their insurance benefits' (Kirschman 1997: 169). Violanti writes in a similar vein and refers to the non-payment of life insurance and similar policies when the cause of the death is suicide.

Violanti and Ramos both highlight that 'misclassification, unstandardized death reports, and subjective criteria for determination' (Violanti 2007: 102) can be verified in accordance with earlier research. Ramos suggests that the claims of misclassification can be corroborated: 'This problem is easily identified by the inaccuracy of documented suicides when the Federal uniform crime reports are compared to the verified suicides documented by the National Police Suicide Foundation' (Ramos 2007: 98). Offering a recommendation with regard to correct classification, Ramos writes that 'Administrators must make it clear that misclassification of suicides is not tolerated and those who file false reports will be disciplined' (ibid.: 24) and that 'Leaders should never tolerate false reports designed to make a suicide look like an accident and should accurately report when an officer commits suicide' (ibid.: 98).

Lack of Systematic Data Collection

In 1982, Reiser suggested that even when deaths have been correctly classified, to ensure statistics are available, there should be greater reporting and more details recorded of police suicides (Reiser 1982: 172). It would appear that his suggestion was ignored. In 1997, Ellen Kirschman described how 'there is no systematic way to collect accurate data' (Kirschman 1997: 169). Ten years later, Violanti similarly commented on the unavailability of such information.

Ramos agrees with these sentiments and notes: 'Police agencies do not have a comprehensive reporting system on completed suicides, suspected suicides, and attempted suicides' (Ramos 2007: 2). To rectify this lack of information, Ramos suggests that there should be a national suicide database: 'Policy changes need to be implemented with regard to reporting suicides. There is a national database for line of duty deaths for police officers. Currently, there is no systematic way of documenting officer suicides across the country' (Ramos 2007: 24). This suggestion accords with Martinez's request that 'All police departments in the nation should be mandated to submit data on police suicides in order for a concrete preventable system to be in place' (Martinez 2010: 79).

Problems of the Risk Ratio

Even when statistics are available, Violanti questions the manner in which they are used. Fundamental to his observations is the use of risk-ratio and relative risk-ratio assessment. He describes how the ratio of one group may be set against the ratio of a second so as to determine the relative risk of one of the groups; 'the ratio of two rates is sometimes called the relative risk' (Violanti 2007: 43).

However, he warns against the danger of assessing the risk of officer suicide by comparing it with the percentage of suicides in the general population. He comments that this may result in a skewed understanding, as the number of suicides within the wider community 'includes the unemployed, institutionalized, incarcerated, and mentally ill' (ibid.: 42). He suggests that suicide numbers in groups such as these may be intrinsically high and that the number of officer suicides could therefore be expected to be lower when compared to the suicide rate in the wider community.

As referenced in Chapter 7 (section entitled 'Unemployment'), the relative risk ratio may be wrongly used within the UK if the number of officer suicides is compared to those within the general community; for example, as Violanti suggests, the suicide rate of salaried officers should be lower than the suicide rate of those who are unemployed.

Further Data Limitations

Reiser, Violanti and Ramos all refer further to a lack of recorded information, which has limited research.

Commenting on 'the dearth of hard data on police suicide' and 'the glaring differences' in the figures offered by different police departments (Reiser 1982: 172), Reiser refers to the multiplex variables associated with suicide. Because of this complexity, which is exacerbated further by different stress factors, Reiser suggests that research needs to be 'evaluated on a department-by-department basis in order to arrive at accurate notions of what the comparative suicide experience is and why' (ibid.).

While Reiser draws attention to departmental research, Violanti and Ramos comment on the dearth of data that could offer a long-term analysis of suicidal ideation. Referring to the distinction between suicide rates and suicide risk, Violanti comments that these two issues are two distinct aspects of mortality and cannot be compared with each other. He suggests that data referring to risk will be more appropriate if determining the possibility that an individual may take their own life, whereas research that refers to rates will seek to determine the frequency at which suicides may occur.

If the risk factor is to be evaluated with some precision, Violanti suggests that this can only be undertaken over a given period of time, due to the complexity of the many factors involved.

Ramos also suggests the need for long-term research. He suggests that qualitative research undertaken by psychological autopsies and interviews should be undertaken alongside qualitative research involving officers at different stages throughout their careers. He suggests that qualitative research into those who had completed suicide 'could be replicated by administering the instrument to a sample of police recruits and measuring a difference in responses later in their career. This would determine if officers become cynical later in their careers' (Ramos 2007: 99).

Statistical Data in the UK

The Office for National Statistics (ONS) makes certain data relating to officer suicide available within the UK. First published by the ONS, Table 5.1 shows the number of deaths of male and female police officers that were classified as 'suicide or undetermined'. Reference is also made in the following section to further statistical data made available in an unpublished research draft paper seen by this author and information in two police-related publications, *Federation News* and *Police Oracle*. In the section immediately following that one, comment is offered with regard to the figures offered by these two publications.

Available Statistics

Table 5.1 offers the number of deaths of male and female police officers that were classified as 'suicide or undetermined'.

Focusing on data from the ONS, an unpublished research paper seen by this author suggested that the suicide rate within the police service had remained steady over recent years and that male officers were not in an occupation that could be considered high-risk when compared to other occupations. Despite this assertion, the report commented that the proportional mortality ratio (PMR) for female police officers in the decade following 1990 revealed they could be at greater risk of suicide than those in other occupations. However, the report commented that due to the small number of female officers involved in the assessment, the PMR rate should be treated with extreme caution.

Table 5.1 Number of deaths of male and female police officers classified as suicide or undetermined intent

England and Wales	Year									
Age	2001	2002	2003	2004	2005	2006	2007	2008	2009	2010
20–24	9	6	9	0	4	8	6	9	6	11
45–74	13	9	7	8	11	12	11	15	9	12
Total	22	15	16	8	15	20	17	24	15	23

Source: ONS[2]

Comment on the Statistics Offered Above

It should be noted that the ONS' recording of numbers of deaths uses data supplied by the next of kin when registering the death. This means that the data offers no precise information regarding when and for how long the police officer served. It is possible that the next of kin, when registering the death, chose an occupation which may have been one among many in which the deceased had been employed. Equally, some next of kin may have chosen not to offer the term 'police officer' when registering the death if they did not wish the deceased to be referred to as an ex-officer; for example, if the officer had been dismissed or left the service for other personal reasons.

Having accessed the data from the ONS, the Police Federation commented that the 'rise in police officers committing suicide could become "pandemic"'.[3] This may be considered an alarmist response. The *Occupational Mortality in England and Wales* report, which examined the PMR of deaths between the years 1991 and 2000, comments that only female police officers are seen to be in an occupation which may have a higher risk of suicide than many other occupations.

When referring to the statistics offered in Table 5.1, the *Federation News* and *Police Oracle* use the phrase 'ended their lives'. This is an ambiguous use of the term, as these figures refer to deaths classified as 'suicide and undetermined intent' and refer to the age range 20–74. Difficulties are numerous here; for example, the age range is extensive and the statistics may include coronial open and narrative verdicts. Suicide cannot be assumed.

In spite of the potential limitations of these statistics, *Police Oracle* stated:

> According to the Fed, serious concerns were highlighted to its health and safety sub-committee 'that police officers were being driven to suicide by their increasing workload which was leading to high levels of stress. The increasing pressure for officers to effectively do more work with fewer resources is having a detrimental impact on their health and wellbeing'.[4]

The *Police Oracle* account provides no information to substantiate the reference to the suggestion that officers 'were being driven to suicide' by an increase in their workload.

Difficulties in Obtaining Accurate Statistics

Not all the difficulties encountered by researchers in the USA to which reference was made earlier will be relevant to the compilation of statistical data in the UK. Nevertheless, they raise certain issues relevant to this research, on which comment is made in the sub-sections that follow.

Coroners' Verdicts

Reference was made earlier to the misclassification of some suicides in the USA. The research found no evidence of deliberate misclassification of officer suicides in the UK. Although there was no evidence of deliberate misclassification, there were two case-studies in which the coronial verdict was possibly surprising. In the first, the coroner gave an open verdict; anecdotally, police colleagues were of the opinion that suicide had occurred. In the second, the coroner offered a narrative verdict despite the fact that the officer had sent 'increasingly desperate and suicidal text messages'.

In spite of the lack of evidence that intentional misclassification occurred in the case-studies, in assessing the accuracy of coronial verdicts there is still reason to be cautious when evaluating the validity of some verdicts generally. Suggestions of potential discrepancies in coroners' verdicts are supported by André Tomlin. In an article entitled 'Physical illness may be the trigger for one in ten suicides', Tomlin refers to situations which may have involved assisted suicide:

> The study also finds wide variation in how verdicts of suicide are recorded by coroners and made available to the public and policymakers. Coroners told researchers they sometimes 'turn a blind eye' when they suspect that a terminally ill person might have had help from a friend or relative in committing suicide. The study recommends that, as part of the Government's ongoing consultation on preventing suicide, they should consider making local suicide audits compulsory and that coroners' duty to share information should be formalised.[5]

It is possible that other instances of coroners' verdicts could result in misclassification. For example, researchers draw attention to potential discrepancies in suicide verdicts according to the sex of the deceased. This possible difficulty is examined in the next section.

Male and Female Verdicts

David Aldridge comments on the inconsistency of male and female suicide verdicts, specifically referring to coroners' reluctance to give a suicide verdict in female deaths. He suggests that the coroners' conclusions may reflect society's tendency to acknowledge that it is more acceptable for men to intentionally complete suicide, whereas attempts made by women 'are perceived as cries for help ... and if completed are examples of accidentally achieving death' (Aldridge 1998: 107). Aldridge continues: 'for men ... death before dishonour appears to be an acceptable description for suicide with no overtones of accident'.

By way of example, Aldridge cites the death of a police officer who fell from a bridge. His death was categorised as suicide: 'nobody suggested that it was a gesture and that he accidentally fell through his own incompetence' (Aldridge 1998: 107). Aldridge concludes that the inconstancy in verdicts 'may account for the greater rate of suicide in men in that suicide is seen as a legitimate solution to insurmountable distress' (Aldridge 1998: 107).

The ratio of recorded female to male deaths by suicide, he comments, may however change as appreciation of female role expectations grows.

The inconsistency in coronial verdicts suggests that care must be taken when using data which differentiates between the two sexes. As important as the data may be when considering different contextual causes of suicide between the two sexes, caution is required.

Suicide Risk Ratio

The unpublished research paper mentioned earlier failed to recognise the danger of using statistics to assess the risk ratio. As noted previously in this chapter, Violanti cautions against such use.

The risk ratio was seen to be high only for females in the decade following 1990 (fluctuating between 6 and 18 per 100,000 officers, with an average of 13: see earlier in this chapter, section entitled 'Available Statistics'). The risk ratio is important, but it should not be used to sustain complacency and limit the urgency of research.

Comprehensive Record-Keeping at Force Level

Reference was made previously to Martinez's comment that officer suicide is often only known about within the departments in which the officer worked. Martinez warns: 'The secrecy that continues to be part of the police culture has been an obstacle in preventing officers from committing suicide' (Martinez 2010: 2–3).

The research revealed a reluctance on the part of UK forces both to make known and to record the suicides of officers within their force.[6] Through conversations during the research, it appeared possible that this was in part because of the perceived stigma that could reflect upon the force. It appeared equally possible that forces were concerned that a verdict of suicide could have legal implications of negligence and liability.

Comprehensive Record-Keeping at National Level

Reference was made previously to Ramos' suggestion that there should be a US national database of officer suicides, as well as to comments by Kirschman and Violanti regarding the lack of a systematic classification of numerical data in the USA. It would appear that this data is also lacking in the UK. If forces were to compile relevant statistical data, this could be done at a national level and thereby offer an accurate assessment of the number of suicides at this level. This information would be invaluable for research purposes and would, for example, enable comparison of officer suicides with suicides in the general community.

Long-Term Statistical Research

In the section of this chapter entitled 'Further Data Limitations', reference is made to Violanti's and Ramos' comments regarding the lack of long-term research in the USA. They advocate that this should be undertaken so as to assist in an identification of possible risk factors. Ramos suggests that this study could be undertaken at different stages in an officer's career. Similarly, Brian Chopko, Patrick Palmieri and Vanessa Facemire comment: 'it is particularly recommended that police recruits be followed from training through their law enforcement careers' (Chopko et al. 2013: 7). No statistical data drawn from a long-term UK study of how individual officers cope with stress during their careers has been identified by this research.

Psychological Autopsies

To understand the context of suicidal ideation, Ramos suggests the need for psychological autopsies. One UK police force commissioned an independent psychologist to undertake such autopsies following a series of suicides in the force, to determine whether there were any common themes to the suicide precipitators. Psychological autopsies are therefore possible, and would appear to be the ideal method of determining underlying causes.

An undertaking of individual psychological autopsies was not within the brief of this research, but such autopsies are suggested in Chapter 11, which offers recommendations for future work.

Concluding Comments

Although in-depth research into officer suicides has taken place over many years in the USA, the suggestion has been made within this chapter that statistical evidence to support this research is nevertheless lacking. It has been further suggested that the some officer suicides in the USA are misclassified and are therefore not recognised in the statistics that are available. While the lack of verifiable data in the US research means it is incomplete, the research offers a significant contribution to the overall understanding of officer suicide and demonstrates the importance of the availability of accurate statistical data.

Some statistical data on officer suicides is available in the UK but, as the analysis has shown, this is limited. Questions of validity have also been raised with regard to some coronial verdicts. Any discrepancy could potentially affect statistics that might be presented.

Further statistical difficulties that impede research have also been identified. These difficulties include the lack of data drawing on long-term research monitoring officers throughout their careers. Such data would be invaluable. Reference has also been made to the risk ratio and how this can be misused to minimise the significance of officer suicides.

Much of the analysis offered throughout this book depends on qualitative research. Quantitative data would offer additional insight. It is regrettable that such data is not compiled and available within the UK. Bearing in mind the absence of statistical data, suggestions are made in Chapter 11 as to how this shortcoming may be remedied.

Having offered an examination of data and literature that seeks to determine the extent to which officer suicide is prevalent, the following two chapters examine suicide precipitators in detail. Chapter 6 offers an examination of the major precipitators, while Chapter 7 offers an analysis of the primary research as it relates to the literature survey.

Notes

1 Reiser does not make it clear to which studies he is referring, but it would appear that they include: Friedman, P. (1968) Suicide among Police: A Study of Ninety-Three Suicides among New York City Policemen 1934–1940. In Shneidman, E. (Ed.) *Essays in Self-Destruction*. New York: Science House, pp. 414–49; Nelson, Z. and Smith, W. (1970) The Law Enforcement Profession: An Incident of High Suicide, *Omega*, November, 293–9; Heiman, M. (1975) The Police Suicide, *Journal of Police Science and Administration*, Vol. 3, No. 3, 267–73; Heiman, M. (1975) Police Suicides Revisited, *Suicide*, Vol. 5, No. 1, 5–20; Danto, B.L. (1976) *Police Suicide*. Paper presented to the American Association of Suicidology, Los Angeles, 1976.
2 www.ons.gov.uk/ons/search/index.html?newquery=Police+suicides; accessed January 13, 2013. Contains public sector information licensed under the Open Government Licence v3.0.
3 *Federation News*, November 2012, available from www.nypolfed.org.uk/assets/uploads/PDFs/Federation_Express_1112.pdf; accessed February 12, 2017.
4 Martis, Royston, *Police Oracle*, 'In figures, the forgotten police suicides', November 8, 2012, available from www.policeoracle.com/news/Comment/2012/Nov/08/Comment-In-Figures,-The-Forgotten-Police-Suicides_57812.html; accessed 17 November 2012.
5 Tomlin, André, 'Physical illness may be the trigger for one in ten suicides", *The Mental Elf*, August 24, 2011, available from www.thementalelf.net/mental-health-conditions/suicide/physical-illness-may-be-the-trigger-for-one-in-ten-suicides/; accessed April 1, 2013.
6 There are 43 different geographical forces within England and Wales.

Bibliography

Aldridge, David (1998) *Suicide: The Tragedy of Hopefulness*. London: Jessica Kingsley.

Chopko, Brian A., Palmieri, Patrick A. and Facemire, Vanessa C. (2013) Prevalence and Predictors of Suicidal Ideation among US Law Enforcement Officers, *Journal of Police and Criminal Psychology*, Vol. 29, No. 1, 1–9.

Coggon, David, Harris, E. Clare, Brown, T., Rice, Simon and Palmer, Keith T. (2009) *Occupational Mortality in England and Wales*. Luton: Office for National Statistics.

Kirschman, Ellen (1997) *I Love a Cop*. New York: Guilford Press.

Martinez, Louis Enrique (2010) *The Secret Deaths: Police Officer's Testimonial Views on Police Suicides and Why Suicides Continue to be Hidden in Police Departments*. Denver: Outskirts Press.

Ramos, Orlando (2007) *A Leadership Perspective for Understanding Police Suicide: An Analysis Based on the Suicide Attitude Questionnaire*. Boca Raton: Dissertation.com.

Reiser, Martin (1982) *Police Psychology: Collected Papers*. Los Angeles: LEHI.

Violanti, John M. (2007) *Police Suicide: Epidemic in Blue* (2nd edition). Springfield: Charles C. Thomas.

6 Suicide Precipitators

Introduction

With the previous chapter having offered an examination of the availability and reliability of statistics relating to officer suicides, this one returns to an analysis of suicide precipitators. Attention was drawn to officer-specific suicide precipitators in Chapter 2. These precipitators were identified primarily by US researchers. In addition to these examples, tangible precipitators, specified within the analysis of the case-studies, were identified in Chapter 4. The current chapter offers an extended and more detailed examination of the suicide precipitators first introduced in Chapter 2, and refers to precipitators suggested by the research of others.

First, the general causes of suicide are explored, followed by further analysis of police-specific precipitators. As well as offering an appreciation of general suicide precipitators to which officers are vulnerable, the analysis within this chapter teases out and examines additional precipitators which are specific to those who work in the police service.

The analysis in this chapter provides a foundation for the analysis in Chapter 7, in which the contextual reality of the case-studies (as identified in Chapter 4) is measured against the identified theories of suicide.

Contextual Factors Leading to Suicidal Ideation in the General Population

Introductory Comments

Referring to suicide and how 'the tragedy of hopelessness may be located within the individual', Aldridge suggests this tragedy may be traced 'through the landscape of personal relationships, family ties and medical treatment where hope is lost' (Aldridge 1998: back cover). Many clinicians have written a wealth of material about the landscape to which Aldridge refers. The examination that follows does not intend to offer a clinical psychological exposition of this suicide landscape, but rather to examine some of the potential precipitators that may lead to suicide and suicidal ideation.

Dalton and Noble offer medical students reasons why people may self-harm. These include:

- to die
- to escape from unbearable anguish
- to get relief
- to change the behaviour of others
- to escape from a situation
- to show desperation to others
- to get back at other people/make them feel guilty
- to get help.

(Dalton and Noble 2006: 171)

The definition of self-harm is broader than that of taking one's own life. However, Dalton and Noble's description of some of the reasons for self-harm equally offers an introduction to some of the possible intentions that may also underlie suicidal ideation.

Psychologist Ronald Mintz, specifically referring to suicide, demonstrates the different factors that may be involved in suicidal ideation. He expands on the apocryphal vignette offered in Chapter 4 (section entitled 'Premeditated or Impulsive') to reveal how suicide is irrational, ambivalent and episodic in terms of the length of time for which the ideation may last. He suggests that the ideation may be irrational in that the suicidal person may have 'no recognition whatsoever that if he dies he will be permanently dead', ambivalent in that the suicidal person may be inconsistent as to his intentions and episodic in that the thoughts may recur but 'each instance is time-limited' (Mintz 1998: 244).

Mintz also refers to the *symptomatic nature* of suicide as a response to 'widely differing emotions'. Defining this response as the *motivation* for suicide, Mintz explains: 'There is no one single motivation of all or most suicidal impulses. Research workers who have studied this question have enumerated about a dozen recurring motivations which clinically often appear in combination' (Mintz 1998: 243).

Mintz continues by offering an extensive list of these motivations. However, he also states that what he describes as a suicidal attempt is not a necessarily a quest for self-destruction. Explaining this alternative possibility, he defines it as the *adaptational function* and suggests:

> The suicide attempt usually represents an effort, however misguided, on the part of a desperately unhappy human being to solve a current, intolerable, personal human problem of living, by bringing some intensely desired change in the external world or in the internal (psychic) world.
>
> (Mintz 1998: 245)

Harry Olin, a psychiatric hospital director, puts forward a similar hypothesis in his essay entitled 'The Third Wish'. When referring to the non-psychotic patient in the pre-suicidal state, Olin explains: 'The consequences of the planned suicide are distorted and minimized. Suicide then becomes a means of dying without terminal death' (Olin 1998: 78). Similarly, Karolynn Siegel, citing Maris (1982), writes: 'paradoxically much suicide is not the wish-to-die, but rather the wish-to-live in some way that is blocked' (Siegel 1998: 98).

General Factors and Mnemonics

Drawing on their medical backgrounds, Dalton and Noble offer specific indicators of those at high suicidal risk and, as also described in Chapter 2, suggest that these indicators may be remembered by the mnemonic SAD PERSON:

- Sex: male > female
- Age: more likely in older people
- Divorced or separated
- Physical illness, especially long-term poor health
- Employment: higher risk in unemployed
- Recurrent attempts
- Socially isolated, living alone
- Other mental illnesses, i.e. depression, alcoholism, schizophrenia
- Note left, to explain the reasons for suicide.

(Dalton and Noble 2006: 172)

MedicineNet.com offers slightly different meanings for (almost) the same acronym, suggesting that SAD PERSONS stands for:

- Sex (male)
- Age younger than 19 or older than 45 years of age
- Depression (severe enough to be considered clinically significant)
- Previous suicide attempt or received mental-health services of any kind
- Excessive alcohol or other drug use
- Rational thinking lost
- Separated, divorced, or widowed (or other ending of significant relationship)
- Organized suicide plan or serious attempt
- No or little social support
- Sickness or chronic medical illness.[1]

As is shown, the sources of both acronyms agree that at greatest risk are: males in specific age groups; those who are divorced or separated; the isolated; those who have sought suicide previously; those suffering from a physical sickness; those who are abusing substances; and the depressed.

In an internet article entitled 'Suicide', Roxanne Dryden-Edwards refers to other risk factors, which include 'single marital status, unemployment, low income, mental illness, a history of being physically or sexually abused, a personal history of suicidal thoughts, threats or behaviors, or a family history of attempting suicide'.[2] The significance of these general precipitators to officer-specific suicides remains to be examined and an analysis of the related relevance of these factors is offered in Chapter 7.

Consideration is now given to potential suicide precipitators as identified by different researchers. The examination that follows is offered in alphabetical order, primarily to avoid suggesting that any of the given precipitators necessarily has any greater significance than another.

Alcohol and Substance Abuse

All of the researchers to whom reference has already been made offer substance abuse, whether involving alcohol or other substances, as a possible contributory factor leading to suicide. Dalton and Noble (2006: 172) describe 'other mental illnesses, i.e. depression, alcoholism, schizophrenia' and Dryden-Edwards and Stoppler refer to 'excessive alcohol or other drug use'.

Kirschman comments that 'people who abuse drugs or alcohol are at risk for many forms of self-destructive behavior, suicide being the most serious' (Kirschman 1997: 172). She expands on this comment by stating: 'some studies predict that fifteen percent of all alcoholics will commit active suicide during their lifetimes' (ibid).

Bereavement

A UK suicide prevention and support group offers the following statement:

> When someone close to you dies, it can totally devastate you. You might not be prepared for the intense feelings you have about the way your world has been turned upside down. Sometimes this can make people wish they too were dead, [because] their world without that person is now too scary, lonely or strange to carry on. They might also think that dying will let them join the person who has died.[3]

The article continues: 'this is a common reaction, and for most people this feeling fades over time.' For some, however, this pain does not fade. Joining the one who has died may appear a welcome alternative to life. This alternative is included by Mintz when he suggests that suicide precipitators include 'rebirth fantasies, including fantasies of reincarnation or of heaven … efforts to rejoin or merge with a dead or lost loved one' (Mintz 1998: 243).

Community Contagion

Not only would it appear that suicidal activity can recur within families, but there are also examples of communities in which suicide has occurred with a given frequency. For example, in an article about the Bridgend suicides, Anne Driscoll and Alex Tresniowski write about 'the feeling each hanging somehow triggered the next – an unstoppable contagion' and how 'some believe[d] the wave of hangings ha[d] made other young people in Bridgend feel hopeless and drawn to a dark and seemingly popular alternative'.[4]

Following the spate of suicides in Bridgend, Carole Cadwalladr wrote an article for the *Observer* entitled 'How Bridgend was damned by distortion'.[5] She referred to research undertaken by sociologist David Phillips, who used the term 'the Werther effect'.[6] Phillips undertook research into the connection between mass media and suicide and suggested that the media can cause suicides to become contagious in a community. Cadwalladr suggested that something similar was taking place in Bridgend. Drawing parallels with earlier research, Cadwalladr wrote:

> In 1998, for example, researchers Etzersdorfer and Sonneck found that after guidelines were introduced to make the reporting of suicides in Vienna's underground less sensational, the number of deaths dropped by 80 per cent. And in 1995 Riaz Hassan in Australia found a 'statistically significant' increase in the number of suicides after prominent newspaper stories. Summing up the evidence in an article for the BMJ in 2002, Professor Keith Hawton, head of the Oxford Centre for Suicide Research, the leading UK institution and probably the world's greatest authority on suicide and the media, describes the evidence for a link between the two as 'overwhelming'.

Cadwalladr also quotes Darren Matthews of the Samaritans, who explains this theory of contagion as being 'as if permission has somehow been given'.

Reference is made to the theory that suicide can become 'contagious' in Chapter 7, when further analysis of the research findings is examined (and also later in this chapter). The theory of contagion would seem particularly relevant to this research, and therefore is now explored in further detail.

Malcolm Gladwell explains the contagion theory at length in his book *The Tipping Point*, which offers an examination of 'fashion trends, the ebb and flow of crime waves ... the mysterious changes that mark everyday life ... [and how] to think of them as epidemics' (Gladwell 2000: 7). He suggests that 'ideas and products and messages and behaviors spread just like viruses do' (ibid.).

Gladwell refers to a long sequence of suicides completed by young males in Micronesia. He explains that suicide in Micronesia was unknown in the 1960s, but by the 1980s, with 160 suicides per 100,000 people, Micronesia had the highest suicide rate in the world. Gladwell further claims that the suicides were for relatively trivial reasons – for example, incidents that would normally be considered elsewhere as minor disappointments. Through the Micronesian experience, Gladwell seeks to show that death by suicide, in certain situations, can become contagious. He comments that 'the idea has fed upon itself ... so that the unthinkable has somehow been rendered thinkable' (Gladwell 2000: 218).

Like Cadwalladr, Gladwell cites American sociologist David Phillips in support of his hypothesis. Phillips' research, Gladwell suggests, claims that following newspaper reports of suicide, 'suicides in the area served by the newspaper jumped. ... In the case of national stories, the rate jumped nationally' (Gladwell 2000: 222). Gladwell also cites Phillips' assertion that following Marilyn

Monroe's death, there was 'a temporary 12 percent increase in the national suicide rate' (Gladwell 2000: 222). Gladwell suggests that the way in which suicide
was completed was also reflected by the suicide means.

Gladwell makes considerable reference to Phillips and comments that 'the
decision by someone famous to take his or her own life has the same effect: it
gives other people, particularly those vulnerable to suggestion, because of imma-
turity or mental illness, permission to engage in a deviant act as well' (Gladwell
2000: 223). Quoting Phillips, Gladwell writes: 'suicide stories are a kind of natural advertisement for a particular response to your problems' (Gladwell 2000:
223). He suggests that following a suicide, others are given permission to follow.
Commenting further, Gladwell writes:

> The 'permission' given by an initial act of suicide, in other words, isn't a gen-
> eral invitation to the vulnerable. It is really a highly detailed set of instruc-
> tions, specific to certain people in certain situations who choose to die in
> certain ways. It's not a gesture. It's speech.
>
> (Gladwell 2000: 224–5)

The Samaritans also refer to this contagion, which they describe as 'copy-cat'
suicide.[7]

Depression

Discussing suicide generally, as opposed to police-specific suicides, Violanti
(2007) makes reference to those who display psychological problems and comments that people suffering with depression are at the greatest risk of taking
their own lives. He contrasts those who are at high risk with those who are
at the least risk, that is, those who have physiological illnesses, which may be
stress-related.

As previously stated, Dalton and Noble include depression as a mental illness, along with alcoholism and schizophrenia (Dalton and Noble 2006: 172),
while Dryden-Edwards and Stoppler refer to 'depression (severe enough to be
considered clinically significant)'.[8] Kirschman refers to what she terms as 'serious
depression' and comments:

> Depressed people may be inwardly punitive, filled with guilt, shame, and
> self-hatred. It is almost as though they have a double life – they appear
> adjusted and successful, but they secretly feel like impostors. The strain of
> covering up or the fear of exposing their inadequacies can precipitate a sui-
> cide attempt.
>
> (Kirschman 1997: 171)

In his essay entitled 'The Prediction of Suicide', George Murphy, the director of
an outpatient psychiatric department, comments on the depression that results in
suicidal behaviour. He states: 'granted that not every depressed patient is suicidal,

a majority have thought of suicide' (Murphy 1998: 55). He explains that suicidal ideation does not come as a sudden realisation, but rather 'Develops, evolves, waxes and wanes. When the depression is substantially relieved the thought of suicide goes underground, not to return until depression returns' (ibid.).

Family History

Commenting on those at greatest risk of suicide, Dryden-Edwards and Stoppler refer to people with 'a family history of attempting suicide'.[9] This is further explored in an article entitled 'Suicide risk runs in families'[10] which states that 'a person is more likely to complete suicide if a family member has taken his or her own life' and that 'those with a family history of suicide were two and a half times more likely to take their own life than were those without such a history'. The article explains how research has shown that 'suicidal behavior in part might be genetically transmitted'. Reference is made to Lanny Berman, executive director of the American Association of Suicidology, who comments: 'with regard to family history of suicide, the pathway may be genetic, biochemical, and/or psychological.' However, the article appears to conclude that further research is required to explore the different theories.

Physical Illness

Physical illness is given as a reason for suicidal ideation by Dalton and Noble (2006: 172), who refer to 'especially long-term poor health'. Meanwhile, Dryden-Edwards and Stoppler highlight 'sickness or chronic medical illness'[11] and the Samaritans refer to 'painful and/or disabling physical illness'.[12]

In an article entitled 'Physical illness may be the trigger for one in ten suicides', *The Mental Elf* reports that the think-tank Demos, in an exploration of the relationship between chronic and terminal illness and suicide, found its research suggested 'that many of the patients studied chose to commit suicide rather than face more severe pain later on in their disease'.[13]

Previous Suicidal Ideation, Parasuicidal Activity or Threats

It would appear that most researchers and writers on suicidal ideation concur with Kirschman's comment that 'it is a myth that people who threaten or attempt suicide will not actually do it' (Kirschman 1997: 173). Violanti explains that each thought of suicide, each plan and each 'attempt' increases the likelihood of suicide being successfully completed, while Mintz states that 'the results of recent studies repeatedly confirm the fact that most persons making suicide attempts communicate their intention to one or several persons in their social environment prior to the actual suicide attempt' (Mintz 1998: 244). Dalton and Noble also suggest that there is a higher risk of suicide among those who have engaged in previous suicidal activity and who may have written letters to explain the cause underlying their action (Dalton and Noble 2006: 172).

Significant Loss – Actual or Threatened

Kirschman refers to the motivation of loss as a suicide precipitator. Such loss may be actual or threatened and, as she explains:

> We will all suffer losses in our lives: loss of friends, family, health, pride, looks, love, confidence, money, work, reputation, dreams, and so on. Everyone copes differently with loss, and every loss is different. Some losses mount up or happen in a series.
>
> (Kirschman 1997: 172)

An example of Kirschman's comment that one loss may be followed by further losses is the way in which an officer facing disciplinary action may also face dismissal and the loss of home and family.

Social Isolation, Divorce or Separation

When referring to the support resources available to people who are vulnerable to suicide, Violanti suggests that those who are socially isolated from family and friends are at greater risk of suicidal ideation than those who belong to a strong social network. Dalton and Noble similarly list those who are socially isolated and those who are living alone as being among the most vulnerable to suicidal ideation. In addition, they refer to those who are divorced or separated (Dalton and Noble 2006: 172).

Dryden-Edwards and Stoppler also focus on those with 'no or little social support' and 'the separated, divorced, or widowed (or other ending of significant relationship)'. Within the same article, the authors furthermore refer to those who are vulnerable following the 'breakup of a romantic relationship'.[14]

Stress

Violanti refers to stress as a contributor to suicidal ideation. The stress factors he describes include both everyday issues and the more significant of life's difficulties. He states further that the possibility of suicide increases with the frequency and number of stressful incidents which may be encountered.

Psychiatrists Eduardo J. Aguilar, Samuel G. Siris and Enrique Baca-García offer a psychological insight into the close relationship between stress and suicidal behaviour:

> Suicide and stress are intimately related. The stress-diathesis model is today the best framework to start to understand the complex mechanisms interacting throughout this relationship. The serotonin and stress systems are also closely related and, together with genetic mechanisms, constitute key biological underpinnings of suicide. Environmental factors interact with these gene and biochemical mechanisms in a lifelong process that may end up in suicidal ideation and behaviour.[15]

Unemployment

Dalton and Noble (2006: 172) and Dryden-Edwards and Stoppler all note that unemployed people are at greater risk than those in employment. Similarly, an article on the Samaritans' website, entitled 'Men and suicide', states that research into a target group of men aged between 25 and 55 (whom the Samaritans identified as the most vulnerable in the UK) found that men from 'poorer backgrounds, those who are unemployed' and the 'long-term depressed due to extended periods of unemployment'[16] were among those who were at higher risk of suicide.

Having examined some of the key suicide precipitators that affect those in society generally, specific police-suicide precipitators are now considered.

Contextual Factors Leading to Police-Specific Suicidal Ideation

Introduction

Chapter 5 of this book examined the difficulty of collecting verifiable statistical data and it is not intended to re-examine this difficulty again. Nevertheless, focusing on this issue once more is helpful in order to understand the context of determining officer-specific suicides as they relate to the broader picture of suicides in the general community.

With reference to officers in the USA, Violanti comments that not all research suggests working as a police officer places an individual at a higher risk of suicide than those within the general population. Forensic psychologist Stephen W. Barron would appear to agree with this view. Nevertheless, in his research, which related to Australia, he referred to research by an Australian researcher named Cantor and other Australian researchers who comment that the police suicide rate was similar to that in the general community. This rate, Barron suggests, is about 20 per 100,000 people.[17] However, Violanti appears to suggest that according to the research presented by Ivanoff in *Police Suicide* (1994), different statistics may conflict with and contradict Barron's assertion.

The American researcher John F. Reintzell suggests:

> Depending on which expert you read, police work is or is not a highly stressed profession, staggering under epic rates of suicide, alcoholism, divorce, and a wide range of psychosomatic disorders[,] or it is merely one of many highly stressed occupations and not very high on the list at that.
>
> (Reintzell 1990: 17)

Whether or not the suicide rate is greater among police officers than in the general community, this research posits that there are specific police-contextual factors that work to the detriment of those within the police community. It is with this understanding that Kirschman asks the all-pervading question:

> How does a person who was once hardy enough to pass a demanding application process, a rigorous psychological screening, and an arduous training

program, become so overwhelmed that suicide is his only out? How does a professional problem solver get so low that suicide seems to be the best solution to her problems?

(Kirschman 1997: 169)

In similar vein, Reintzell asks his readers to consider response officers on a shift pattern that interrupts the sleep routine and asks:

Are his judgment and abilities impaired to the extent that he constitutes a threat to the citizens he serves? Have these effects, for years, contributed to accident-frequency rates? Are they somehow contributing to medical-leave usage, alcohol abuse, marital separations and divorce rates? Are they a factor in apprehension and clearance rates? Or do they contribute to a suicide rate among police officers higher than most other occupations?

(Reintzell 1990: 15)

Barron offers further similar comments and suggests that the officers who experienced suicidal ideation had been:

Usually fit, had undergone some structured screening for mental illness and problematic behaviours which may hinder their performance … these officers usually worked with other colleagues, closely and usually had supportive peer relationships, they were also employed by an organisation with well developed human resource systems.[18]

However, Barron suggests, 'Somehow, the system failed these officers' and 'their colleagues failed to recognise and report a growing range of problematic behaviours, such as deteriorating personal relationships, increased alcohol abuse and problematic behaviour and performance in the workplace'.[19]

Violanti writes about assessing the impact of the police officer's role and context in relation to suicide. He suggests that even though there may be no proven direct link, the work and the ensuing lifestyle pressures on the officer give significant cause for concern.

While it would seem difficult to separate the police-specific contributory factors to suicidal ideation, it would appear that within police work there are specific contributory causes to suicide. Primarily, it is researchers in the USA who have examined specific factors. Violanti refers to Ivanoff's *Police Suicide* (1994), which examined New York officers' perceptions of suicidal ideation, and reports that Ivanoff ranked the possible reasons for officer suicide, in descending order, as follows:

- Depression
- Relationship conflicts or losses
- Access to firearms
- Drug/alcohol abuse
- Financial difficulties

- Involvement in corruption investigations
- Difficulty with police organization.

(Violanti 2007: 157)

Barron appears to refer to the same research by Ivanoff and offers the same list of possible causes, but substitutes 'Difficulty with police organization' with 'Organisational issues such as corruption and management decisions'. Barron also refers to research undertaken by others and writes that 'shift work and the resultant loss of family time and family disruption, ineffective communication and lack of support from administration as being areas which contributed to the range of individual factors in suicide'.[20]

Martinez offers a slightly different list of 'signs and factors that law enforcement officials should look for when trying to identify officers who might be potentially at risk for committing suicide' (Martinez 2010: 64). The list he offers has been taken from National Police Suicide Foundation papers:

- Excessive use of alcohol
- Break up of a relationship or marriage
- Stagnated careers
- An officer under investigation
- Rise in officer's complaints
- The officer writes a will
- A change in personality
- Starts giving away prized possessions.

(Martinez 2010: 65)

It would appear that there are many potential causes; as Kirschman comments, 'there are likely as many reasons and combinations of reasons as there are officers who kill themselves' (Kirschman 1997: 169). In the analysis that follows, the intention is to examine some of these many potential causes. Much of this analysis relies primarily on research work undertaken in the USA, as this is where, as previously stated, the greatest amount of research and analysis has been undertaken.

Accumulative Factors

As will be demonstrated by the qualitative research undertaken in this exploration of police suicides (see Chapter 7), there is rarely a single cause that leads to suicide. The literature researched agrees with this premise. As Violanti comments, 'suicide can result not from a single major crisis but from the accumulation of apparently minor life events' (Violanti 2007: 158).

Barron appears to affirm the suggestion that suicide may be due to an accumulation of factors, stating, with reference to research work undertaken by Hawton in 1987:

Factors which were identified in their study included: alcohol problems (found in more than 50% of cases), psychiatric symptoms, domestic problems, associated physical injuries/illnesses, and police disciplinary issues were represented in the majority of the suicides examined. Overall, their results were consistent with similar findings in general community suicide studies.[21]

Chae and Boyle are clearer than Barron in stating their understanding of what they refer to as the 'cumulative interaction' of suicide precipitators. They write that 'Prominent themes in the risk category include: organizational stress, health problems linked to shift work/sleep restriction, traumatic stress symptoms, problems with interpersonal relationships, alcohol use as a maladaptive coping method, and the cumulative interaction of these variables' and explain further the importance of accumulated factors as opposed to any one single precipitator; it is the intensity of several precipitators, they suggest, that raise the possibility of suicidal ideation (Chae and Boyle 2013: 108–9).

With the understanding that there will often be a number of combined contributory causes of officer suicide, as well as various complex contextual factors, an examination now follows of specific factors which may be part of the causal web. As causes of suicide in the general community were examined in alphabetical order, so are the police-specific factors. This, again, is to avoid offering a mistaken assumption that any one factor may have a greater effect than another.

Alcohol and Substance Abuse

With regard to alcohol abuse, Louis Martinez writes, citing the National Vital Statistic Reports of 2004, that 'There is a relationship between alcoholism and suicide. The risk of suicide in alcoholics is fifty to seventy percent higher than the general population' (Martinez 2010: 80). Alcohol and substance abuse may not be among the direct causes of suicide, but certainly such abuse is a symptom of the stress under which suicidal officers may be working and which, at times, is closely associated with those who take their own lives.

Referring to alcohol abuse, police officers and the causes of suicide, Violanti comments that alcohol abuse is deemed to be problematic for some officers. Similarly, referring to 1989 work carried out by the researchers West and West, Terry Beehr, Leanor Johnson and Ronnie Nieva comment that 'drinking seems to be part of the macho culture of police and has been nominated as a behavioral symptom of police stress' (Beehr et al. 1995: 11).

Violanti offers a further explanation, suggesting that officers may use alcohol after a traumatic event and when experiencing PTSD; such usage may, he believes, curb the effects of endorphin withdrawal (Violanti 2007: 64). By way of offering an example of a negative coping mechanism, Chae and Boyle similarly comment that officers may engage in alcohol abuse to overcome workplace anxieties (Chae and Boyle 2013: 108). Further reference is made to alcohol and PTSD later in this chapter.

Availability of the Means

Chicago police officer Louis Martinez writes: 'Whether having access to a weapon increases the risk of suicide still needs more research. The Officers I interviewed both agreed and disagreed with the accessibility of a gun being detrimental to the police officer committing suicide' (Martinez 2010: 46).

Despite this inconclusive statement, Martinez appears to think that access to the means is a significant factor in suicide completion. He cites Paul Quinnett,[22] who states: 'I think the ease of gun access to be a major contributing factor' (Martinez 2010: 47). Martinez continues by referring to seven further police-suicide researchers, six of whom suggest that access to guns increases the risk of officer suicides.

A clear majority of researchers in the USA, and Barron (2007) in New South Wales, appear to suggest that access to firearms proactively contributes to the deaths of those who wish to take their own lives; for example, Beehr et al. comment that 'the likely existence of a handy means for suicide (officers' service revolvers, if not their own weapons in addition) make[s] suicide especially easy to implement' (Beehr et al. 1995: 11).

Violanti and Barron both refer to Ivanoff's 1994 research and rate access to firearms high on the list of the possible causes of officer suicide. Barron makes several references to such access throughout his report and Violanti clearly states that it is one of the relevant factors underlying officer suicides.

Community Contagion

Reference was made earlier in this chapter to the theory of 'copy-cat' suicides. Gladwell, referring to a string of suicides, used Phillips' analogy of pedestrians crossing on a red light:

> When I'm waiting at a traffic light and the light is red, sometimes I wonder whether I should cross and jaywalk … then somebody else does it and so I do too. It's a kind of imitation. I'm getting permission to act from someone else who is engaging in a deviant act.
>
> (Gladwell 2000: 223)

No literature was identified by this research that referred to the suicide of one officer leading to the suicide of another as a copy-cat action. However, later in this study, analysis of the research suggests that within one police force, at least, the suicide of officers 'gave others permission' to take the same action; it is for this reason that this theory is re-stated here.

Control Mechanism

Violanti states:

> Suicide may be an attempt of police officers to restore feelings of strength, courage, and mastery over the environment after exposure to a traumatic incident. Such deaths may be prompted by a perceived loss of coping abilities, and a feeling of vulnerability not experienced prior to the incident.
>
> (Violanti 2007: 24)

Violanti explains this opinion by suggesting that some officers will discover their coping mechanisms are stretched to the limit by the stresses they encounter, while others may not have the resources to cope either emotionally or mentally.

Violanti further explains that a precipitant of suicide may be a desire on behalf of the officer to exert authority over a situation. He cites McCafferty et al. (1992), who describe how suicide offers control when other such avenues are denied (Violanti 2007: 55). Violanti emphasises this point later by repeating himself and suggesting that other researchers have made the same observations relating to suicide as a control mechanism.

Criminal or Internal Investigation

The researchers to whom reference has been made comment widely on the vulnerability to suicide of officers under criminal or internal investigations. For example, Miller comments:

> Officers who are under criminal or administrative investigation, especially if this represents the culmination of an otherwise shameful episode in the officer's career, may fear the loss of status and identity of the police role and, for some emotionally-invested officers, this may be too much to bear.
>
> (Miller 2006: 188)

In their respective lists of suicide precipitators, Violanti includes 'involvement in corruption investigations' (2007: 157) and Martinez refers to 'an officer under investigation' (Martinez 2010: 65).

Violanti suggests some of the underlying pressures on officers facing allegations. These include censorial disciplinary procedures, which are perceived to be biased against the officer. Martinez, by way of expanding on investigations that act as a catalyst to suicidal ideation, refers to a common complaint made by the officers with whom he has spoken: 'They are unappreciated and that they always have to be on their guard, not from the criminal element, but from the department officials who are always ready to punish instead of reward' (Martinez 2010: 32). Barron comments on the length of time investigations take, writing that the difficulties officers face as a result are 'compounded ... by protracted and time consuming investigations'.[23]

Death Fantasy

Kirschman comments on officers who may have what she refers to as 'a death fantasy':

> Cops who are extreme risk takers may be hoping to die in a 'blaze of glory' or cover up their suicide so that it looks job-related. Unfortunately, some of these officers are praised for their bravery when they should be counseled

about their intentions ... A lot of suicidal cops, particularly angry ones, have [a] kind of death fantasy.

(Kirschman 1997: 174)

Violanti also refers to the possibility of officers deliberately placing themselves in situations in which their safety will be severely compromised. He includes examples whereby officers may put themselves in confrontational situations or take risks that endanger their lives.

Denial of Help

Martinez states that 'troubled officers want to be rescued, but do not want to ask for assistance or [know] what specific help to request' (Martinez 2010: 80). Similarly, with reference to Ivanoff's 1994 research, Violanti comments that many officers appeared unwilling to look for support from either colleagues or other sources.

Violanti later re-asserts this view, commenting that traditionally, and invariably, police officers will hold back and avoid asking for help, regardless of their situation. He explains that there may be a number of reasons to explain this lack of action on the part of the officer. This behaviour may, in part, be due to the officer wishing to be seen as a 'tough guy': someone who is invulnerable and the one who resolves other people's difficulties. Martinez comments on officers' disinclination to seek assistance from programmes designed to prevent suicide, noting that they are 'usually private people' and that 'many have macho man syndrome and are not open for discussion when it comes to their private lives' (Martinez 2010: 68).

Depression

Violanti ranks depression, as stated earlier and with reference to Ivanoff (1994), as the greatest officer-suicide precipitator. Ramos refers to depression in officers and comments that loss of control is an important factor in officers' depression. Offering other examples of loss, Ramos suggests the loss of a loved one, the loss of control within work issues and the loss of police identity. He explains that these losses can create 'anger, frustration, and depression for police officers' (Ramos 2007: 19).

Violanti also perceives the loss of control as an important factor leading to depression. Furthermore, he suggests that the different stresses experienced by officers will leave some vulnerable to the effects of psychological draining and comments that 'incidents such as witnessing death, encountering abused children, and street combat weigh heavily as precipitants to depression, alcohol use, and suicide' (Violanti 2007: 43). Referring to response-officer work, he cites previous research which reveals a connection between depression and the long-lasting consequences of trauma and experiences of dangerous situations.

Depression may also be associated with other precipitators discussed in this chapter, such as alcohol abuse, PTSD and stress.

Dichotomised Decision-Making

Referring to the psychological vulnerability of officers, Ramos comments on decision-making processes:

> Officers take control of their emotions, actions, dangerous situations, and become the consummate problem solvers. A career filled with solving others' problems leaves an officer hopeless when they feel they cannot resolve their own.
>
> (Ramos 2007: 19)

Violanti also suggests that officers may tackle their personal problems in the same way that they approach their work-related situations. He refers to this trait as 'dichotomised decision making' (Violanti 2007: 13). He explains that officers can come to regard work-related situations in terms of good or bad, right or wrong, black or white, with no 'grey' area in between. This work-orientated philosophy is one which officers may then apply to themselves and situations in their own lives, leaving little room for compromise. He suggests that this style of problem-solving is not helpful, as the officer contemplating suicide is unable to identify other choices of action.

Possibly parallel to what Violanti refers to as dichotomised decision-making, Martinez and Beehr et al. refer to action-orientated officers and problem-focused activities. Martinez comments:

> Many individuals that seek police careers have a personality that is necessary to a successful career in law enforcement. This 'action-oriented' personality is important for dealing with traumatic situations. However, this personality can also be a liability for the individual because recent suicide theories indicate that people with 'action-oriented' personalities are more likely than others to act upon their suicidal thoughts.
>
> (Martinez 2010: 62)

Beehr et al. note, meanwhile, that 'Suicide thoughts were assessed for police … and they were apparently affected by the officers' emotion-focused coping activities … and perhaps also by the problem-focused activities' (Beehr et al. 1995: 15).

Financial Difficulties

Even though financial difficulty is described as a key suicide precipitator by Kirschman, Violanti and Ramos, little, if any, further discussion can be found directly relating to this precipitator. This is unfortunate, as such comment would elucidate some of the contextual financial pressures leading to suicidal ideation. The lack of discussion may be because financial difficulties are a consequence of other precipitators faced by the suicidal officer. The complex matrix of issues involved, which may embrace financial difficulties, will be demonstrated in

Chapter 7 when an examination of the researchers' theories is placed against the empirical results of the case-studies.

High Standards

Both Martinez and Violanti suggest that the shame of failure can contribute to suicidal thoughts on the part of officers. They both refer to the high standards officers set for themselves and the impact that failure can have on their self-perception. Violanti refers to the potential shame officers may feel when realising their vulnerability and suggests that this realisation may also heighten an officer's sense of anxiety.

Martinez also refers to the self-perception of shame following officers' erroneous actions: 'lawsuits, bad press, shame to their families, the thought of going to prison … [officers] are held to a higher standard and a mistake or a bad judgement is looked [on] as a crime' (Martinez 2010: 49). Furthermore, Martinez suggests that 'an officer's negative portrayal in the media, a lack of support from the community, and a criminal justice system that values expediency over equity all contribute to the officer's sense of frustration' (Martinez 2010: 16–17).

Invulnerability

Martinez and Violanti both note how officers' feelings of invulnerability can contribute to suicidal ideation. Martinez writes that an important theme throughout his research findings is the officers' fear of being perceived as weak 'because police officers are cultured never to show weakness' (Martinez 2010: 55). He comments: 'I remembered as a recruit in the academy, I had apologized for doing something wrong in training and instantly was corrected by one of my instructors that police officers never apologize because it shows weakness' (Martinez 2010: 55). Martinez suggests that weakness is seen as vulnerability and consequently works against the officer's well-being, in that the officer will seek to repress this potentially perceived weakness.

Violanti comments on officers' perceptions of vulnerability. Whereas they may consider themselves to be invulnerable, the incidents that they witness and experience may challenge their original self-perception. He describes at length the feeling of invulnerability inculcated in officers. Included in his observations is the following comment:

> The strong socialization which occurs in police training and experience instills in officers a sense of superhuman emotional and survival strength to deal with adversity. From the very first day in the police academy, recruit officers are told that they are someone unique, far different from the average citizen and certainly beyond psychological harm.
>
> (Violanti 2007: 59)

He goes on to refer to the negative emotional response caused by this realisation of vulnerability and comments that for some officers, suicide may be a way in which this realisation can be faced. Violanti explains that this may be due to the aggression which officers face 'on the streets', a growing realisation of their vulnerability and a realisation of their own impermanence, which hitherto they have either ignored or denied.

Isolation from the Non-Police Role

Officers and staff, ingrained in the police role and culture, may become isolated from their other roles in family and community life. Violanti and Ramos comment at length on this issue.

Violanti explains that officers can become so entrenched in the police work and culture that they become isolated in that role, and thereby emotionally vulnerable. He suggests that the pressures on officers may result in them assuming a monochromatic police perspective on life. This is a process, he warns, in which officers can lose their own identity and individuality.

Violanti considers that this loss of identity will restrict the officer's ability to respond to stress generally and limit the officer's skills in social relationships, both of which are factors considered to contribute to suicide. Violanti reaffirms this position in his statement that when an officer has been absorbed into the police culture to such a degree, it is increasingly difficult for the officer to make personal decisions and 'the potential for suicide may increase' (Violanti 2007: 18).

Ramos first refers to young officers, explaining how this process of isolationism begins:

> Young officers become addicted to the rush of adrenaline faced in daily work related scenarios. Life outside of the uniform becomes less interesting and boring sometimes. Officers feel they cannot relate to others who are not police officers, and they lose trust in anyone who is not a cop. The role identification of an officer has a snowball effect. The more time an officer has in the profession, the more cynical, isolated, and defensive they become.
>
> (Ramos 2007: 18)

He suggests that this absorption can be damaging to the officer's well-being and that this may leave the officer susceptible to undue stress. He explains that the intense assimilation can create confrontational relationships and act as a 'stimulus of an "Us-versus-them" mentality' (Ramos 2007: 19):

> Soon an officer's social circle becomes narrowly filled with mostly other officers. The investment in the police role is a 24-hour obligation. Officers are required to carry a firearm and police identification off duty. The identification of the police role takes precedent over other roles such as parent, spouse, sibling, and friend.
>
> (Ramos 2007: 19)

Referring also to the constant tension involved in responding to stressful incidents and the isolation from family and friends that is experienced, Ramos writes: 'Over time this constant exposure to critical incidents, death, frustration, and high levels of stress eventually takes a toll physically and mentally. As identification with this coveted role grows, the officer becomes more isolated from family and friends' (Ramos 2007: 18).

He reaffirms this theory later in his report:

> Officers have a tendency to isolate themselves from previous friends, loved ones, and the community. This social isolation is a defense mechanism that keeps officers safe in the line of duty from perceived dangers [and] societal rejection, and often causes them to become suspicious of others.
>
> (Ramos 2007: 96–7)

Organisational Structures, Procedures and Culture

Emphasising the impact of organisational structures, procedures and culture on officer-suicide ideation, Violanti draws attention to Ivanoff's citation of 'Difficulty with police organization' as a major precipitator of officer suicide (Violanti 2007: 157). These difficulties are demonstrated by Martinez when he repeats the comments of two respondents to his research enquiries: one officer's partner commented, 'My husband came home more screwed up with department problems than with anything he encountered on the streets' (Martinez 2010: 31), while an officer stated: 'I believe most of the stresses come from the bosses [rather] than any criminal or job tasks' (Martinez 2010: 52).

The stress of organisational pressures that is described by Martinez was referenced by others in preceding years. In 1982, Reiser wrote: 'Organizational and role pressures also routinely impinge on the officer, contributing to his total stress load. ... The stresses of hierarchy and peer group are exceedingly strong and influential' (Reiser 1982: 169). Some 30 years later, Mark Chae and Douglas Boyle similarly commented:

> Further, structural aspects of the police organization (e.g. bureaucratic leadership) can be a source of chronic anxiety and tension. Factors such as minimal support from supervisors, few opportunities for advancement, and poor working conditions contribute to feelings of isolation and despair – factors that predict suicidal ideation.
>
> (Chae and Boyle 2013: 109)

Violanti writes at length about organisational pressures when referring to the 'social acquisition of the police role' (Violanti 2007: 16). He suggests that the pressure of working in the police environment, with its administrative culture and structure, can limit an officer's individual approach; the officer can develop a monochromatic interpretation and act accordingly. This can be at the expense of officers forfeiting their own particular abilities and talents.

Violanti also offers examples of the organisational pressure that can lead to suicidal ideation. These include the way in which the police establishment will seek to secure its own standing in the community at the expense of an officer's reputation. Other examples given by Violanti include censorious disciplinary procedures, a lack of managerial/organisational support and officers' inability to contribute to the decisions that affect their day-to-day work.

Partner Relationships

Once again, Violanti refers to Ivanoff's (1994) listing of suicide precipitators and draws attention to what Ivanoff refers to as 'relationship conflicts or losses'. These are described as among the prime causes of suicidal ideation (Violanti 2007: 157). Clearly the causes of these losses will include bereavement and other relationship difficulties, but primarily it would seem that the researchers are referring to breakdowns in partner relationships and divorce. According to Kirschman, 'an angry separation or divorce will be the most common precipitating event' (Kirschman 1997: 172).

Martinez also emphasises the importance of the breakdown of partner relationships and quotes a police officer who, referring to colleagues who had taken their own lives, explains:

> The main circumstance was that they were depressed over their personal domestic situation. Not so much that they were getting divorced, but that their spouse was leaving them or had left them ... A police officer has to be in control when they are on duty. When their personal lives become out of control, desperation occurs.
>
> (Martinez 2010: 52–3)

Violanti makes wide reference to interpersonal difficulties that officers may experience which can lead to the breakdown of relationships and marriages, and describes some of the causes of these difficulties. He refers to officers' emotional detachment and explains how this work-mode requirement can transfer into the officer's home and social lives. Officers can find it difficult to respond with the appropriate emotions to home, family and social engagements; they may become entrenched in the workplace-dominant role that they display 'on the streets'. He suggests that 'Police officers are socialized into not expressing emotion, to put up an emotional barrier to protect themselves from the human misery they witness' (Violanti 2007: 20).

Violanti also suggests there are other contributors to this emotional detachment, such as 'the type of work assignment, sleep deprivation due to long hours and shift work' (Violanti 2007: 119). All of this can lead to aggression in the home. He also explains how an officer's understanding of required force in a work situation can be transferred to the home context; the officer can become vulnerable to perpetrating abuse, in its many forms, against partner and family members.

Violanti suggests that the many traumas faced by the officer will also have an effect on that individual, and that one of the effects will be that the officer looks for increased stimulus in impetuous activities that are out of character. Further, not only can emotional detachment lead to a breakdown in relationships and suicide, but this breakdown can have greater consequences. He comments that an officer can become addicted to violence, and that this violence can be displayed in abuse and in an officer's suicide preceded by murder.

Examples of murder–suicide are offered in Chapter 7 when the analysed case-studies are placed alongside the analysis of the literature survey (section entitled 'Murder/Attempted Murder/Assisted Suicide').

Peer Pressure

Miller and Violanti both make reference to the heightened sense of pressure officers may feel when they think that they have let their colleagues down. This perception of failure on the part of the officer involved might follow an incident 'on the streets' or an inappropriate action at work or in the personal life of the officer.

Miller suggests that 'officers may … become despondent because they feel they let their fellow officers down in a crisis situation, "froze" during a dangerous encounter, or failed to "pull their weight" on an assignment' (Miller 2006: 188). He also writes that the perceived disgrace felt by the officer is greatly exaggerated if 'the presumed lapse of performance led to the injury or death of another officer' (Miller 2006: 188).

Violanti also refers to police peer relationships and comments that the characteristic constraints of the officer's role may influence relationships with colleagues. Citing Durkheim's reference to 'altruistic suicide' (Violanti 2007: 21), Violanti suggests that officers' commitment to their peers can be of significant importance. If officers feel their actions have brought dishonour on their colleagues and the police unit in which they work, a sense of disgrace may be uppermost in their minds. As Violanti's reference to Durkheim indicates, both he and Miller regard this perceived pressure to contribute to suicidal ideation.

Post-Traumatic Stress Disorder

Violanti refers to the work of previous researchers and comments that such research has suggested a link between officer suicides and traumatic incidents, offering examples of the incidents an officer will encounter that may cause post-traumatic stress.

As Martinez explains, post-traumatic stress may occur when officers have 'been exposed to a distressing situation in which the individual is confronted with an event or events that involve injuries, death, or a threat of physical integrity to oneself or others' (Martinez 2010: 36–7). Martinez continues: 'police work is comparable to the same stresses that a soldier would have in military conflict. Studies have shown that a twenty-year veteran police officer shows similar signs of stress as a soldier fighting in a war' (Martinez 2010: 37).

However, Carlier et al. question the root cause of this stress, suggesting: 'it appears that the traumatic event may not be the event itself, but rather the organization's response to the officer, making them feel isolated, unsupported, disempowered, and ultimately, traumatized' (Carlier et al. 1997: 501).

Whether it is the event or the lack of support after the event that causes the traumatic response, the response to the trauma is real and may be linked to other precipitators. Chae and Boyle, for example, comment on the association of post-traumatic stress and officers' use of alcohol. They suggest that officers may use alcohol to minimise the effects of their past negative and difficult experiences. Reference was made earlier in this chapter to the potential link between PTSD and alcohol.

Retirement

American researchers suggest that retirement may be a precipitator for US police officers. Reintzell offers the following vignette:

> Sitting alone in his furnished room [the officer] contemplates his best friend, a .38, in the knowledge that everything in his life: family, friends, are now gone. So he eats his best friend. And therein, with more drama than reality, nevertheless, is underscored an important point. Membership in the informal police group cannot continue past retirement. It is ended then and all the time invested, all the laughs, all the beers, all the scrapes and all the stories told, equal nothing.
>
> (Reintzell 1990: 93)[24]

Violanti suggests that retirement is more difficult for officers than it is for members of the general community. He refers to previous research into suicide and offers an example of the suicide risk of officers in Detroit compared with that of those in the wider community (Violanti 2007: 163). He comments that many officers will retire at a relatively young age, fear losing the security of belonging to the police culture and may feel ill-equipped for new employment.

Kirschman offers similar comments and also focuses specifically on those who have been medically retired:

> Cops who lose their jobs because of an injury face a double whammy. They have lost health and vigor as well as an identity, a purpose in life, and companionship. This kind of transition stirs up significant emotional turmoil, and cops need a lot of support during this time, especially if they feel retirement has been forced on them by medical doctors or administrators.
>
> (Kirschman 1997: 172)

'Rugged Individualism'

Beehr et al. refer to the dangers of 'rugged individualism', which may be used as a coping mechanism, and write that they found 'no evidence that this could be helpful in coping with police stress' (Beehr et al. 1995: 19). They suggest that this characteristic, far from supporting the officer, can be detrimental to the officer's welfare. They suggest that 'rugged individualism' may instead be 'a harmful coping mechanism' and, if found to be so, should be subject to specific research: 'If its source is in stable personal inclinations of police officers, this suggests that selection could be improved. If its source is post-hiring socialization, then training might be advocated' (Beehr et al. 1995: 19).

Because of the psychological barriers that officers create around themselves, Violanti (as referenced earlier in this chapter) suggests that officers' personal relationships can be inhibited and that an officer's natural ability to empathise outside the workplace can be repressed by their work ethos. Furthermore, he suggests that the officer role can be a safe retreat, a place which denies an expression of true identity. All in all, this inability to release important emotions and relate to those who are close without using police techniques may become a prime cause of relationship difficulties.

Martinez also refers to the 'rugged individualism' of the officer. In addition to his description of officers experiencing 'macho man syndrome' (Martinez 2010: 68; as referenced in Chapter 2), Martinez quotes a police officer's comments regarding the way in which officers portray themselves as 'tough guys': 'I think the main reason officers contemplate suicide is because they are too proud to ask for help being they are always "the tough guys" giving the help' (Martinez 2010: 56).

Significant Loss – Actual or Threatened

'Significant loss' can refer to many different situations, including bereavement and divorce, to which reference has already been made. Nevertheless, with reference to a comment made by Kirschman, it seems correct that reference is made to significant loss as an issue in its own right.

Kirschman comments that 'many people, especially cops, push themselves to recover from a loss before they are ready. Sometimes this comes back to haunt them later on' (Kirschman 1997: 172). The cause of this determination to recover prematurely from the loss may be, for example, the officer's dichotomised decision-making process and/or the officer's 'rugged individualism', both of which were referenced earlier in this chapter.

Shift Work

Reintzell describes the difficulty that can arise out of shift work: 'shift work inhibits efficiency and good performance and is a well-documented source of physical and mental harm' (Reintzell 1990: 15). Violanti comes to the same conclusion. He describes the intrinsic pattern of shift work as being detrimental to the officer, as a disturbed sleep pattern will impair the officer's ability to respond to stress. Chae and Boyle also support this theory on the basis of their own investigations and write that other quantitative research has shown a strong possibility that there is a connection between suicidal ideation, constantly changing shift duties and varying sleep patterns.

Stress

In 1982, Reiser commented on the stress encountered by the police officer: 'Police work is a high stress occupation. It affects, shapes, and, at times, scars the individuals and families involved. Some of the typical stresses are related to environmental work factors such as danger, violence and authority' (Reiser 1982: 169).

Some years later, in 1995, Beehr et al. – specifically referring to suicidal ideation, alcohol abuse and difficulties in partner relationships – noted that 'empirical research on these three potential outcomes of job stress, whether in police or other work, has been minimal' (Beehr et al. 1995: 10) and further suggested that these stressors were 'worthy of further investigation as strains affecting police in future research' (ibid.: 20).

Violanti notes the difficulty of researching the effects of stress and suicide because of past research anomalies and the many different ways in which different officers may respond to different stressors, but nevertheless suggests that although there may be many contributory factors leading to the suicide of officers, workplace stress may be a significant contributor. He describes the manifold causes of stress and offers a list of stressors that range from situations that can be anticipated by the officer to those that cannot be expected or predicted.

Martinez also comments on the varied stressors that can impact on officers, noting that 'Police officer stress has long been attributed to the long hours, shift changes, military hierarchy, arbitrary disciplinary procedures, and a promotional system that caters to individuals with political clout' (Martinez 2010: 31). McCafferty et al. also offer their opinions on the effect of the stress faced by officers, stating: 'The stress that the individual police officer encounters is extraordinary. The effect of this overwhelming stress on the police officer is a demoralization and brutalization in which former values become meaningless' (McCafferty et al. 1992: 234). They explain that this is primarily because:

> The exposure to carnage, death, and hostility results in a loss of one's sense of immortality, with the consequent development of an expectation of a foreshortened future. There is also a concomitant development of the sense that one is not immortal, a recognition of the possibility of dying or of being maimed as a result of police work. The denial of one's mortality becomes progressively more difficult, and the erosive effect of constant confrontation with hostile people takes its toll.
>
> (McCafferty et al. 1992: 234)

In addition to their observations on the general stress facing an officer, Violanti, Martinez, Reiser and Chae and Boyle offer comments on a number of specific stressors, including:

- promotional aspirations;
- working as a response officer;
- the response of the community to officers at work;
- organisational processes.

Referring to promotional aspirations, Violanti comments that promotions can be viewed by officers as being unfair and influenced both internally and externally by biased procedures. Referring to the stress of working as a response officer and the way in which waiting to respond and being on constant alert can itself cause stress, Violanti remarks that boredom and a lack of new stimuli can be detrimental to work-related satisfaction. Martinez offers similar comments on the work-related stress of a response officer:

> No evidence suggests that the job of an officer is continually strenuous … most of the time the job is routine and uneventful, not as television or the media portrays it to be. Again I must stress that boredom does not put the officer at ease.
>
> (Martinez 2010: 38)

> The fact is that although an officer is not always involved in traumatic situations, the potential for any situation to escalate is prominent. This alone puts officers in a constant alert mode and stress levels are evaluated constantly.
>
> (ibid.: 37)

Reiser also comments on the community response to officers at work:

> Behavior related to the police officer's symbolic significance is an often overlooked but important factor that generates stress and operates at a largely unconscious level. His symbolization of authority elicits the dormant and active ambivalence that many people feel toward authority figures perceived as potentially threatening or punitive. Individuals whose conflicts are significant and largely unresolved typically react to authority symbols with resentment, hostility and aggression.
>
> (Reiser 1982: 169–70)

Referring to the impact of organisational processes, Violanti comments on the frequency with which officers feel unsupported by an organisation that is indifferent to their simple requests.

Chae and Boyle offer a similar opinion to Violanti's when commenting on the impact of organisational processes. They question the notion that 'police stress and symptoms of poor psychological functioning are a direct result of exposure to trauma and critical incidents', suggesting instead that research points to the stressful impact of 'administrative inefficiency, poor management, and work related stressors in routine policing' (Chae and Boyle 2013: 93).

Stress may have many different causes. However, it should be acknowledged that stress is not necessarily and always a suicide precipitator. Explaining how stress may affect people differently, Violanti cites McCafferty et al. (1992), who state that stress is not always harmful and that different people will respond to a given stressful situation in different ways; to one person a particular stress may be insufferable, while to another it may be experienced as positive.

This is a useful reminder that stress may not lead to suicide. However, it would appear that there is overwhelming evidence that stress can and does lead to suicidal ideation for certain officers.

Training

Violanti refers on several occasions to the ways in which officers' initial training can contribute to later suicidal ideation. He comments that 'from the very first day in the police academy, recruit officers are told that they are someone unique, far different from the average citizen and certainly beyond psychological harm' (Violanti 2007: 59). He continues, as noted in Chapter 2, by suggesting that their training encourages them to believe that, given the many forms of protection they can access (body armour, self-defence training, the ability 'to talk people down'), they are 'far different from the average citizen and certainly beyond self harm' (Violanti 2007: 14).

Violanti makes further similar comments on recruit training, suggesting that the initial induction 'attempts to instill a sense of superhuman emotional strength in officers' (Violanti 2007: 14) and that 'the strong socialization which occurs in police training and experience instills in officers a sense of superhuman emotional and survival strength to deal with adversity' (Violanti 2007: 59). (Comment on the potential dangers of training can also be found in Chapter 2, section entitled 'Police-Specific Causes of Suicidal Ideation'.)

Concluding Comments

The researchers to whom reference has been made within this survey of relevant literature indicate that there can be differing psychological contexts in which the suicidal may seek to kill themselves. According to Mintz, for example, suicide and suicidal ideation can be irrational, ambivalent and episodic. The suggestion has also been offered that suicide may also have a root cause that is genetic or biochemical.

Whatever the physiological cause, it has been also demonstrated within this chapter that there are many different contextual precipitators leading to suicide, and that these precipitators can be manifold in one person – a complex web, with one precipitator working alongside, if not aggravated by, another.

Many of the key suicide precipitators identified have been shown to be present both in members of the general community and in those who work as police officers. These precipitators include alcohol abuse, depression, significant loss, social isolation, difficult partner relationships and stress. Researchers have identified other precipitators in the general community, but no reference has been found to indicate that they are relevant to those working in the police community. Among these precipitators, several researchers have identified drug abuse, bereavement, community contagion, family history, physical illness, history of parasuicide and financial difficulties. Dryden-Edwards and Stoppler also refer to single marital status, unemployment, low income, mental illness and a history of physical or sexual abuse. In addition, the Samaritans identify yet other contextual situations, including the situations of those who come from poorer backgrounds and those who have experienced long-term depression due to extended periods of unemployment. None of these precipitators were identified by the researchers as being relevant specifically to officers.

Furthermore, with the exceptions of drug abuse and unemployment, when citing officer-specific precipitators one might expect these researchers to have made reference to bereavement, physical illness, previous parasuicidal activity and financial difficulties. However, this is not so. The lack of reference to financial difficulties would also seem an important omission; financial difficulty is one of Ivanoff's key precipitators, and it is on Ivanoff's investigations that researchers base many of their comments.

As has been demonstrated in this chapter, and as will be demonstrated when further analysis of the case-studies is undertaken in Chapter 7, bereavement, physical illness, previous parasuicidal activity and financial difficulties are in fact significant in the context of officer suicides. Equally, the examination of the precipitators examined in this chapter demonstrates that there are key officer-specific precipitators which are significantly different from the precipitators of those who take their own lives in the wider community. It would therefore appear that Barron is mistaken when he comments that 'the risk factors [for police officers] appear similar to those within the general community'.[25] His statement would not appear to be verified by the research of others.

The police officer-specific precipitators which have been identified in the analysis offered in this chapter, in alphabetical order, are as follows:

- control mechanism
- criminal and internal investigations
- death fantasy
- denial of required support
- dichotomised decision-making
- easy access to firearms
- high standards
- invulnerability
- isolation from the non-police role
- organisational structures, procedures
- peer pressure
- 'rugged individualism'
- shift work
- stagnated careers
- training.

The above list of precipitators has been drawn primarily from research within the USA, where officers have easy access to firearms. Access to firearms is the only precipitator which is not relevant to the majority of officers in the UK police service, although some UK officers will have relatively easy access.

It could be suggested that of the above listed precipitators, some would apply equally to those working in other occupations, such as those in the armed forces. This is a valid comment, although, as Violanti suggests, the work of a police officer is unique. He comments that the pressure of working in the police environment, with its administrative culture and structure, can limit an officer's individual approach; the officer assumes a monochromatic view and acts accordingly.

Working in the police service may not involve responding to situations that are quite as exceptional as Violanti suggests. However, the above listed officer-specific precipitators are issues which the vast majority of police officers could potentially face at different times during their careers. In spite of Violanti's view that there can be no *verifiable* direct link between the officer's work and suicide, examination of the possible causes suggests that there is a direct link between the two and that the officer's role is 'very likely part of the causal chain of suicide' (Violanti 2007: 50).

What Violanti refers to as a causal chain, Chae and Boyle refer to as 'cumulative interaction'. This is an interaction to which Mintz also refers, explaining: 'There is no one single motivation of all or most suicidal impulses. Research workers who have studied this question have enumerated about a dozen recurring motivations which clinically often appear in combination' (Mintz 1998: 243). It is the conclusion of this analysis that these recurring motivations can work as a damaging, toxic cocktail for officers, leading to suicidal ideation for the most vulnerable.

Having considered the different theories leading to suicidal ideation, the examination of the suicidal ideation of those who work within the police service continues in Chapter 7 by placing the suggestions of the examined researchers against the harsh reality of the case-studies.

Notes

1 Author Roxanne Dryden-Edwards and editor Melissa Conrad Stoppler, 'Suicide', n.d., *MedicineNet.com*, available from www.medicinenet.com/suicide/article.htm; accessed March 13, 2013.

2 Ibid.

3 'When someone dies – feeling suicidal', n.d., available from www.rd4u.org.uk/personal/when/suicidal.html; accessed March 17, 2013.

4 Driscoll, Anne and Tresniowski, Alex, 'A tragedy in Wales: a small town mystery', *People*, May 14, 2012, available from www.people.com/people/archive/article/0,,20595753,00.html; accessed March 16, 2013.

5 Cadwalladr, Carole, 'How Bridgend was damned by distortion', *Observer*, March 1, 2009, available from www.guardian.co.uk/lifeandstyle/2009/mar/01/bridgend-wales-youth-suicide-media-ethics; accessed March 16, 2013.

6 Ibid. Cadwalladr writes: 'Phillips coined the term after the hero of an 18th-century novel by Goethe which was supposed to have inspired copycat suicides around Europe, and his work suggested that 58 additional deaths were reported in the wake of a front-page story about suicide.'

7   Samaritans, 'Best practice suicide tips', n.d., available from www.samaritans.org/media-centre/media-guidelines-reporting-suicide/advice-journalists-suicide-reporting-dos-and-donts; accessed February 9, 2017.
8   Dryden-Edwards and Conrad Stoppler, 'Suicide'.
9   Ibid.
10   *HealthyPlace*, 'Suicide risk runs in families', n.d., available from www.healthyplace.com/depression/articles/suicide-risk-runs-in-families/; accessed March 15, 2013.
11   Dryden-Edwards and Conrad Stoppler, 'Suicide'.
12   Samaritans, 'What to speak to us about', n.d., available from www.samaritans.org/how-we-can-help-you/what-speak-us-about; accessed April 1, 2013.
13   Tomlin, 'Physical illness may be the trigger for one in ten suicides'.
14   Dryden-Edwards and Conrad Stoppler, 'Suicide'.
15   Aguilar, Eduardo J., Siris, Samuel G. and Baca-García, Enrique (2009) 'Stress and suicidal behavior', available from www.researchgate.net/publication/287539565_Stress_and_suicidal_behavior; accessed February 7, 2017.
16   Samaritans, 'Men and suicide', n.d., available from www.samaritans.org/media-centre/samaritans-and-network-rail-campaign-2010/men-ropes-about-campaign;   accessed March 15, 2013.
17   Barron, Stephen W. (2007) *Police Officer Suicide: A Review and Examination Using a Psychological Autopsy*, October 2007, www.barronpsych.com.au/research/Police%20suicide%20in%20NSW.doc; accessed February 12, 2017 (p. 9).
18   Ibid., p. 21.
19   Ibid.
20   Ibid., p. 8.
21   Ibid., p. 9. Hawton's comment that police suicides 'were consistent with similar findings in general community suicide studies' is contested later in this book.
22   Quinnett, Paul (1998), *Police Suicide Prevention*, FBI Law Enforcement Bulletin, 00145688, Vol. 67, No. 7, July.
23   Barron, *Police Officer Suicide*, p. 21.
24   This vignette was first presented by Joseph Wambaugh: 'In his book, *The New Centurions*, Joseph Wambaugh depicted the ultimate result of alienation in the characterization of Andy Kilvinski, former cop's cop, now retired' (Reintzell 1990: 93).
25   Barron, *Police Officer Suicide*, p. 21.

Bibliography

Aldridge, David (1998) *Suicide: The Tragedy of Hopefulness*. London: Jessica Kingsley.

Barron, Stephen W. (2007) Police Officer Suicide: A Review and Examination Using a Psychological Autopsy, October 2007, available from www.barronpsych.com.au/research/Police%20 suicide%20in%20NSW.doc; accessed February 12, 2017, p. 9.

Beehr, Terry A., Johnson, Leanor B. and Nieva, Ronie (1995) Occupational Stress: Coping of Police and Their Spouses, *Journal of Organizational Behaviour*, Vol. 16, No. 1, 3–25.

Carlier, I., Lamberts, R. and Gersons, B. (1997) Risk Factors for Posttraumatic Stress Symptomology in Police Officers: A Prospective Analysis, *Journal of Nervous and Mental Disease*, Vol. 185, No. 8, 498–506.

Chae, Mark H. and Boyle, Douglas J. (2013) Police Suicide: Prevalence, Risk, and Protective Factors, *Policing: An International Journal of Police Strategies & Management*, Vol. 36, No. 1, 91–118.

Dalton, H.R. and Noble, S.I.R. (2006) *Communication Skills for Final MB*. London: Elsevier.

Gladwell, Malcolm (2000) *The Tipping Point: How Little Things Can Make a Big Difference*. London: Abacus.

Ivanoff, A. (1994) *The New York City Police Suicide Training Project*. New York: Police Foundation.

Kirschman, Ellen (1997) *I Love a Cop*. New York: Guilford Press.

Lesse, Stanley (Ed.) (1998) *What We Know about Suicidal Behavior and How to Treat It*. Northvale: Jason Aronson.

McCafferty, F.L., McCafferty, E. and McCafferty, M.A. (1992) Stress and Suicide in Police Officers: A Paradigm of Occupational Stress, *Southern Medical Journal*, Vol. 85, No. 3, 233–43.

Maris, R. (1982) Rational Suicide: An Impoverished Self-Transformation, *Suicide and Life-Threatening Behavior*, Vol. 12, No. 1, 4–16.

Martinez, Louis Enrique (2010) *The Secret Deaths: Police Officer's Testimonial Views on Police Suicides and Why Suicides Continue to be Hidden in Police Departments*. Denver: Outskirts Press.

Miller, Laurence (2006) *Practical Police Psychology: Stress Management and Crisis Intervention for Law Enforcement*. Springfield: Charles C. Thomas.

Mintz, Ronald (1998) Psychotherapy of the Depressed Suicidal Patient. In Lesse, Stanley (Ed.) *What We Know about Suicidal Behavior and How to Treat It*. Northvale: Jason Aronson, pp. 241–64.

Murphy, George (1998) The Prediction of Suicide. In Lesse, Stanley (Ed.) *What We Know about Suicidal Behavior and How to Treat It*. Northvale: Jason Aronson, pp. 47–58.

Olin, Harry (1998) The Third Wish. In Lesse, Stanley (Ed.) *What We Know about Suicidal Behavior and How to Treat It*. Northvale: Jason Aronson, pp. 77–84.

Ramos, Orlando (2007) *A Leadership Perspective for Understanding Police Suicide: An Analysis Based on the Suicide Attitude Questionnaire*. Boca Raton: Dissertation.com.

Reintzell, John F. (1990) *The Police Officer's Guide to Survival, Health and Fitness*. Springfield: Charles C. Thomas.

Reiser, Martin (1982) *Police Psychology: Collected Papers*. Los Angeles: LEHI.

Siegel, Karolynn (1998) Rational Suicide. In Lesse, Stanley (Ed.) *What We Know about Suicidal Behavior and How to Treat It*. Northvale: Jason Aronson, pp. 85–102.

Violanti, John M. (2007) *Police Suicide: Epidemic in Blue* (2nd edition). Springfield: Charles C. Thomas.

7   An Analysis of the Primary Research as It Relates to the Literature Survey

Introduction

The literature examination offered in Chapters 2 and 6 details many underlying causes and precipitators of suicidal ideation with reference to officers primarily in the USA. The researchers whose work is considered offer a source of information that contributes to an overall understanding of officer suicide. However, it is inappropriate to draw specific principles or conclusions from these sources. The theories that have been offered by the relevant literature can only be provisional; they 'need to be checked out against the actual data, and never accepted as fact' (Babbie 2001: 284).

It was on the basis that the referenced researchers 'provide a rationale and context' (Leedy and Ormrod 2005: 141) that primary qualitative research and analysis was undertaken focusing on officer suicides in the UK. As explained in Chapter 3, this research was undertaken according to grounded-theory principles so as to offer the greatest possible flexibility of research and 'pursue areas of investigation that might not have been foreseen or planned' (Denscombe 1998: 97). It was necessary 'to discover the key components or general principles ... so that these can be used to provide a clearer understanding' (ibid.). The results of this investigative research were presented and examined in Chapter 4.

As the research analysis proceeds in the chapters that follow by investigating and recommending preventative measures, it is important that 'theories should be useful at a practical level and meaningful to those on the ground' (ibid.: 91). To achieve this and to determine the clearest possible understanding, this chapter scrutinises both the primary research case-studies and the surveyed literature to determine:

- contextual trends which these two different sources have in common;
- suicide precipitators which can be identified in both sources;
- precipitators identified in one source only.

The contextual analysis of these sources uses the primary research case-studies as the baseline and determines the extent to which the issues and precipitators identified within the surveyed literature correspond to those identified within the primary research. The possible correlation of the two sources offers the foundation for the analysis of the preventative measures examined in the three chapters that follow.

Contextual Trends which the Two Different Sources Have in Common

General contextual factors are considered first. Reference is made to:

- the suicide ratio of officers to staff;
- the suicide ratio of male to female;
- the ages at which the suicide or suicidal ideation occurred.

The Ratio of Officers to Staff

The police-specific suicide researchers to whom reference was made in Chapter 6 refer invariably to the suicidal ideation of officers rather than staff.[1] Furthermore, these researchers make no apparent reference to police staff who had previously worked as officers.

Of those who had completed suicide, the primary research also identified officers rather than staff (Chapter 4, section entitled 'Officer and Staff Ratio'). However, the primary research also identified:

- retired officers working as police staff;
- officers who had recently left the service under difficult circumstances, for example because of disciplinary issues;
- retired officers who had retired because of health and other related issues.

From the primary research, it would appear conclusive that the suicide precipitators relevant to the research pertaining to the suicide of officers and staff are predominantly specific to those who have worked as officers rather than staff. Therefore the issues that are further examined within this chapter are those that relate to serving and past officers.

The Ratio of Male to Female

Reference has been made previously (Chapter 6, section entitled 'General Factors and Mnemonics') to data suggesting that within the general population, the suicide rate is greater in males than in females (Violanti 2007; Dalton and Noble 2006). One possible contributory reason for this difference relates to the possibility that coroners more readily offer suicide verdicts for males than for females; specific suggestions in this were discussed earlier in the book (Chapter 5, section entitled 'Male and Female Verdicts'; see also Aldridge 1998).

However, as previously stated, the *Occupational Mortality in England and Wales* report (Coggon et al. 2009), which examines the proportional mortality ratio (PMR) of deaths between the years of 1991 and 2000, identifies only female police officers as being in an occupation which may involve a higher risk of suicide than many others (see Chapter 5, section entitled 'Available Statistics'). In spite of this UK data, those researchers to whom reference has been made (primarily within the USA) fail to differentiate between the suicides of males and females. The primary research revealed that the majority of officer suicides reported by the media were predominantly male. (However, as reported in Chapter 4, section entitled 'Data Relating to the Different Sexes', this ratio could change in the future due to the increased number of recruited female officers.)

The Ages at which the Suicidal Ideation Occurred

With regard to the wider community, several references within the literature survey indicate and agree that suicide is more likely to occur in older people (Dalton and Noble 2006: 172; Violanti 2007: 156; see Chapter 6, section entitled 'General Factors and Mnemonics'). Dryden-Edwards and Stoppler offer further comment, suggesting that suicide is more likely to occur specifically in those who are younger than 19 years of age or older than 45 (Chapter 6, 'General Factors and Mnemonics').[2]

The only apparent comment made by a researcher with regard to officers' age was that of Reintzell (Chapter 6, 'Introduction' to the section entitled 'Contextual Factors Leading to Police-Specific Suicidal Ideation'), who poses the question as to whether working to a shift pattern over many years may 'contribute to a suicide rate among police officers higher than most other occupations' (Reintzell 1990: 15). His assertion with regard to the occupational suicide rate would not appear to be correct (Chapter 5, section entitled 'Available Statistics'), although the ages and service lengths of those featured within the primary research possibly support his query concerning the shift pattern.

The primary research reveals that the ages of those concerned range from 27 to 62, with significant concentrations of suicides between the ages of 37 and 38 and between the ages of 45 and 49 (Chapter 4, section entitled 'Age at which Suicidal Ideation Occurred'). As has been previously stated, there is a significant difference between sexes with regard to age. With the exception of one female, who was aged 44, the suicidal ideation of females occurred at the age of 38 or before. This contrasts with male suicidal ideation, which took place at the age of 34 or after, with the one exception of a male suicide at the age of 27. As was also previously stated, the analysis of the primary research indicates that younger female officers are more vulnerable to suicide in their late twenties and early thirties, whereas their male counterparts are more vulnerable in their late thirties or mid- to late forties.

The average age at which new officers are recruited appears to be increasing and consequentially there may be a change in the ages at which officers are most vulnerable to suicidal ideation, but this will only become apparent with the passage of time and future research.

Precipitators Common to Both the Literature Survey and the Primary Research, and Those which Stand Alone

A comparison of suicide precipitators suggested by the primary research on the case-studies is now measured against the precipitators suggested by the researchers to whom reference was made in the survey of relevant literature. This examination is undertaken in three parts:

- General and police-specific precipitators identified within the literature survey that do not correlate with the results of the primary research.
- Correlation between precipitators identified within both the primary research and the references to police-specific precipitators offered by the literature survey.
- Primary research precipitators not identified by the literature survey as being police-specific.

General and Police-Specific Precipitators Identified within the Literature Survey that Do Not Correlate with the Results of the Primary Research

As demonstrated, the researchers to whom reference has been made comment on wide-ranging precipitators of suicide. Several of these were not identified as officer-specific precipitators by the primary research according to grounded-theory principles; therefore, after a brief examination within this section, no further attention is paid to these precipitators.

They are:

- unemployment
- death fantasy
- drug abuse
- ambivalence
- availability of the means – firearms
- stagnated careers
- retirement.

There are four further areas of concern which were not identified within the primary research but were identified by the literature survey as potential contributory factors. These factors would not necessarily be recorded at an inquest as they are not easily identifiable. For this reason, in addition to consideration in this section, these factors are further discussed in the analysis of preventative measures in Chapters 8 and 9.

They are:

- invulnerability
- peer pressure
- shift work
- training.

Unemployment

Several analysts, for example Dalton and Noble (2006) and Dryden-Edwards and Stoppler,[3] refer to the unemployed being at greater risk of suicide than those in employment (Chapter 6, sections entitled 'General Factors and Mnemonics' and 'Unemployed'). As stated in Chapter 6, the Samaritans also state that men from 'poorer backgrounds, those who are unemployed' and the 'long-term depressed due to extended periods of unemployment'[4] are among those who are particularly vulnerable to suicide.

The fear of unemployment is a different issue and a brief reference is made to this as a precipitator in the first case-study cited in this chapter, but within the primary research long-term unemployment was not an issue leading to suicide even for those who had left the police service.

If – as the above references suggest – unemployment is one of the greatest suicide precipitators in the UK, and this precipitator does not apply to officers, it would seem that greater significance is assumed by the PMR of officers taking their own lives, compared to the national average (Chapter 5, section entitled 'Statistical Data in the UK').

Death Fantasy

Kirschman refers to the way in which the reckless behaviour of some officers can be an indication of a 'death fantasy' (Chapter 6, section entitled 'Death Fantasy'), but this issue was not identified within the case-studies as being relevant to this research.

Drug Abuse

Some researchers – for example Kirschman and Dryden-Edwards and Stoppler – refer to drug abuse as a precipitator (Chapter 6, sections entitled 'General Factors and Mnemonics' and 'Substance Abuse' and the 'Introduction' to the section entitled 'Contextual Factors Leading to Police-Specific Suicidal Ideation'). No officers within the primary research were identified as suffering from problems involving drug abuse.[5] Reference to alcohol abuse is made later in the present chapter.

Ambivalence

As noted in Chapter 6, Mintz refers to suicidal ideation being ambivalent, stating that 'it is a clinical fact that the suicidal person is usually highly ambivalent about committing suicide' and 'it is worthwhile to reflect on the fact that most persons surviving a suicide attempt do *not go* on to ultimately kill themselves' (Mintz 1998: 243).

There is no clear evidence that the majority of those featured in the case-studies within the primary research were ambivalent with regard to their intentions. None of those who hanged themselves, shot themselves or stood in front of a fast-moving train could survive death by these means and the case-studies offered no evidence that their suicides were actions of ambivalence. It would appear that the majority of the suicides in the case-studies were well planned, with forethought (Chapter 4, section entitled 'Premeditated or Impulsive').

Availability of the Means

The majority of the researchers to whom reference has been made, such as Violanti and Barron, support the theory that access to firearms increases the risk of suicidal ideation (Chapter 6, particularly section entitled 'Availability of the Means'). There is no evidence within the primary research to suggest that this is true of those featured in the case-studies. Death by firearm was the second highest means by which officers within the primary research took their own lives, and certainly one death by firearm was reported as involving a handgun withdrawn from the armoury where the officer worked. However, only a few of the other officers who died in this way worked, or had previously worked, with firearms, and the firearms with which suicide was completed were acquired by a number of means. One officer, for example, had borrowed the firearm; another officer reportedly belonged to a gun club; yet another kept firearms legally for country pursuits.

Stagnated Careers

Commenting on stress, the unpublished draft report on suicidal ideation that was first mentioned in Chapter 5 reported that some officers had 'concerns with the promotional process'. Violanti comments, in reference to promotional aspirations, that the system can be viewed by officers as being unfair and influenced both internally and externally by biased factors and procedures. Martinez also suggests that a stagnated career could be a suicide precipitator (see Chapter 6, 'Introduction' to section entitled 'Contextual Factors Leading to Police-Specific Suicidal Ideation'). However, this was not an identifiable precipitator in the primary research.

Retirement

Reintzell, Violanti and Kirschman all refer to retirement, particularly enforced retirement, as a precipitator (see Chapter 6, section entitled 'Retirement'). This was not identified as a precipitator by the primary research in the way suggested by Reintzell and Violanti. Kirschman's reference to a connection with retirement on health grounds may have been reflected in one of the case-studies, although any direct connection is tenuous, particularly as Kirschman was referring to physical injury while at work. One may suggest that the arrangements for enforced retirement in the UK police service are currently different from those in the USA. Kirschman perhaps illustrates this difference in arrangements when she writes:

> Unfortunately, many cops ignore the serious emotional losses that go with retirement. They laugh it off – perhaps to avoid thinking it could happen

to them too and kid the retiree about faking problems and conning the employer. Some folks envy and greatly overrate the disabled cop's tax-free income, and it keeps them from seeing things through the retiree's eyes.

(Kirschman 1997: 172)

Invulnerability, Peer Pressure, Shift Work and Training

These four issues identified within the literature survey were not identified as precipitators by the primary research.[6] However, it would be difficult to measure the contribution that each of these potential precipitators might make to suicidal ideation. They are not the type of issues to which reference would necessarily be made at a coronial inquest. In spite of the difficulty of identifying these issues, because of the comments made by other researchers on each of these issues, it is the suggestion of this research that they are potential powerful precipitators in their own right. Reference is made to the possible precipitators of invulnerability, peer pressure, shift work and training in the following chapters examining preventative measures. Reference is also made to stress of a general nature later in this chapter.

Suicide Precipitators Identified in Both the Primary Research and the Literature Survey

Within the case-studies of the primary research, a range of precipitators and issues relating to officer suicide were identified which accord with those identified within the literature survey. These are now examined in sections addressing:

- accumulated factors
- emotional and psychological issues
- workplace issues
- personal issues.

Accumulated Factors

As previously stated, the researchers and analysts to whom reference has been made comment that there are often many combined contributory factors and precipitators leading to suicide (see Chapter 6, section entitled 'Accumulated Factors'). Violanti's comment that 'suicide can result not from a single major crisis but from the accumulation of apparently minor life events' (Violanti 2007: 158) has already been noted. Barron's comments on the interaction of precipitators have also been offered, but in addition to earlier discussion of an accumulation of precipitators, he also comments:

Occupational stress, alcohol use and abuse, frustration and impulsivity, the presence of some mental health problem and firearm accessibility all feature in the lives of the officers in this study ... this study did indicate that many of these officers did not have supportive, positive and productive personal relationships. Others who appeared to have such positive relationships with family, children and peers had poor organisational relationships and were subject to management action in some form.[7]

Within the primary research, only eight case-studies were reported in which there appeared to be a single precipitator leading to suicide (see Chapter 4, sections entitled 'Premeditated or Impulsive' and 'Single Contributory Factor' and 'Introductory Comments' to section entitled 'Possible Links to Key Precipitators Leading to Suicidal Ideation'). These single causes included potential criminal investigation, internal investigation, extra-marital affair, health concerns, suicide following an assisted suicide and depression/stress. In each of these case-studies there may have been factors that have not been reported by the media; however, it remains possible that there was only a single precipitator, especially, for example, when the precipitator was health-related. Nevertheless, the majority of suicides within the primary research, as examined in Chapter 4, revealed a multiplicity of accompanying factors, as described by the researchers to whom reference has been made.

The multiplicity of precipitators within the primary research, as examined in Chapter 4, reveal no clear common pattern, although there were strong underlying themes in that one precipitator could be seen either to initiate a series of ensuing factors or exacerbate other factors. From the primary research, three examples of a complex web of precipitators are offered:

Case-study 1

An officer's partner was involved in an extra-marital affair, which caused the officer to become involved in actions resulting in an internal investigation. Following the investigation, the officer was dismissed and faced unemployment. The consequence of these circumstances was that the officer faced losing his home and was subject to significant financial difficulties.

Case-study 2

An officer who had abused alcohol over a long period of time and suffered from long-term depression also experienced partner and family difficulties. At the same time, the officer felt that he was being bullied and that there was a lack of support in the workplace.

Case-study 3

An officer suffered from significant health issues which caused short-term depression. At the same time the officer was facing severe difficulty in his relationships with his partner and family.

Emotional/Psychological Issues

Some of the precipitators identified in both the primary research and the literature survey relate to the inner disposition of the officer concerned; that is, the precipitators are of an emotional/psychological nature. The nature of these emotional precipitators that are common to both sources is now scrutinised.

CONTROL MECHANISM

McCafferty et al. (1992) and Violanti (2007) refer to the theory that suicide may be an attempt to take control over feelings of powerlessness at a given time and in a given situation (see Chapter 6, section entitled 'Control Mechanism'). It is suggested in Chapter 4 that the number of suicides within the primary research that were premeditated, carefully planned and wilfully carried through is a clear indication of the control that at least some officers took as they considered their apparent choices. Some of the comments made after the suicides of some of those featured in the case-studies (Chapter 4, section entitled 'Premeditated or Impulsive') are typical. They reveal a certain sense of control exercised by the officers and include the following statements:

- 'He left all his affairs in order.'
- 'He planned his death meticulously.'
- 'He was very strong-minded and once he had made his mind up about something, nothing anyone could say could stop him.'
- 'He seemed "at peace" and very calm.'

The apparent control exercised by officers in taking their own lives was seen to be particularly significant with regard to health issues, alleged criminal offences, bereavements and a breakdown in partner/family relationships.

The issue of control mechanisms adopted by officers would appear to relate to the way in which officers are vulnerable to the process of dichotomised decision-making (discussed later in this chapter).

DEPRESSION

Violanti (2007) and Ramos (2007) are clear in their comments describing depression as a suicide precipitator. Both describe how depression can be caused by an officer's sense of a lack of control. Violanti, as previously described, also refers to the depression which can be caused by the stressful events of working as a response officer (Chapter 6, section entitled 'Depression').

As the primary research demonstrated (Chapter 4, section entitled 'Emotional Context'), many of the media reports referred to the depression that preceded the officers' suicides. As previously noted, some of the case-study subjects within the primary research were said to have experienced long-term depression over many years, whereas other officers suffered from short-term depression following a specific incident in their lives.[8] As has also been reported, this depression accompanied a range of issues: partner relationships/family difficulties, bereavement, work-related issues, financial concerns, PTSD, investigations and physical health concerns.

The age of those officers suffering with long-term depression may be significant: it would appear that older male officers, that is, those aged 40 years and older, are more vulnerable to depression than younger officers (Chapter 4, section entitled 'Depression').

DENIAL OF HELP

As previously noted, Martinez (2010) and Violanti (2007) refer to officers' reluctance to request or accept support. As explained in Chapter 6 (section entitled 'Denial of Help'), this reluctance can be for a number of different reasons – for example, an officer's reluctance to be seen as weak. Equally, as explained in Chapter 6 in the section entitled '"Rugged Individualism"', some officers wish to be seen as 'tough guys' and are too proud to ask for help.

The primary research identified eight case-studies in which the officer either failed to share their problems and concerns with their families or failed to engage with support agencies after being advised to do so. As previously stated in Chapter 4 (section entitled 'Unwillingness to Accept Help'), it would appear that in general the officers' independence prohibited them from showing weakness to themselves, their families or their work colleagues. Comments about the officers in Chapter 4 include:

- 'He was very proud and private about his inner thoughts and feelings and would not want to show weakness to others.'
- 'I personally did not feel that he was ready to go back to work … he did his best to hide it from me.'
- 'He was not good at seeking help from others.'

DICHOTOMISED DECISION-MAKING

As detailed in Chapter 6 (section entitled 'Dichotomised Decision-Making'), Violanti (2007) and Ramos (2007) refer to dichotomised decision-making, Martinez (2010) refers to action-orientated officers and Beehr et al. (1995) refer to problem-focused activities. Whatever terminology is used, these researchers are noting that officers who spend their lives taking control of the difficult dilemmas they face in the workplace and in the lives of others become less able to make considered decisions regarding their own personal lives.

The primary research did not identify this issue as a specific precipitator in its own right; however, the difficulty officers may face in making decisions with regard to dilemmas within their own personal lives may be displayed in the symptomatic emotions of anger, negative self-perceptions and depression (all considered in Chapter 4 under the heading 'Emotional Context'). Alcohol abuse would also appear to be an activity that can mask the decision-making process (considered in Chapter 4 under the same heading and that of 'Alcohol Abuse and Depression'). These symptoms were manifestly revealed by officers within the primary research, as detailed in Chapter 4.

HIGH STANDARDS

As previously detailed (Chapter 6, section entitled 'High Standards'), Martinez (2010) and Violanti (2007) refer to the sense of shame officers may feel when they are perceived, either by themselves or by others, to have failed to maintain high standards in their actions. Martinez refers further to the added pressures of potential 'lawsuits, bad press, shame to their families, the thought of going to prison' (Martinez 2010: 49). Violanti comments that officers are surprised by their vulnerability and the ensuing sensations of shame and fear (Chapter 6, section entitled 'Invulnerability').

In at least six case-studies in the primary research, the media reports indicated that the officer's negative self-perception at the time of their death contributed to their suicide (Chapter 4, section entitled 'Negative Self-Perceptions'). Low self-esteem, shame and feelings of worthlessness were among the descriptions offered by the media. The families interviewed as part of the primary research corroborated that those who died had these feelings.

As was also stated in Chapter 4 (section entitled 'The Acknowledged Calibre of Officers'), many of the officers who took their own lives were highly regarded and commended by colleagues and/or members of the community. Violanti notes that 'some police suicides may therefore be based on shame or inability to fulfill role expectations of the organization, police peers, the public, or oneself' (Violanti 2007: 22).

ISOLATION

Martinez (2010), Violanti (2007) and Ramos (2007) all refer at some length to the process of isolation that can affect police officers in what is potentially a close-knit community (Chapter 6, sections entitled 'Isolation from the Non-Police Role' and 'Social Isolation, Divorce or Separation').

Becoming isolated is not a development that can easily be quantified, and therefore it is not surprising that it is not stated as a contributory factor to suicide within coronial inquests. However, isolation remains a factor that is easily understood and can be identified by those working within the police service.

The effects of being or feeling isolated may be demonstrated in the breakdown of relationships between certain officers and their partners/family units (Chapter 4, section entitled 'Difficulties within the Home and Family Context').

Feelings of isolation from peers may be also a further contributory precipitator. Isolation, for example, may be particularly significant when an officer has been suspended as a result of a disciplinary inquiry; the officer may be cut off from friends and colleagues who have, over the years, become part of a natural support group (Chapter 4, sections entitled 'Criminal Investigation Issues', 'Internal Investigations for Professional Misconduct', 'Lack of Welfare and Colleague Support').

STRESS

Reiser (1982), McCafferty et al. (1992), Beehr et al. (1995), Violanti (2007), Martinez (2010) and Chae and Boyle (2013) each refer to the general stress that police officers face in their daily work and routine (Chapter 6, section entitled 'Stress'). This general stress is not to be confused with the stress related to organisational structures and procedures that is detailed in this chapter.

Only three officers in the case-studies were reported to be suffering from work stress of a general nature (Chapter 4, section entitled 'Pressure of Work-Related Stress') as opposed to stress caused by specific incidents, as referenced elsewhere in this chapter.

POST-TRAUMATIC STRESS DISORDER

Comments by Violanti and Martinez indicating the direct connection between post-traumatic stress and suicide were highlighted previously (Chapter 6, section entitled 'Post-Traumatic Stress Disorder'). In the same section, attention was drawn to the suggestion by Carlier et al. that 'the traumatic event may not be the event itself, but rather the organization's response to the officer, making them feel isolated, unsupported, disempowered, and ultimately, traumatized' (Carlier et al. 1997: 501).

Isolation, a lack of support and a lack of control are themselves precipitators to which reference has been made in previous chapters (for example Chapter 6, section entitled 'Isolation') and in this one. Chae and Boyle and Violanti further assist in an understanding of the complexity of accumulated precipitators by linking the effects of PTSD with other precipitators, and specifically with alcohol abuse.

Within the primary research, three officers were reported to be suffering from PTSD. However, only in one case was this directly due to police work (Chapter 4, section entitled 'Post-Traumatic Stress Disorder (PTSD)').

Workplace Issues

In terms of workplace issues, both the primary research and the literature survey identified the following precipitators:

- organisational structures and procedures
- criminal or internal investigation.

The nature of these precipitators common to both sources is now examined.

ORGANISATIONAL STRUCTURES AND PROCEDURES

Reiser (1982), Violanti (2007), Martinez (2010) and Chae and Boyle (2013) each refer to the stress caused by organisational structures and procedures (Chapter 6, section entitled 'Organisational Structures, Procedures and Culture'). These stresses are additional to others referenced within this chapter, such as general work stress and stresses relating to criminal and internal investigations. Reiser notes that among these, 'the stresses of hierarchy and peer group are exceedingly strong and influential' (Reiser 1982: 169–70).

Violanti refers to the way in which the pressure of working in the police environment, with its administrative culture and structure, can limit an officer's individual approach; the officer assumes a monochromatic view and acts accordingly. This can come at the expense of officers forfeiting their interpersonal skills and aptitudes. He also offers examples of the organisational pressure that can lead to suicidal ideation. These embrace the way in which the police establishment will seek to secure its own standing in the community at the expense of an officer's reputation. Other examples that Violanti gives include censorial disciplinary procedures, which are perceived to be biased against the officer; a lack of managerial/organisational support; and officers' inability to contribute to the decisions that affect their day-to-day work. The quotes from officers that Martinez offers include: 'I believe most of the stresses come from the bosses [rather] than any criminal or job tasks' (Martinez 2010: 52).

Chae and Boyle list a number of organisational pressures:

- bureaucratic leadership
- minimal support from supervisors
- few opportunities for advancement
- poor working conditions.

(Chae and Boyle 2013: 109)

Whereas some of the above pressures may be known to some officers generally and may well contribute to suicidal ideation, they are not directly identified as stress precipitators within the case-studies. Among the stresses identified within the case-studies that contributed to suicidal ideation (Chapter 4, section entitled 'Workplace Issues') were the following precipitators:

- lack of general communication;
- lack of information concerning future re-deployment posts;
- being overworked;
- pressure from targets and paperwork;
- a monitoring regime;
- fear of transfer to other stations for failure to perform as expected;
- the re-assignment of the working role;
- lack of understanding regarding health issues;
- lack of welfare and colleague support.

CRIMINAL OR INTERNAL INVESTIGATIONS

Investigations may be carried out for many different reasons. An officer might be investigated for an alleged criminal offence or for a non-criminal action which, for example, has brought the force into disrepute, or indeed the officer might face both a criminal and internal investigation. Anecdotally, officers refer to this as 'double jeopardy'; that is, after an officer is cleared of a criminal charge, the officer may still face an internal investigation for, for example, inappropriate conduct (see Chapter 8, section entitled 'Investigations: Complaints and Discipline').

Within the realm of internal investigations, there is also a distinction between misconduct and gross misconduct. Allegations and investigations of gross misconduct are the more serious of the two, the consequence of which could be dismissal.

Miller (2006), Violanti (2007), Barron (2007) and Martinez (2010) all write at length about the vulnerability of officers under investigation (Chapter 6, section entitled 'Criminal or Internal Investigation'). The vulnerability about which they write was well demonstrated within the primary research: approximately half of those who suffered suicidal ideation were under measures by which they had been, were currently or were waiting to be investigated (Chapter 4, sections entitled 'Criminal Investigation Issues' and 'Internal Investigations for Professional Misconduct').

It is not possible to draw specific links between the gravity of the internal/criminal investigations (pending or otherwise) of the primary research and suicide, as many of the facts pertaining to the alleged offences were not disclosed. However, the seriousness of the allegations may not be acutely relevant, as the stress of how particular investigations affect different officers cannot necessarily be measured. What may be stressful to one officer may not be to another, and vice versa (Violanti 2007: 55; Chapter 6, section entitled 'Stress'). The primary research suggests that investigations of any order may lead some officers to suicidal ideation.

Personal and Other Issues

Some of the precipitators identified by both the literature survey and the primary research relate to issues which might be described as being of a personal nature:

- alcohol abuse
- financial difficulties
- murder/attempted murder/assisted suicide followed by the suicide of 'the offender'
- partner relationships.

The nature of these precipitators common to both sources is now examined.

ALCOHOL ABUSE

Alcohol abuse was identified within the literature survey as a major suicide precipitator in both the general community and the police community (Chapter 6). It is discussed, for example, in the research of Dalton and Noble (2006), Dryden-Edwards and Stoppler,[9] Kirschman (1997) and Violanti (2007).

Eight officers within the primary research experienced alcohol-abuse problems. Furthermore, as previously referenced in Chapter 4 (section entitled 'Alcohol Abuse'), the officers within the primary research who abused alcohol were also suffering with long-term depression.

As previously noted, with reference specifically to PTSD, Violanti suggests that alcohol may be a substitute for the effects of endorphin withdrawal that may occur following a traumatic incident. Three officers in the primary research were suffering from the effects of PTSD, but according to explanations offered concerning their suicides, only one officer was suffering from alcohol-abuse problems.

FINANCIAL DIFFICULTIES

Of the researchers to whom reference has been made, it would seem that only Kirschman includes financial difficulties as a key precipitator (Chapter 6, section entitled 'Financial Difficulties'). However, financial difficulties were identified in the analysis of four of the case-studies (see Chapter 4).

MURDER/ATTEMPTED MURDER/ASSISTED SUICIDE

Violanti comments on officers who commit murder before taking their own lives (Chapter 6, section entitled 'Partner Relationships') and suggests that the officer's role may manifest itself in behaviour which is impetuous and outside the officer's natural character. He suggests that the manifestation of anger is such an attribute, commenting that 'the expression of anger and rage progresses over time with increases in amount and severity. Such interactions can ultimately result in murder-suicide' (Violanti 2007: 119).

In Chapter 4 (section entitled 'Anger') it was noted that nine of the officers within the case-studies displayed a high level of anger. However, only one of these officers had demonstrated periods of anger and went on to commit murder. In two of the case-studies where murder was attempted, the individuals showed no previous signs of anger. There were two further deaths caused by officers who intended to kill, but the officers were not reported to have exhibited previous patterns of anger (Chapter 4, sections entitled 'Anger' and 'Criminal Investigation Issues').

PARTNER RELATIONSHIPS

As has been previously noted (Chapter 6, section entitled 'Partner Relationships'), Violanti refers to Ivanoff (1994) and appears to agree that difficult partner relationships are one of the greatest precipitators of officer suicide. Kirschman also comments that 'an angry separation or divorce will be the most common precipitating event' (Kirschman 1997: 172), and Martinez emphasises how difficult relationships between the officer and their partner can lead to suicide (Martinez 2010: 52ff.).

Within the case-studies, it would appear that one of the major contributing precipitators of suicidal ideation is related to the breakdown of relationships within the family. Such difficulties were revealed in 24 case-studies. Important information may not necessarily be offered by the media reports, but the case-studies, as earlier reported, offered examples of the difficulties within partner/family relationships and the family unit (Chapter 4, section entitled 'Difficulties within the Home and Family Context').

As reported in Chapter 4, the context of the difficulties varied considerably:

- partners had simply grown apart;
- officers or their partners were involved in physical relationships with a third person;
- officers had become estranged from their children.

In the above situations, many of the officers were also experiencing other difficulties within either their personal or their working lives, such as disciplinary investigations. Furthermore, some partners described the officers as people who were unwilling to accept support. The analysis of the case-studies suggests that those officers experiencing difficult partner and family relationships are among the most vulnerable to suicidal ideation.

Primary Research Precipitators Not Identified by the Literature Survey as Police-Specific

The primary research, carried out in accordance with grounded-theory methodology, revealed a number of precipitators not referenced by the researchers in the literature survey as being police-specific. However, some were identified by other researchers as precipitators for suicide within the general community. The primary research identified deaths which suggest that these precipitators have contributed to the suicide of some within the police community. An examination of these precipitators is therefore now offered.

Bereavement

None of those writing on police suicides appear to mention bereavement as a key precipitator, although some psychologists – Mintz, for example – suggest it can be a precipitator for those in the wider general community (Chapter 6, 'Introductory Comments' to section entitled 'Contextual Factors Leading to Ideation in the General Population'; section entitled 'Bereavement'). Bereavement was evident in at least eight case-studies within the primary research (Chapter 4, section entitled 'Bereavement') and in six of the case-studies bereavement was a cause of depression (Chapter 4, section entitled 'Long-Term Depression').

Bullying, Harassment and Victimisation

Alleged bullying, harassment and victimisation were not apparently specified as precipitators by the researchers to whom reference was made within the literature survey, and yet reports of these allegations were to be found in nine of the case-studies (Chapter 4, section entitled 'Alleged Bullying, Harassment, Victimisation').

Community Contagion

Community contagion has been referenced within the literature survey as a precipitator within the general community (Chapter 6, section entitled 'Community Contagion'). Community contagion is also referred to by other names, for example 'the Werther effect' or 'copy-cat suicides'.

The primary research indicated that a high number of suicides had taken place in specific forces within a given time period. This number would appear to be disproportionate when compared to the suicides in other forces. Within one relatively small force, for example, six suicides occurred in a two-year period.

It is difficult to determine whether community contagion is significant without collating figures at force level, but anecdotally the argument for community contagion would appear feasible, both within the different forces and nationally.

Family History

Suicide analysts (for example, Dryden-Edwards and Stoppler) refer to those who have a family history of suicide as being at particular risk (Chapter 6, section entitled 'Family History'). The reasons for this, as previously indicated, may be genetic, biochemical and/or psychological.

This risk factor was not apparently specified by the researchers to whom reference has been made, but a history of suicide within the family was present in five of the case-studies within the primary research (Chapter 4, section entitled 'History of Suicide within the Family').

Lack of Welfare Support

Several of the researchers refer to a lack of support, but it would appear that they are referring primarily to a lack of general support from the institutional organisation.

Barron refers to a 'lack of support from administration as being areas which contributed to the range of individual factors in suicide'[10] (also see Chapter 6, 'Introduction' to section entitled 'Contextual Factors Leading to Police-Specific Suicidal Ideation'). Violanti comments on the lack of organisational support and the organisation's indifference to basic and sometimes simple requests with regard to the general needs of the officer (Chapter 6, section entitled 'Stress'). Chae and Boyle refer to 'minimal support from supervisors' (Chae and Boyle 2013: 109; Chapter 6, section entitled 'Organisational Structures, Procedures and Culture'). Martinez comments on 'the lack of support' from the community following traumatic incidents (Martinez 2010: 36ff.; Chapter 6, section entitled 'Post-Traumatic Stress Disorder').

The primary research revealed that the families of three officers felt there was a clear lack of welfare support from within the organisation (Chapter 4, section entitled 'Lack of Welfare and Colleague Support').

Physical Illness

Although physical health does not appear to be an issue in the work of the police-specific researchers (possibly because of enforced retirement in the USA), the researchers who commented on suicide in the general community regard physical illness as a precipitator (Chapter 6, section entitled 'Physical Illness'). As previously shown in Chapter 4 (section entitled 'Health Concerns of a Physical Nature'), health-related factors were an important element in four of the case-studies.

Concluding Comments

As has been demonstrated within this chapter, a number of issues and precipitators relating to officer suicide that were raised within the literature survey are not identified within the analysis of the case-studies. Because much of the literature surveyed was primarily written by US researchers, an underlying cause of this discrepancy may be, in certain cases, differences in police community practices (for example, the availability of firearms) and police organisational processes (for example, retirement arrangements and stagnated careers).

Further reasons for these discrepancies may relate to the simple fact that some of these issues and precipitators are not relevant to officers – unemployment, for example. Equally, ambivalence was identified as a suicide precipitator for those in the community at large, but it was not evident that this was a police-specific suicide precipitator within the case-studies.

Within this chapter, other issues and precipitators were identified within the primary research case-studies but not by the literature survey. All of these issues, one might suggest, are universal in nature – bereavement, community contagion and family history, for example. Therefore, one might have expected the researchers to whom reference has been made to have identified these precipitators as being relevant to officers.

In spite of the areas in which there was a lack of correlation between the two research sources, there was significant agreement between the primary research and the literature survey on a wide range of other contextual issues and precipitators. Examination of preventative measures therefore continues in the chapters that follow by focusing primarily on the issues identified within the section of this chapter entitled 'Suicide Precipitators Identified in Both the Primary Research and the Literature Survey'.

In addition to these issues, the following chapters focus on issues and precipitators identified solely by the primary research. The analysis of the case-studies, for example, reveals a predominance of male suicides. The analysis also identified the most vulnerable ages for completion of suicide, including a difference in the ages of male and female suicides. As well as responding to the identified key pre-cipitators, reference is made in the following chapters to the hidden precipitators of invulnerability, peer pressure, shift work and training. These precipitators are not easily identifiable but may have a significant impact on officers' vulnerability to suicidal ideation.

Resourced by the information determined in this and the preceding chapters, the investigation which continues identifies ways in which the catalogued risk factors may be reduced by the intervention of appropriate prevention measures. Certain measures and safeguards are already in place to support officers who may be vulnerable to suicidal ideation. However, if these processes can be enhanced and further measures implemented, it will be to the benefit of all who work within the police service, their families and others associated with the service.

The intervention measures to which reference is made in Chapters 8, 9 and 10 focus on safeguards that can be introduced not only at organisational and per-sonal levels, but also by family members, close friends and colleagues of officers.

Notes

1 The term 'staff' is used for those who work in what are termed 'civilian' or 'support' staff roles; that is, those who are not 'sworn' officers.
2 Author Roxanne Dryden-Edwards and editor Melissa Conrad Stoppler, 'Suicide', n.d., *MedicineNet.com*, available from www.medicinenet.com/suicide/article.htm; accessed March 13, 2013.
3 Ibid.
4 Samaritans, 'Men and suicide', n.d., available from www.samaritans.org/media-centre/samaritans-and-network-rail-campaign-2010/men-ropes-about-campaign; accessed March 15, 2013.
5 A comprehensive system of random drug (and alcohol) testing is undertaken within the UK police service. Details of this are given in a Home Office publication first published on April 30, 2012, 'Circular: testing police officers for substance misuse', available from www.gov.uk/government/publications/testing-police-officers-for-substance-misuse; accessed April 25, 2016.
6 Chapter 6, sections entitled 'Invulnerability'; 'Peer Pressure'; 'Shift Work'; 'Training'.
7 Barron, Stephen W. (2007) *Police Officer Suicide: A Review and Examination Using a Psychological Autopsy*, October 2007, www.barronpsych.com.au/research/Police%20 suicide%20in%20NSW.doc; accessed February 12, 2017 (p. 34).
8 Having read the accounts of those suffering from long- and short-term depression, the analysis defines short-term depression as lasting a few weeks or months only and long-term depression persisting over a longer period.
9 Dryden-Edwards and Conrad Stoppler, 'Suicide'.
10 Barron, *Police Officer Suicide*, p. 8.

Bibliography

Aldridge, David (1998) *Suicide: The Tragedy of Hopefulness*. London: Jessica Kingsley.
Babbie, Earl (2001) *The Practice of Social Research* (9th edition). Belmont: Wadsworth/ Thomson Learning.
Barron, Stephen W. (2007) Police Officer Suicide: A Review and Examination Using a Psychological Autopsy, October 2007, available from www.barronpsych.com.au/ research/Police%20 suicide%20in%20NSW.doc; accessed February 12, 2017, p. 9.

Beehr, Terry A., Johnson, Leanor B. and Nieva, Ronie (1995) Occupational Stress: Coping of Police and Their Spouses, *Journal of Organizational Behaviour*, Vol. 16, No. 1, 3–25.

Carlier, I., Lamberts, R. and Gersons, B. (1997) Risk Factors for Posttraumatic Stress Symptomology in Police Officers: A Prospective Analysis, *Journal of Nervous and Mental Disease*, Vol. 185, No. 8, 498–506.

Chae, Mark H. and Boyle, Douglas J. (2013) Police Suicide: Prevalence, Risk, and Protective Factors, *Policing: An International Journal of Police Strategies & Management*, Vol. 36, No. 1, 91–118.

Coggon, David, Harris, E. Clare, Brown, T., Rice, Simon and Palmer, Keith T. (2009) *Occupational Mortality in England and Wales*. Luton: Office for National Statistics.

Dalton, H.R. and Noble, S.I.R. (2006) *Communication Skills for Final MB*. London: Elsevier.

Denscombe, Martyn (1998) *The Good Research Guide for Small-Scale Social Research Projects*. Maidenhead: Open University Press.

Ivanoff, A. (1994) *The New York City Police Suicide Training Project*. New York: Police Foundation.

Kirschman, Ellen (1997) *I Love a Cop*. New York: Guilford Press.

Leedy, Paul D. and Ormrod, Jeanne Ellis (2005) *Practical Research*. New Jersey: Pearson Education International.

Lesse, Stanley (Ed.) (1998) *What We Know about Suicidal Behavior and How to Treat It*. Northvale: Jason Aronson.

McCafferty, F.L., McCafferty, E. and McCafferty, M.A. (1992) Stress and Suicide in Police Officers: A Paradigm of Occupational Stress, *Southern Medical Journal*, Vol. 85, No. 3, 233–43.

Martinez, Louis Enrique (2010) *The Secret Deaths: Police Officer's Testimonial Views on Police Suicides and Why Suicides Continue to be Hidden in Police Departments*. Denver: Outskirts Press.

Miller, Laurence (2006) *Practical Police Psychology: Stress Management and Crisis Intervention for Law Enforcement*. Springfield: Charles C. Thomas.

Mintz, Ronald (1998) Psychotherapy of the Depressed Suicidal Patient. In Lesse, Stanley (Ed.) *What We Know about Suicidal Behavior and How to Treat It*. Northvale: Jason Aronson, pp. 241–64.

Ramos, Orlando (2007) *A Leadership Perspective for Understanding Police Suicide: An Analysis Based on the Suicide Attitude Questionnaire*. Boca Raton: Dissertation.com.

Reintzell, John F. (1990) *The Police Officer's Guide to Survival, Health and Fitness*. Springfield: Charles C. Thomas.

Reiser, Martin (1982) *Police Psychology: Collected Papers*. Los Angeles: LEHI.

Violanti, John M. (2007) *Police Suicide: Epidemic in Blue* (2nd edition). Springfield: Charles C. Thomas.

8 Organisational Preventative Measures

Introductory Comments

Having offered an analysis of primary suicide precipitators in the case-studies and examined how these precipitators relate to the precipitators identified by earlier researchers, in this chapter the study focuses on the possible implementation of preventative measures.

As indicated previously (particularly in Chapter 2, section entitled 'Identifying and Responding to the Potential Suicide of Police Personnel'), certain suicide-intervention measures are currently in place within the police service. Through these intervention measures, many suicides will be averted, both by formal and informal processes. However, these averted suicides will rarely be identified. George Murphy draws attention to this when he comments on the lack of recorded data concerning suicides that have been prevented by medical intervention:

> Primary prevention occurs both at the level of removing a substrate of suicidal thinking and at the level of direct interruption of the developed thought. If it is successful, the patient will live. A suicide will have been prevented. Yet to quantify this effect is impossible. It is important to realize that *the absence of a suicide generates no data.* Thus, we can never prove what has been accomplished. Yet we can hardly doubt that it occurs.
>
> (Murphy 1998: 55)

In spite of the suicides which have been averted, officer suicide continues to occur at regular intervals. Indications of those who may be more vulnerable were offered in Chapter 4 (in particular the section entitled 'Analysis of the Primary Research'), where reference was made to the age, length of service, calibre and sex of the most vulnerable officers. As helpful as these indicators may be, the possibility that all officers may be vulnerable to suicidal ideation is a justifiable starting point when seeking to ensure that preventative measures are in place to safeguard the well-being of police officers.

As the results of this and earlier research have shown, the manifold potential contributory causes of suicide make identifying potential suicides an almost insurmountable task. Martinez comments that there can be no set configuration to predict officer suicide. Nevertheless, he suggests:

> We as a nation should do whatever necessary to understand why and who are more vulnerable to suicidal tendencies, and if we can understand this dynamic of vulnerability, then we can put in motion measures that will prevent this from happening.
>
> (Martinez 2010: 17)

The 'dynamic of vulnerability' was considered in the previous chapters. Before recommendations are offered in Chapter 11, this and the following two chapters identify and examine preventative measures that might be adopted by:

- the police organisation (current chapter)
- officers themselves (Chapter 9)
- family, close friends and colleagues (Chapter 10).

The recommendations to reduce suicidal ideation that are set out in Chapter 11 are drawn from the examination of the preventative measures primarily provided in these three chapters, supported by evidence drawn from the previous chapters.

As with much of the previous analysis of literature relating to officer suicide, the prevention measures to which reference is now made (alongside reference to the case-studies wherever possible) come primarily from the USA, with some reference to work undertaken in Australia. This is principally because, as previously stated, there is a lack of written resources within the UK. It is the suggestion of this research that this is in itself an indication of the lack of attention paid to the prevention of officer suicides within the UK.

Responsibility for suicide prevention is a shared concern of officers, family and community support agencies. However, specific responsibility also lies with the police organisation as the employer, and it is with organisational preventative measures that this examination commences. Within this chapter, an examination is offered that focuses on the aspects of preventative measures that might be introduced at an organisational level and considers:

- training
- welfare support within and initiated by the organisation
- investigations: complaints and discipline
- identification of officers at risk
- bullying, harassment and victimisation
- an assessment of shift patterns.

Training

Introductory Comments

The three media accounts offered below underline the necessity of quality training as a response to stress and suicide.

Rebecca Pocklington writes:

> Thousands of police officers called in sick for stress, anxiety and depression last year and bosses are blaming harsh cuts to their budget. Figures show the number has increased over three years as police groups warn officers could end up 'burning out' because of huge workloads.[1]

Royston Martis reports:

> According to the Fed,[2] serious concerns were highlighted to its health and safety sub-committee 'that police officers were being driven to suicide by their increasing workload which was leading to high levels of stress'. That is worth repeating – there are concerns that 'police officers are being driven to suicide by their increasing workloads'.[3]

In a further article, Robert Verkaik reports that 'more than half of senior police officers are suffering from anxiety and depression'. Verkaik quotes Tim Hollis, Chief Constable of Humberside and ACPO Vice-President: 'High quality leadership training throughout the service is essential if we are to meet the complex demands made of us without people feeling poorly managed or led.'[4]

The above media accounts suggest reasons for the stress and anxiety experienced by officers. However, the causes of officer stress have already been examined in the earlier chapters; the following investigation therefore now turns to the importance of training as a proactive response to stress and anxiety. Reference is consequently made to:

- recruitment and initial training
- in-service training
- content of training programmes
- family participation in training
- leadership commitment.

Recruitment and Initial Training

Barron (2007) comments that the suicide risk factors of officers recruited from the New South Wales community may mirror the same ones present in the community from which they have been recruited, but nevertheless hopes that 'the prevalence and severity [of the risk factors] may be reduced due to the screening process that many recruits undergo in the first stage of training and probationary duty'.[5] Violanti (2007) also emphasises how important it is for the selection process to involve identifying officers who are both emotionally robust and able to undertake the role of an officer.[6] As important as the selection process may be in the USA, Violanti is critical of the initial training that American officers receive: as previously noted, he highlights that 'from the very first day in the police academy, recruit officers are told that they are someone unique, far different from the average citizen and certainly beyond psychological harm' (Violanti 2007: 59).

Ramos agrees with these sentiments and comments on the formal training of police recruits:

> This training has an underlying theme of officer survival. The officers are educated in self-defense, physical fitness, firearms training, impact weapons, and pepper spray. All of these subjects are designed to keep an officer alive. Surprisingly, very few agencies teach their officers about the mental demands of the profession, the physical and psychological implications of stress, and the dangers of suicide.
>
> (Ramos 2007: 20–1)

Violanti affirms this description of the initial training and describes how the officers acquire what he refers to as a 'false personalization' (Violanti 2007: 16). He describes the consequence of this characteristic by suggesting that, in taking on the prescribed identity of the police culture, the officer's own identity and personality can be overwhelmed. Violanti links this instilled sense of false personalisation with early 'socialization in the police role', in so far as the initial training 'attempts to instill a sense of superhuman emotional strength in officers' (Violanti 2007: 14).

Violanti's and Ramos' descriptions of the consequences of the initial training suggest that it is at this early point in the officer's career that officers first acquire the 'rugged individualistic' attributes described in earlier chapters (for example Chapter 6, '"Rugged Individualism"'). If this is the case, then a comment made by Beehr et al. with regard to 'rugged individualism' is highly significant: they note that 'If its source is post-hiring socialization, then training might be advocated' (Beehr et al. 1995: 19).

Martinez helpfully illustrates the danger of 'rugged individualism' created by false personalisation and the social acquisition of the police role in his previously noted citation of an officer's comment: 'I think the main reason officers contemplate suicide is because they are too proud to ask for help being they are always "the tough guys" giving the help' (Martinez 2010: 56).

The content of initial training programmes is crucial in the development of new officers. The researchers to whom reference has been made above identify the potential consequences of bad practice, but also offer a number of recommendations concerning the training content which, they advocate, will offer a greater awareness and understanding of suicide.

As early as 1982, Reiser suggested that 'it seems desirable to have the recruit training on mentally ill, suicidal persons and family disputes'; this, he added, should be undertaken 'jointly by a professional psychologist and an experienced police instructor' (Reiser 1982: 35).

Training on the aspects identified by Reiser would form an ideal base to ensure new recruits understand that, as Larned expounds, 'seeking help is a strength, not a weakness'; he adds that 'the knowledge that help is available, if needed, is vitally important' (Larned 2010: 69). As Larned also states, 'it's never too early to start learning basic intervention techniques that can be used to help those in trouble and to understand the myths, misinformation, warning signs, and available support groups' (ibid.).

Violanti affirms this view, commenting that such training should begin as early as possible to encourage new officers to understand that seeking support is not a sign of weakness. Such support may prove invaluable as personal dilemmas ensue and suicidal ideation becomes a reality. Ramos expands on this recommendation, suggesting that the training might be offered at three different levels and that 'in the police academy, new officers should be made aware of the impact their role can have on personal relationships, the community, and themselves' (Ramos 2007: 22).

Research analysis suggests that Ramos' reference to personal relationships highlights an important issue. This is demonstrated clearly by the many comments that have been previously referenced, for example, with regard to the potential isolation of many police officers and the difficulties experienced in partner and family relationships (both discussed in Chapter 6). This is a theme on which Violanti also comments; he suggests that training programmes for new officers should emphasise the importance of creating and maintaining relationships and friendships outside the police service.

In-Service Training

Just as the initial training which police recruits receive on matters relating to suicide awareness is of great importance, so too is the in-service training that officers might receive throughout their careers.

The unpublished research paper seen by this author that was referenced in Chapters 5 and 7 examines officer-suicide ideation and comments on the organisational factors that can lead to stress and burnout. Among these factors, the report includes 'poor training'. As Waters and Ussery (2007: 184) note, training which responds to the practicalities of police work must be readily available.

Commenting on factors leading to the suicide of officers in New South Wales, Barron also refers to the issue of organisational stress and focuses on training, with specific reference to an understanding of self-harm. He comments that documents and statements of the families, friends and colleagues of officers who completed suicide reveal that 'a number of organisational factors may have featured in the development of the suicidal behaviour(s) leading to suicide', and that one of these organisational factors was 'an absence of training in the recognition and assessment of self-harming behaviours'.[7]

Violanti is of the same opinion and highlights the absence of officer training in suicide awareness. This absence may be surprising, considering that as early as 1982 Reiser had referred to the importance of primary prevention training, commenting that this was offered through a number of different avenues throughout an officer's career.

To create a greater awareness of suicidal ideation, Barron suggests that 'internal police training courses over the "career life" of the police officer provide more opportunities to address personal, professional and medical issues if they are detected'.[8] Violanti also writes at length concerning the value of training courses related to suicide prevention. He refers to training officers and line-managers understanding the psychological factors which may lead to suicide, and the importance of training in stress awareness.

Yet another officer-researcher, Ramos, suggests that suicide-awareness training 'should include recognizing risk factors, identification of warning signs, and positive coping mechanisms. Stress reduction techniques can supplement physical fitness training and promote an overall wellness' (Ramos 2007: 22). In his analysis of factors leading to officer suicide, Ramos affirms the benefit of training in stress management and comments that 'through training, officers can learn to reduce stress in their life and recognize dangerous conditions in themselves and co-workers' (Ramos 2007: 22).

In addition to stress-management training for officers generally, Waters and Ussery comment on the importance of stress-management training for supervisors (Waters and Ussery 2007: 184). However, they suggest that supervisors may not be trained to identify the signs of stress in others and, even if trained, may not respond in an ideal way (Waters and Ussery 2007: 179–80).

Models of Training

Referring to the research of others, Chae and Boyle advocate that police bodies should adopt 'psycho-education and suicide prevention programs' (Chae and Boyle 2013: 101). In the abstract to their article, they suggest that the introduction of such programmes will help to decrease suicidal ideation as they 'assist police personnel in developing active coping styles, identify and access available social support systems, as well as utilize community-based services'.

Commenting on the impact of prevention programmes, Violanti cites Ivanoff's 1994 research (Violanti 2007: 157) and states that there is sufficient evidence to indicate the important benefits of suicide-awareness training. This training has been seen to be of benefit to the officers themselves and to their appreciation of the psychological difficulties that colleagues may face. However, referring to the work of Robert Douglas of the Police Suicide Foundation, Ramos states that in the USA in 2006, 'less than two per cent of American law enforcement agencies [had] a formal police suicide awareness training program' (Ramos 2007: 7).

Nevertheless, it would appear that successful programmes were available that could have been, and still could be, adopted. Martinez refers to the existence of such programmes and commends their benefit. Discussing alcohol or substance-abuse problems, he offers the comments of one officer: 'The programs are designed to target the problem and help the individual recover; ensuring them their job will still be available to him' (Martinez 2010: 68).

An early suicide-awareness programme, and one commended by Violanti, is that undertaken by the New York City Police Foundation to enable officers to be more aware of and able to respond to issues concerning officer suicide. Violanti refers to previous research focusing on a programme which included a video entitled *By Their Own Hand*, produced by Jonathan David. Violanti reports that the video offered three examples of suicide and the events that preceded these deaths.

Ramos also refers to available programmes, writing that 'there are several suicide prevention models available' (Ramos 2007: 22). As well as commenting on a programme adopted by the FBI (Ramos 2007: 21), Ramos notes: 'A model that has been nationally recognized is QPR. QPR stands for question, persuade, and refer. This prevention program is known as the QPR for officer suicide. The premise behind the QPR program is to be your brother's keeper' (Ramos 2007: 22–3).

Chae and Boyle also affirm the availability of successful programme models and comment on the increasing number of police bodies which have successfully introduced stress management, psycho-education and prevention training programmes (Chae and Boyle 2013: 106). They refer to work undertaken by the organisation Cop2Cop and a programme which includes successful peer-counsellor training. (Reference is made to peer counselling later in this chapter.)

In spite of the availability of prevention programmes, Martinez warns of the difficulty that some officers may have with this type of support. He cites the comments of two officers: 'This is problematic to an officer and the department because if officers feel an iota of mistrust toward preventive programs the program will be a failure' (Martinez 2010: 80); 'There are programs but I think I will never use them because you may lose your job' (Martinez 2010: 67).

The above comments raise the dilemmas of confidentiality and whether involvement in the programmes should be mandatory or optional. The issue of confidentiality is examined later in this chapter. With regard to the extent to which the programmes should be compulsory or optional, analysis suggests that preventative programmes should surely involve all officers, as programmes are designed to ensure that all officers have the necessary resources to deal with potential stresses.

Content of Training Programmes

Those who have written on the necessity of suicide-awareness training make various suggestions as to the content that might be included in training programmes. As early as 1982, Reiser referred to programmes that included

> The availability of mental health services, stress factors in police work and the application of psychological principles to field situations … A variety of workshops and seminars focused on the areas of stress management, smoking, weight reduction, parenting skills and the problems of police officers' wives … A program to train sergeants in the early warning signs of emotional distress and in techniques of brief crisis intervention and referral.
>
> (Reiser 1982: 172)

More recent writers offer a broad range of suggestions. Waters and Ussery suggest training in marital difficulties, parenting techniques and retirement planning (Waters and Ussery 2007: 184), while Ramos talks of a programme that 'also includes adopting a community policing philosophy to minimize officer isolation' (2007: 21) and states that 'Officers should be encouraged to participate in activities outside of the police agency' (ibid.: 20); 'Training should include identification of resources available inside and outside of the police agency' (ibid.: 21–2); 'Mid-level management can build on the recruit training and learn how to identify danger signs of suicide and be well versed on available resources' (ibid.: 22); and 'Administrators and command staff need to be trained on handling of high-risk officers, funeral protocols, and dealing with survivors of suicide' (ibid.: 22).

Larned comments:

> It is incumbent upon the administrators in the law enforcement community to educate officers in the nature of mental illness, depression and addiction. Through education and open discussion, the law enforcement community can provide a supportive culture that allows officers to admit problems, discuss solutions and seek help.
>
> (Larned 2010: 69)

Larned also refers to the importance of an awareness of emotional intelligence as part of a training programme and states:

> In the end, as a way to help those in crisis, we can utilize 'emotional intelligence'. Emotional intelligence centers on empathy and an understanding of others' feelings and perspectives and takes an active interest in their concerns as well as developing and building bonds with others and bolstering their abilities while listening openly, working with others toward shared goals and finally, creating group synergy in pursuing collective goals.
>
> (Larned 2010: 71)

Violanti similarly recommends appropriate training to enable officers to be more emotionally self-aware and to introduce personal skills that will assist officers in being emotionally strong.

A considerable list of possible areas of study on which training programmes can focus may be drawn from the above recommendations. It would be feasible to create a training programme which includes the above suggestions and is designed for officers at intermittent levels throughout their career. Such a programme will assist all officers in understanding their vulnerability and the resources that are available to them.

Family Participation

The training programmes to which reference has been made are not only advocated for officers; it is also suggested that they should be made available to officers' families. In support of this proposition, Ramos notes that 'the FBI recommends training police officers, their spouses, supervisors, and administrators' (Ramos 2007: 21), while Violanti recommends that there should be joint training for new officers and their families and suggests that, working together in this way, they can begin to understand some of the pressures of the work in which the officers are going to be involved.

Larned also believes that awareness programmes should offer training to family members. He regards this as essential, as:

> Providing training and information to family members and significant others on the demands and pitfalls of police work early on can offer departments and officers allies for encouraging officers through difficulties, and offers additional eyes and hands to help identify struggling officers.
>
> (Larned 2010: 71)

Clear indication was offered in the case-studies (Chapter 4, section entitled 'Difficulties within the Home and Family Context') to demonstrate the potential usefulness of family participation in relevant training programmes.

Leadership Commitment

If families are to be involved in the training sessions, as suggested above, it will be through their goodwill and desire to participate. Equally, if suicide-awareness training programmes are to be part of the training curriculum, then this will come about through the commitment of chief officers and those who have responsibility for officer welfare.

Ramos describes the commitment which leaders should make to training programmes, writing: 'the leaders of the organization at all levels must support training. It would be difficult to implement a successful training curriculum if the line members knew that the program was not fully backed by the leadership' (Ramos 2007: 25). Later he returns to this subject and comments: 'strong leadership and mandatory suicide prevention training are the keys to a successful suicide prevention model, which may reduce officer suicide rates in America' (ibid.: 84).

One might assume that leaders would be willing to give their commitment to suicide-prevention programmes. However, if leaders are not prepared to acknowledge that the suicide of officers is an issue of organisational concern, as has been previously suggested (Chapter 2), then commitment to such programmes through robust human resources policies will not be forthcoming.

Concluding Comments

As demonstrated, the psychological welfare of police officers will be more positively secured if their future emotional needs are taken into account at the commencement of the selection process and in the initial monitoring and early training phases. At this early point in their careers, great care will be taken to ensure that new officers are both suitable and equipped with the necessary emotional qualities to respond to what will be required of them in the traumas of their day-to-day work.

It is of equal importance that the ethos of this initial training should continue throughout the officers' careers, through the inclusion of 'psycho-education and prevention training programs' (Chae and Boyle 2013: 106ff.). These programmes would run parallel to the varied range of training programmes essential to the day-to-day work of the officer. This training would enable officers to have a wider perspective and understanding of their holistic identity, both within and outside the police service, especially if partners and family members were encouraged to participate. As well as offering a better understanding of relevant family issues, this participation would offer partners a greater awareness of the pressures on officers.

The value of training programmes, whether at an initial stage or as part of the in-service training curriculum, cannot be overestimated. The previous chapters have demonstrated that suicide precipitators are wide-ranging and include emotional and psychological issues (for example, depression, anger and dichotomised decision-making), home issues (for example, divorce, bereavement and financial difficulties) and workplace issues (for example, pressure of work-related stress, alleged bullying and organisational procedures). Training alone may not assist officers in avoiding some of these issues, but it can enable their awareness of the prime ones, which include:

- their vulnerability;
- the vulnerability of colleagues;
- how to identify signs of severe stress in themselves and in colleagues;
- when support is essential;
- how to seek that support.

Training can also help officers understand that an acceptance of their potential vulnerability, or a request for support, is not an indication of their weakness but rather a sign of their strength. The recognition and knowledge of coping mechanisms that can be adopted will be to the benefit of officers, the organisation and all concerned.

With reference to training in the USA, Ramos concludes that, 'based on the results of the study, it appears that leaders have much room for improvement with respect to implementing training, and effective policy for suicide prevention' (Ramos 2007: 84). This research analysis suggests that there is equal room for such improvement in the UK police service. This will have financial implications for the police service, but the potential costs should be measured against potential losses. At best, these losses will be incurred through illnesses relating to stress; at worst, through the scenario of suicidal ideation. The potential financial loss to the organisation offers a further, and pragmatic, reason why the inclusion of prevention programmes requires the commitment of senior commanders and their policy makers.

Welfare Support within and Initiated by the Organisation

Introductory Comments

A *Police Oracle* report from the UNISON Police and Justice Conference reported that occupational health units across the police service 'are falling short of properly addressing many of the mental health issues that stressed personnel are suffering from due to a lack of resources'.[9] The report includes the following comments made at the UNISON conference:

> Occupational health units [are] overwhelmed as numbers of police personnel suffering mental health issues from stress soars.

> Occupational health units are lacking the resources and manpower to deal with officers and staff suffering mental health issues due to soaring stress levels.

> Severe cuts to forces' budgets have been blamed for health issues for remaining police officers and staff who are being asked to take on more work due to redundancies and reductions in numbers.

As occupational health units are the main thrust of occupational support for police officers, the report suggests a worrying scenario, especially as the police service's financial restrictions limit the external sources that might supplement the support required for suicidal officers. The mental health issues discussed at the UNISON conference contribute to so many of the precipitators identified in the case-studies, and a consideration of the welfare support that forces are able to offer now follows. The following issues are examined:

- confidentiality
- psychological support and counselling
- peer support
- 24-hour crisis support lines
- a process to identify risk.

Confidentiality

The case-studies revealed the importance of officers having people in whom they could confide. This importance of confidentiality was particularly demonstrated in Chapter 4 (section entitled 'Unwillingness to Accept Help') and in Chapter 7 (section entitled 'Denial of Help'). It is also an issue on which considerable comment has been made by the relevant researchers.

Violanti considers where the officer may turn for support, whether this can be found within the work or home context and the extent to which the officer can trust that support to be confidential. Commenting on the confidentiality of appropriate intervention measures, Kirschman states, 'if there is a common thread … it is the doomed officer's inability to ask for or find confidential help before small problems snowball into a tidal wave of torment' (Kirschman 1997: 169). According to the researchers to whom reference has been made, the fear that access to welfare support provided by the police organisation is not confidential is an issue of serious concern to officers. Reiser explains: 'Some men feel suspicious and distrustful and hesitate to use a helping resource within the department' (Reiser 1982: 65).

Martinez describes confidentiality as the most important issue (Martinez 2010: 80) and offers a number of comments made by officers:

> One male officer with eight years on the job stated that, 'Anonymous support would alleviate the stress of the stigma brought about by thoughts of suicide or an attempt'.
>
> (Martinez 2010: 81)

> Another officer, a female with five years on the job wrote, 'I think that if the department created programs that would be 100% confidential they would probably be more successful'.
>
> (ibid.)

Duncan Chappell, who undertook research in Australia, reports similar comments, stating: 'all those I spoke to were nervous about being identified' (Chappell 2010: 296).

As well as raising concerns about the lack of confidentiality, researchers suggest reasons for the officers' mistrust. Martinez cites an officer's comment that 'I think officers who come forward are afraid about losing their jobs and what they discuss may not be kept confidential' (Martinez 2010: 81).

Within the Australian policing community, Chappell suggests that the officers' fear of disclosing their stress is partly because 'the topic of mental illness still remain[s] clouded by stigma and suspicion' (Chappell 2010: 296–7). Chappell also comments that officers are fearful of accessing support from within the organisation because 'this fact alone would be documented in their personnel files and affect their future chances of promotion' (Chappell 2010: 297). Ramos similarly suggests that this nervousness is in part due to a fear of 'organizational retribution from the administration' (Ramos 2007: 23).

Many of the above suggestions were contextually reflected in the analysis of the case-studies. The process of dichotomised decision-making (discussed in Chapters 6 and 7) may deter officers from recognising the need for support in the first place. If the need for support is acknowledged, officers may either be unwilling to accept help (Chapter 4) or deny the help that is offered (Chapters 6 and 7). There may be a number of reasons for this; it would appear that one such reason is a fear that the support will not be confidential.

The fear of being seen as weak by peers (Chapters 6 and 7), the notion of invulnerability (Chapters 6 and 7) and the characteristic of 'rugged individualism'

(Chapter 6) will also deter officers from revealing feelings related to suicidal ideation in potentially non-confidential situations. Officers who feel betrayed by management (Chapter 4) will fear a lack of confidentiality related to the organisational structures, procedures and culture (Chapters 6 and 7). Depression may bring anxiety about a fear of losing control (Chapter 7). All these attributes will be exacerbated if the officer is isolated from either family or others (Chapters 4 and 6).

In spite of the comments regarding the fear that welfare-support services will not offer confidentiality, the researchers to whom reference has been made strongly recommend the development of internal police welfare-support systems.

Violanti recommends that such support systems should be made available to all officers regardless of the size of the force, as all officers confront comparable difficulties. Furthermore, he proposes that every effort should be made to progress confidential support mechanisms; access to these should be possible through non-formal means. He suggests that if such intervention mechanisms are in place, the potential for suicide should be reduced. With regard to confidential support, Martinez agrees with Violanti and states that 'police departments should not be able to know when an officer uses a department counsellor' (Martinez 2010: 80). With reference to 'departmental counsellors', Chappell also affirms that officers continue to mistrust 'in-house psychologists and counsellors' (Chappell 2010: 297).

Reiser, in his role as a psychologist working within a police department, refutes the basis of this mistrust, asserting that the confidential relationship between psychologist and client-officer is maintained. He suggests that this is because much of the counselling involves issues 'of a personal nature, whether marital, job related or family' (Reiser 1982: 65) and that there exists what he defines as 'a privileged counselor-client relationship' (ibid.). He supports this assertion by stating that 'If there are no criminal activities involved and the person is in control, rational, and capable of self-care, there is no problem about maintaining the confidentiality of the relationship' (ibid.)

Reiser's above statement, however, possibly demonstrates why an officer may be apprehensive about approaching a psychologist/counsellor appointed by the force; for example, the officer may well have good reason to ask who determines the level of rationality, self-care and self-control required before the officer's force is informed and, if the force is informed, what knowledge will be shared and with whom. These questions will consequently reinforce the officer's fear of a loss of control (Chapter 6, section entitled 'Depression').

Reiser highlights the potential for further raising an officer's concern over a lack of confidentiality when he continues: 'If the individual is psychotic, destructively acting-out, engaged in serious criminal activity, suicidal or homicidal, then the need for confidentiality is overridden by the greater need to protect the individual and the community' (Reiser 1982: 65). He is correct that this is in accordance with 'the ethical principles of psychiatrists, psychologists and social workers' (ibid.) in private practice, but questions remain as to where those who may wish to talk about suicide may safely turn for a confidential discussion.

With regard to overcoming the issue of mistrust, Chappell offers an observation from his research. As the psychologists and other staff involved in helping with mental health issues became more integrated into mainstream policing, mistrust and suspicion diminished (Chappell 2010: 297). By way of example as to how this was achieved, Chappell refers to the way in which a psychologist attended regular meetings 'with personnel working in "high stress/risk" areas like accident and homicide investigations, sexual offence inquiries including child pornography; and coronial work' (ibid.). Similarly, Martinez offers an officer's suggestion that it would be a positive move if 'more people from the counseling center attend roll-calls and give out handouts with phone numbers a couple of times a year' (Martinez 2010: 67).

In spite of all these possible safeguards, a further dilemma pertaining to confidentiality concerns the number of people who may be called upon to support a single 'client'. The most vulnerable of officers will be supported by a number of different individuals, and a difficulty that can arise lies in the amount of information that those in support roles are free to share with each other. This difficulty was demonstrated following the death of a Deputy Chief Constable. An HMIC report of a review following his death commented: 'The review found that there was considerable welfare provision available ... however responsibility for providing this was shared between a number of individuals ... it is acknowledged that confidentiality arrangements made it extremely difficult to share information.'[10]

Further reference is made to this dilemma later in this chapter.

Psychological Support and Counselling

The literature survey reveals the importance of the potential support of psychologists and trained counsellors. Barron writes, for example, that 'Police community approaches ... and supportive clinical care are essential strategies in any attempt to reduce the incidence of suicide amongst police officers'.[11] This importance was reinforced by analysis of the case-studies. However, it would appear that, following the reduction of central-government funding to local UK forces, the financial resources to offer such clinical support may be increasingly unavailable in the UK, as reported earlier in this chapter.

Finding the funding for such support may be equally challenging in the USA: Rostow and Davis describe 'the difficulty of finding and engaging police-knowledgeable treatment providers' and explain that 'securing payment for treatment' can be problematic (Rostow and Davis 2004: 123). However, according to Waters and Ussery, certain funding can be made available from state, federal and other agencies (Waters and Ussery 2007: 177).

As challenging as the identification of financial resources may be, the argument for the necessity of clinical support is overwhelming. Referring to the importance of quality in-force psychological support and counselling, Reiser claims that this has significantly contributed to 'the relatively low suicide rate for Los Angeles police officers' (Reiser 1982: 171). Other researchers offer similar comment: 'Having meaningful, supportive relationships and a therapeutic alliance with a mental health professional greatly reduces a person's risk for suicide' (Kirschman 1997: 176); 'Peer and professional counseling must be made immediately available' (Larned 2010: 69); 'Police departments should have a psychologist and a chaplain for the officers available at all times' (Martinez 2010: 80, quoting an officer). Violanti also strongly recommends having a team of trained professionals who can respond to referrals. Furthermore, he suggests that these professionals should be conversant with the police role and culture. Such comments are affirmed by Waters and Ussery, who comment that police psychologists are not only available to support officers, but also to offer counselling to officers' partners and their children (Waters and Ussery 2007: 177).

Peer Support

The importance of colleague support and/or the lack of it is well illustrated in the analysis of the case-studies in Chapter 4 (see section entitled 'Lack of Welfare and Colleague Support'). Conversely, within the same chapter, reference is made to an officer who 'had attempted to take his own life just four months earlier but on that occasion was stopped after colleagues intervened' (Chapter 4, section entitled 'Premeditated'; case-study 10). Within the same section, reference is made to colleagues who 'became concerned about the welfare of [the officer] after taking a series of increasingly desperate telephone calls from him' (case-study 12) and to another officer who 'had spoken of suicide to colleagues who said that he had later changed his mind' (case-study 20).

The context of officers under investigation is worthy of special reference with regard to peer support (see Chapter 4, sections entitled 'Criminal Investigations' and 'Internal Investigations for Professional Misconduct'.) Those under investigation may have many close colleagues, but the latter may be unable to express their support because of the institutional contact restrictions placed upon them. Furthermore, if there is a criminal or internal investigation, close colleagues may be fearful of becoming personally involved in the investigation and may distance themselves from the situation. The officer will therefore feel ostracised and isolated. If the officer is allowed to remain in the workplace, there may be a constant feeling that colleagues are talking behind the officer's back, regardless of whether or not this is an accurate perception.

The research analysis demonstrates the valuable contribution that proactive peer support can provide in many different contexts. Miller, after using the analogy of officers being taught how to offer fellow officers cardiopulmonary resuscitation, asks: 'shouldn't the same emphasis on psychological lifesaving techniques be part of the training of all officers' (Miller 2006: 183). Violanti lists peer support as one of three levels of intervention and, affirming its value, suggests that greater use should be made of this support mechanism. He explains: 'It is easier for troubled officers to talk to other police officers. ... These counselors would not be expected to be psychologists but support persons primarily there as someone to talk to' (Violanti 2007: 162).

Ramos suggests that trained peer-support groups and critical-incident response teams might be created, which would complement outside counselling (Ramos 2007: 25), and Larned states that peer counselling 'must be made immediately available' (Larned 2010: 69).

The success of peer support is described by Chae and Boyle, who comment that, time-wise, it may be more expedient to arrange a meeting with a peer counsellor than to make an appointment with a counsellor working in a busy professional practice. However, they also comment that 'to date, only a handful of effective and reliable peer counseling programs for law enforcement officials have been established' (Chae and Boyle 2013: 106). One peer-group counselling system which they claim has had success provides access to peer counsellors using a 24-hour telephone hotline. Reference is made to this system in the next section.

A 24-Hour Crisis Support Line

Chae and Boyle refer to a peer-support programme offered by the New York Police Department and report that 'preliminary evidence indicates that Cop2Cop has served as an important source of support for law enforcement personnel dealing with various life and work-related stressors' (Chae and Boyle 2013: 106). Cop2Cop is a system of peer support undertaken solely by telephone and is commended by Waters and Ussery, who make in-depth comments on the Cop2Cop peer-support system, detailing both the general and assessment guidelines of the approach to be followed by the peer counsellor. They state that the general guidelines are as follows:

1. plan and conduct a crisis assessment (including measures of lethality);
2. establish rapport and a therapeutic relationship;
3. identify the caller's major problems including the precipitating events;
4. deal with feelings. Be an active listener and validate the caller's emotions;
5. generate and explore alternative coping strategies and skills;
6. develop and formulate an appropriate action plan; and
7. establish a follow-up plan and agreement.

(Waters and Ussery 2007: 184)

Waters and Ussery explain that because the hotline call-takers are retired officers, they are able to develop a constructive relationship with the officer making the request for support and help. This, they suggest, is because call-taker and caller will have many experiences in common, and a shared knowledge of policing (Waters and Ussery 2007: 185).

Waters and Ussery continue by describing how the volunteers, using their existing knowledge, will assess:

1. the nature of the support required by pursuing answers to the following questions:
2. the nature of the presenting problem;

3. the severity of the situation and the length of time that the problem has existed;
4. the actual impact on the officer's ability to function on the job and at home;
5. the precipitants of the situation or the immediate cause of the problem;
6. any past history or current substance abuse;
7. other relevant aspects of past history;
8. previous inpatient and/or outpatient psychiatric history; and
9. current medical problems and medical history.

(Waters and Ussery 2007: 185)

After presenting the initial approach taken by the volunteer call-takers, Waters and Ussery offer a comprehensive account of how the peer counselling is structured over a period of time and will only be concluded by the peer counsellors when they believe that the person seeking support has overcome the crisis and is ready to move forward with confidence.

Martinez and Violanti both commend the availability of a 24-hour hotline telephone system. Martinez offers the comment of an officer, who states:

> The true reality is that if someone's life is in danger and they are calling the hotline that means they really want help. Hotlines are beneficial to a certain extent, you could probably talk someone out of it or you can send some help by tracing the number to the location of the call.

(Martinez 2010: 81)

Violanti explains the importance of an officer being able to easily access support and suggests that a 24-hour phone service offers such support. He details how such a scheme could work using a generic telephone number which would offer totally confidential support in that the call-taker would, initially, receive calls anonymously. If further intervention was required and acceptable to the call-maker, then one-to-one support could be arranged. Violanti considers that this confidential method would succeed in being readily available to many and would be economically viable.

Larned offers a word of caution in that, as valuable as any immediate response may be – whether by telephone or through counselling – further strategies are required to ensure that support is offered 'at periodic intervals and around anniversary dates of traumatic incidents [to remind] officers they are not alone and help is close at hand' (Larned 2010: 69).

A Process to Identify Risk

Research indicates that support designed to determine those who might be at risk following a critical/traumatic incident is to be encouraged.

The University of Maryland Medical Center defines a traumatic event as 'An experience that causes physical, emotional, psychological distress, or harm. It is an event that is perceived and experienced as a threat to one's safety or to the stability of one's world'.[12] In a similar vein, a trauma risk management (TRiM) document published by Suffolk Police states: 'A traumatic incident is any event that can be considered to be outside of an individual's usual experience and causes physical, emotional or psychological harm.'[13]

Violanti offers examples of traumatic incidents that officers face in their work on the streets. Referring to the work of a response officer, as stated in Chapter 6 (section entitled 'Depression'), he cites earlier research which reveals the close relationship between depression and the long-lasting consequences of trauma and experienced dangerous situations. Furthermore, Violanti states that the possibility of suicide increases with the frequency and number of stressful incidents encountered by officers.

Robert Verkaik reports on this relationship between traumatic incidents and depression experienced by officers in an article for the *Independent*; commenting on a survey of officers, he states that officers had spoken of how 'stress and depression could be triggered by the exposure to traumatic incidents they encountered during their work'.[14]

The overriding presence of either long-term or short-term depression was identified in many of the case-studies (see Chapter 4, sections entitled 'Depression' and 'Emotional Context – Depression'). The causes of the depression were manifold, but the accumulative effects of depression and trauma were identified particularly in case-study 6 in Chapter 4, section entitled 'Bereavement' – the officer was suffering from grief when a further traumatic incident occurred, and the coroner commented that these factors had 'a cumulative effect'.

To identify and thereby minimise the effects of stress, depression and anxiety, a number of UK forces have introduced a programme – briefly referred to earlier in this chapter – entitled TRiM. TRiM is designed to encourage officers to work through the critical incident they may have witnessed.[15]

As a Suffolk Police TRiM document explains:

> The intent is to capitalise on the natural processes that occur after traumatic events, such as; meeting in groups; talking the event through and looking after each other. It should help towards keeping people working and prevent long-term loss of resources through psychological injury by identifying psychological problems at an early stage.[16]

The purpose of the TRiM process accords with Ramos' comment (see Chapter 2, section entitled 'Police-Specific Causes of Suicidal Ideation') that 'Literature shows that the previous method of suppressing or compressing the emotional feelings associated with exposure to critical incidents is detrimental to officers over extended periods of time' (Ramos 2007: 25).

In responding to the need for this expression of feelings, as the Essex document explains, 'TRiM is not classed as a preventative measure, but must be seen as an early intervention that identifies possible harmful reactions and addresses them appropriately'.

Those who facilitate the TRiM programme are referred as TRiM practitioners. They are peer officers or staff who are trained to work according to a prescribed system designed to assess the officer's traumatic risk. The trained practitioners are required to meet the officer(s) within 24 hours of the given incident and explain the process. After this initial meeting there are two further meetings, the final one of which is 28 days after the incident. The Essex document explains:

> All individuals that prove to still need intervention at the 28 day point should be referred for assessment and possible treatment to the OH&W Department where they will be assessed by a Welfare Adviser and Occupational Health Adviser where necessary.

Those who work with the TRiM process speak highly of its effectiveness and would advocate its benefit to officers and therefore the police service also, although some interviewed officers felt that TRiM had been of no value to them personally.

Concluding Comments

As the analysis of the case-studies demonstrates, the suicidal ideation experienced by officers is complex and the precipitators may be manifold. Consequently, the welfare support provided will need to be multi-faceted. Waters and Ussery refer to the need for this multi-dimensional response in commenting that, as the personality of each officer is unique, all officers will have individual needs. An officer will therefore need to select an approach, or indeed a combination of approaches, that is pertinent to that individual (Waters and Ussery 2007: 184).

Reference has been made within this section to preventative programmes and post-traumatic briefings. For some officers at least, these programmes and briefings may be helpful – although in one officer's words, offered by Martinez, 'Many officers would not go to preventative programs because they are usually private people ... many have macho man syndrome and are not open for discussion when it comes to their private lives' (Martinez 2010: 68).

Ramos suggests that following traumatic situations, 'policy can be created to make employee assistance programs mandatory for exposure to critical incidents' (Ramos 2007: 25). Whether compulsory or not, it is possible that officers may choose not to express their feelings in these contexts, for reasons previously given, including the lack of confidentiality.

This fear of disclosing information which could be detrimental to the officer's career or the personality which the officer wishes to portray to colleagues may deter the officer from accessing the required support. However, if a range of support services can be offered to officers, the greater is the chance that officers will avail themselves of those support mechanisms. As referenced within this chapter, the welfare support provided might include a full range of psychological services and counselling, peer support and immediate access to those who can offer empathy through their knowledge of the police service.

These intervention measures will include initiatives at 'peer, supervisory, and administrative' levels which, as Violanti suggests, 'should be evaluated separately as well as together to determine effectiveness' (Violanti 2007: 158). The need for constant evaluation and monitoring was demonstrated by the suicide of Audrey Fagan in 2007.[17] Chappell explains that Fagan had been referred for psychiatric support and that, as a member of the Australian Federal Police (AFP), she had access to 'an extensive "well-being service" for its personnel, staffed by eight staff psychologists, five counsellors and four family liaison officers' (Chappell 2010: 296). In spite of this range of potential support, Fagan still took her own life.

There will always be situations that cannot be foreseen in which officers experiencing suicidal ideation may complete suicide. However, this does not minimise the need for the provision of extensive welfare-support systems that are constantly monitored to ensure their effectiveness.

As noted in the concluding comments to the section of this chapter entitled 'Training', and as mentioned elsewhere in the chapter, the cost of welfare provision weighs heavily on the police's financial budget at a time of financial constraint, but the consequential cost of poor welfare provision must also be taken into account.

Investigations: Complaints and Discipline

Martinez refers to 'arbitrary disciplinary procedures' as a precipitator contributing to officer suicides (Martinez 2010: 31; Chapter 6, section entitled 'Stress' under the section 'Contextual Factors Leading to Police-Specific Suicidal Ideation'). In a similar vein, Violanti comments on the stress involved in working in an organisation which is controlling by nature and which is perceived by some to be biased against its officers in disciplinary matters (Chapter 6, section entitled 'Criminal or Internal Investigation'). Similarly, Barron comments that 'the complaint management system viewed problematic behaviours as a discipline/management issue and further compounded problems by protracted and time consuming investigations'.[18]

The issues referenced above were closely identified within the primary research undertaken. The earlier analysis of the case-studies revealed that in a large percentage of officer suicides – more than 50 per cent – the officers were or would have been involved in investigations of either a criminal or internal nature at the time of their deaths (Chapter 4, sections entitled 'Criminal Investigation Issues', 'Criminal Investigations', 'Internal Investigations for Professional Misconduct').

As analysis of some of the case-studies demonstrated, the stress that officers faced was exacerbated by the notion of 'double jeopardy'; that is, when officers are found innocent of all criminal charges and yet still face an internal police investigation, with a possible formal disciplinary hearing. *Police Oracle* explains this scenario and draws attention to the contributory pressures, citing the comments of a Police Federation spokesperson:

> Federation official argues officers are subject to double standards by police watchdog despite being acquitted at court. … Officers who are cleared of

wrongdoing in the courts are subject to 'double standards' if they then have to face a misconduct hearing, a Police Federation official has said. … Mike White, Chairman of the Wiltshire branch board questioned the public interest in pursuing a professional standards investigation or misconduct hearing if an officer has been held to account and cleared of wrongdoing at court. … There appears to be double standards for police officers. When MPs and politicians are found not guilty in courts that is enough but it is not the case for officers. … It could make a difference in the way the force reacts to possible complaints and they could go to the 'nth' degree when investigating, which could have an impact on the officers subject to such an investigation.[19]

Whether the officer faces a situation of double jeopardy or a single charge, the pressure involved will be substantial. The pressures faced by officers under disciplinary measures are described in a Metropolitan Police internal document:

The Metropolitan Police Service's (MPS) Department of Professional Standards (DPS) understands and acknowledges that the notification of formal investigation or misconduct proceedings against a member of staff or a police officer, is a significantly stressful time for the individual and their family. They may face long periods of uncertainty while the case is progressed through the different stages. These include the investigation, the evidential review, a legal assessment for the Appropriate Authority, the final determination (whether the conduct alleged is Gross Misconduct or not) then the formal Misconduct proceedings.[20]

As the above document states, the initial investigation period is lengthy. During this initial period of investigation, during which officers may be suspended, they are unlikely to be able to obtain free legal advice through their professional bodies, such as the Federation or the Superintendents' Association. If legal advice is available through a professional association, it will not be made available until after what is termed as the 'disclosure' has been made; that is, when the officer is given a detailed account of the charges. During this period, there is likely to be a lack of general communication (Chapter 4, section entitled 'Workplace Issues'), a lack of confidential welfare support (Chapter 4, sections entitled 'Unwillingness to Accept Help') and a lack of colleague support (Chapter 4, section entitled 'Lack of Welfare and Colleague Support'; Chapter 7, section entitled 'Lack of Welfare Support').

To illustrate some of the pressures faced by officers under investigation, the following scenario is offered. The scenario is a compilation of case-studies to which reference has been previously made:

Without warning, officer colleagues, some of whom are long-standing friends, arrive at the family home late in the evening and arrest the officer; the officer's partner is also arrested (neither are eventually charged). The family home is searched thoroughly by the officer's colleague friends. The officer and partner are taken under arrest to separate custody units, where they are interviewed. Their children are taken into the care of others, with no contact allowed between the parents and their children. Items are taken from the home as possible evidence for charges to be brought, including family photographs and all the family/children's computers.

The officer concerned will feel degraded both by the allegations made and by the arrest procedure, especially when this is undertaken by colleagues. Furthermore, the officer will feel acute guilt, genuine or perceived, for the ordeal their partner has had to endure.

This is the initial situation. To describe the situation as the investigation continues, a further typical scenario is offered. The scenario is again drawn from the case-studies.

The officer is suspended and told that there can be no contact with colleagues. The officer's colleagues are similarly informed that there can be no contact with the officer under investigation. Consequently, the officer is isolated from those with whom the officer has worked and socialised.

If the officer is suspended, a welfare contact is appointed, but this welfare contact acts on behalf of the force and is expected to report on the officer to line-managers and those involved in carrying out the investigation.

Policy guidelines acknowledge the stress faced by officers and suggest that an officer-colleague should be appointed as a Welfare Support Officer. The Metropolitan Police (MPS) guidelines[21] state that the role of the Welfare Support Officer is to:

- Provide support and guidance to the individual by providing information about the MPS Support Services.
- Assist with access/referrals to officers if required.
- Clarify a 'contract' of expectations with the individual.
- Set boundaries. These may include: acceptable hours and methods of contact, the limits of confidentiality, the protocol for out-of-hours contact and whom to contact if the Welfare Support Officer is off work.
- Carry out regular dynamic risk assessments on the individual.
- To monitor & review the welfare of an individual facing formal misconduct proceedings by offering regular contact.
- Manage & maintain a comprehensive contact log.
- Report any risk, lack of engagement, identified concern or change in circumstances to the (B) OCU [Operational Command Unit] Commander or the (B) OCU's Professional Standards Champion. (PSC). They will inform the individual's DPS Case Manager.
- Take necessary action to ensure line management and supporting services are made aware of any identified risk or concern.

The guidelines also state:

> The Welfare Support Officer is NOT there to:
>
> - Provide counselling services. (This can be arranged via OH [Occupational Health].)
> - Advise the individual on the progress of their case.
> - Discuss or advise on the Misconduct allegation(s).

As comprehensive as these guidelines may be, it will be noted that the role is not one that offers any sense of confidentiality, nor is it one that specifically offers welfare support. It appears that, primarily, the role involves attempting to ensure that impartial contact is maintained between the officer and managers within the force. As confidentiality cannot be offered by the welfare contact, trust between that contact and the officer will be limited, especially if the officer no longer trusts the force and is aware of reporting-back procedures.

As the investigation into the officer's conduct commences, in all probability a referral will be made to Occupational Health. Their support, and the additional support of the counselling agencies to which referrals may be made, cannot be over-estimated. However, the officer's confidence in the occupational health unit may be limited (see, for example, case-studies 7 and 8 in Chapter 4, section entitled 'Unwillingness to Accept Help', under section entitled 'Identified Causes of Suicidal Ideation'). Furthermore, if the officer is screened by occupational health personnel (and others) for suicidal ideation, that individual will more than likely be well versed in responses designed to offer the appearance that their emotions are under control (Chapter 4, section entitled 'Premeditated or Impulsive', case-study 23).

An appointed Federation representative (or the appropriate staff association) will also offer assistance. Their concern will be for the individual officer and they will support in whatever manner they are able, but primarily the association's expertise will be used to advise the officer on the appropriate courses of action in relation to the investigation.

As can be seen from the *Guidance for Welfare Support Officers* cited earlier in the chapter, various avenues of support will be available to the officer (see the discussion of Audrey Fagan's case earlier in this chapter). It should be noted again, however, that these many different support mechanisms may nevertheless be limited by a lack of coordination because of their confidentiality codes (see the comments regarding the death of the DCC earlier in this chapter).

To summarise the above, investigations are lengthy and the process unwieldy, during which communication about the process can be lacking; as *Lessons Learned* comments in relation to the investigation of the DCC, 'there was a lack of clear communication around how the misconduct process operated [and] its timescales'.[22]

As the analysis of the case-studies demonstrates, throughout this period of investigation the officer will envisage many different possible consequences, all of which can lead to further fears – some of which may be irrational but may nevertheless become real in the officer's thoughts. For example, officers may fear the loss of the role which they have known for many years, financial ruin, the loss of the home, the loss of their spouse/partner, the loss of family (Chapter 4, section entitled 'Difficulties within the Home and Family Context'), a court case and possibly prison.

As well as fear, the officer will experience many other additional emotions. The officer will cease to trust individuals in the organisation, and the organisation itself. Lack of communication will leave the officer feeling that he has been, as expressed in the context of a case-study, 'hung out to dry'. There will be distress at the possibility of losing the status and identity involved in the police role. Furthermore, the officer will be embarrassed to belong to an organisation that is seemingly uncaring and hypocritical in its dealings. During this time the officer will receive unsolicited advice from friends and family, which is likely to include pressure from home and friends to leave the work and the organisation for which the officer has lived and worked.

The sum total of all these pressures leads to a complete lack of self-esteem and self-confidence. This again in turn may lead to depression, which in turn may lead to physical illness, alcohol abuse or other negative behaviour patterns, such as anger and aggression. All of this will be compounded by a loss of self-respect and the respect of colleagues and friends (Chapter 4, section entitled 'Negative Self-Perceptions'). Again, as analysis of the case-studies reveals, officers under investigation become increasingly confused as to their future in an ever-increasing spiral of stress. Because of officers' feelings of invulnerability (Chapters 6 and 7), 'rugged individualism' (Chapter 6) and dichotomised decision-making (Chapters 6 and 7), they may be fundamentally ill-equipped to be able to respond to their stress.

The welfare support of officers under investigation is generally underestimated by those who have responsibility for their welfare. The pressures faced can become overwhelming and lead to suicidal ideation. Consequently, it is the conclusion of this research that significant changes should be made to the welfare arrangements of those being investigated; appropriate recommendations as to changes in procedures are made in Chapter 11.

An Identification of Officers at Risk

Barron recognises the limitations to predicting which officers may be the most vulnerable to suicidal ideation and comments that 'there exists no management system which can accurately assess and identify officers who are at risk of suicide'.[23] Furthermore, he suggests that 'the development of a risk profile for police officers who may, in some circumstances, commit suicide is a subtle part solution only to the problem of police officer suicide'.[24] Research suggests that a risk profile is of little use if effective prevention measures are not in place.

Nevertheless, Barron refers to specific risk factors, which include 'depression, relationship problems, financial problems, substance abuse, alcohol abuse, and access to firearms, organisational issues such as corruption and management decisions'. He continues:

> other risk factors ... include: one or more diagnosable mental or substance abuse disorders, impulsivity, history of alcohol abuse, adverse life events, family history of suicide, physical and sexual abuse, a prior suicide attempt, and exposure to other suicidal events (contagion effect).[25]

Kirschman also discusses the warning signs that may indicate vulnerability to suicide, which she lists as serious depression, a significant loss – actual or threatened, substance abuse, previous suicide attempts or threats, marked change in personality, giving things away, reckless behaviour, anniversary reactions and reunion fantasies (Kirschman 1997: 171–4).

The analysis of the case-studies indicate that it is possible to identify which officers might be at greatest risk, and the contexts in which officers might be particularly vulnerable (Chapter 4). However, in spite of the indicators of suicide precipitators, the case-studies reveal that these indicators are at times missed or not recognised. As Barron writes: 'somehow, the system failed these officers, their colleagues failed to recognise and report a growing range of problematic behaviours, such as deteriorating personal relationships, increased alcohol abuse and problematic behaviour and performance in the workplace'.[26] In seeking to overcome this failure, Martinez suggests, 'it is important that supervisors are capable of identifying officers who might be contemplating suicide' (Martinez 2010: 80).

Single precipitators (Chapter 4, section entitled 'Single Contributory Factor') and precipitators in combination offer valuable information as to officers' vulnerability to suicide. In addition, perhaps even greater vigilance might be considered following one or more suicides in a particular force, or following an officer suicide that has high-level media attention. Line-managers should be aware of the possibility of community contagion (Chapter 6, section entitled 'Community Contagion'). Risk factors should be clearly understood and known by colleagues and line-managers of all levels (as discussed earlier in this chapter) and thereby identified. Without the development and effective utilisation of a risk profile, there may be no application and implementation of successful prevention measures.

Bullying, Harassment and Victimisation

In 2009, the *Independent* reported that 'nearly 40 per cent of officers reported that senior management's approach to managing performance was "harsh and unhelpful", and nearly a third said chief constables showed "bullying behaviour"'.[27]

Police Oracle also offered a report concerning bullying:

> More than half of police officers and staff have suffered bullying in their forces – and more than a quarter face bullying from colleagues on a regular basis, a commission on the future of policing has said. Fifty-three per cent of

officers said they had encountered bullying at some stage, while 20 per cent said they suffered bullying either all or some of the time. Meanwhile, 24 per cent of PCSOs and 22 per cent of other police staff said they faced bullying on a regular basis. Only 47 per cent of officers, 40 per cent of PCSOs and 43 per cent of other police staff said they never suffered bullying.[28]

Alleged bullying, harassment and victimisation (Chapters 4 and 7) was identified within the analysis of the case-studies as a suicide precipitator. Examples of alleged and proven bullying, harassment and victimisation can be readily found in various media reports. One example was reported by *Police Oracle*:

> The Metropolitan Police has failed to overturn an employment tribunal ruling that stated a gay, black officer was 'harassed and victimised' out of his job. Former counter-terrorism officer Kevin Maxwell claims racism and homophobia 'are still rife' in the force following allegations that he suffered bullying while serving at Heathrow's Terminal Five.[29]

Police Oracle also reported the force's response:

> In a statement, the Force said it was 'disappointed' with the latest judgement and would consider it in more detail. It added: 'Mr Maxwell's claims relate to events in 2009 and 2010. Since that time there have been changes across a number of areas including how to report wrongdoing and managing employees on sick leave. Any other learning opportunities identified from this case will be taken forward'.[30]

As can be seen, according to the *Police Oracle* account, the reported harassment and victimisation occurred prior to various changes. Furthermore, the *Police Oracle* account reported the force's assertion that 'any other learning opportunities identified from this case will be taken forward'. It would be appropriate for these learning opportunities to be shared across the forces to minimise the potential effects of bullying, harassment and victimisation.

Stress Caused by Shift Patterns

The analysis of the case-studies did not identify rotating shift patterns as a suicide precipitator. However, the stress of shift patterns is a potential factor that would not necessarily be quantifiable, and therefore would not be considered at a coroner's inquest. Various researchers have nevertheless commented on the potential strain of working according to a challenging shift pattern and the need for an assessment of its impact on stress.

Martinez refers to the vulnerability created by working on a changing shift pattern (Martinez 2010: 31), while Reintzell states that 'shift work inhibits efficiency and good performance and is a well-documented source of physical and mental harm' (Reintzell 1990: 15). Similarly, Violanti comments that the pattern of shift work is detrimental to an officer's well-being, as a disturbed sleep pattern will impair the officer's ability to respond to stress.

It is not only a rotating shift pattern that is claimed to cause stress; in addition, Royston Martis reports comments by Chris Jones, secretary of West Midlands Police Federation, stating that stress levels are increased by 'shifts being constantly changed at short notice' due to 'the way they are being managed as a result of the staffing levels'.[31] These comments were made in response to research undertaken by Dr Jonathan Houdmont of Nottingham University, who carried out research into work-related stress on behalf of West Midlands Police Federation.

Some months later, *Police Oracle* offered further reference to Houdmont's report. Cliff Caswell reported that according to Houdmont, 'a common and popular custody shift pattern is showing signs that it could be shattering the health of officers and should be examined', and that

> 70 per cent of those on 12-hour shifts, of four days on and four off, were showing that they could be at risk of burning out … which amounted to emotional exhaustion – [and] could have serious consequences for the health of individuals and organisational effectiveness … the academic highlighted that some 40 per cent of custody sergeants in both surveys had shown signs that they were suffering psychological stress – and would be likely to be diagnosed with disorders such as anxiety if they were assessed by health professionals.[32]

According to *Police Oracle*, Houdmont's report was welcomed by the national custody lead, Assistant Chief Constable (ACC) Dawn Copley, who said that the results of the study would be taken 'extremely seriously'. She went on:

> It was important that the service took action to mitigate the risks. … It is important we do something tangible. … I welcome this work which gives a picture of custody sergeants across the service. Those officers that completed the survey have given us a consistent message.[33]

The ACC's comments would surely be welcomed by Waters and Ussery, who comment on the potential dangers of rotating shift patterns and advise that there should be a reconsideration of the shift system (Waters and Ussery 2007: 184). The analysis suggests that stress caused by difficult shift patterns should be given due consideration.

Concluding Comments

Throughout this chapter, analysis has been provided which demonstrates the need for an organisational response to officers who are vulnerable to suicidal ideation. The organisation and the role requirements can lead to officer stress, which in turn can become a suicide precipitator. Among the stress factors are disciplinary procedures, the promotional system, the authoritarian organisational structure, poor management practices and inadequate communication. Barron summarises such precipitators when he describes the service as 'an unfeeling organisational culture which could lead to suicide'.[34]

The earlier analysis of the case-studies drew attention to many difficulties within the organisational processes to which the comments above relate, including situations related to:

- criminal and internal investigations (Chapter 4, sections entitled 'Criminal Investigation Issues', 'Internal Investigations for Professional Misconduct', 'Criminal Investigations');
- bullying (Chapter 4, section entitled 'Alleged Bullying, Harassment and Victimisation');
- welfare support (Chapter 4, section entitled 'Lack of Welfare and Colleague Support');
- the perceived failures of management (Chapter 4, sections entitled 'Lack of Communication', 'Re-Assignment of Working Role', 'Pressure of Work-Related Stress').

The ways in which these precipitators may interrelate were further examined in Chapters 6 and 7. The need to implement intervention measures at an organisational level has been clearly demonstrated, both in this chapter and in preceding ones.

The importance of prevention measures cannot be overestimated, for, as Barron reports, 'studies have shown that suicide prevention measures are successful in reducing the likelihood and incidence of suicide'.[35] Within this chapter, a broad range of organisational strategies have been examined and advocated. These include:

- the selection and initial training of officers;
- in-service training;
- welfare support from managers, peers and internal support mechanisms such as occupational health;
- support during criminal and internal investigations;
- the elimination of bullying;
- an identification of officers at risk;
- an assessment of shift patterns;
- a debriefing process following traumatic/critical incidents.

Within these strategies, a wide range of important issues have been identified. These include:

- the need for confidentiality;
- the socialisation of the officer's identity to dismiss the 'false personalisation' that can occur;
- leadership commitment;
- the role of welfare officers.

Some of these strategies and issues may have cost implications, but certainly not all; for example, there can be virtually no cost in ensuring:

- open communications between officers and supervisors;
- opportunities for meaningful input into departmental decisions whenever possible;
- constructive feedback on job performance;
- opportunities for 'debriefing' sessions at the end of the shift.

(Waters and Ussery 2007: 184)

Equally, the cost implications of peer support to develop departmental, 'confidential help resources' (Violanti 2007: 158) would be negligible, especially if peer-support mechanisms are used.

Other support mechanisms, such as psychological counselling, will have cost implications, and at a time of financial constraint and limited resources, prevention measures may become a secondary consideration. An officer in need of psychological support would hope that the situation which Chappell describes in Australia would not occur in the UK:

> This informant also said that the number of professional staff available to assist with counselling and advice was severely limited, with priorities going elsewhere to 'frontline' police needs rather than to what was seen by most as a peripheral area of police responsibility.
>
> (Chappell 2010: 297)

The finances and potential financial liability of a US police department led Reiser to comment that 'particular attention is paid to those officers whose behavior or psychological state presents a potential liability to the Department or to the City' (Reiser 1982: 172). More recently, in a case in New South Wales,[36] the vulnerability caused by injury and stress to officers was examined; Barron reported that the implications of the Court decisions may necessitate 'a review of assessment, intervention and treatment for officers considered or determined to be at risk of self harm, suicide ideation or suicide'.[37]

It is the proposal of the research analysis that organisational support mechanisms should be implemented in the UK police service due to an acknowledged responsibility of care for officers rather than a fear of litigation; however, as Chappell comments, referring to the fear of litigation, 'it is likely that similar legal trends are occurring in comparative jurisdictions elsewhere in Australia and abroad' (Chappell 2010: 297).

Whether because of a fear of litigation or a recognition of the value of human life, the police service and the individual forces have a responsibility to sustain current, and implement new, intervention measures. These intervention measures are referred to in Chapter 11, where appropriate recommendations are made.

Notes

1　Pocklington, Rebecca, 'Thousands of police took sick leave due to stress "brought on by government cuts"', *Mirror*, November 10, 2013, available from www.mirror.co.uk/news/uk-news/thousands-police-took-sick-leave-2716619; accessed November 20, 2013.

2　'The Fed' is an abbreviation for the Federation, to which UK constables, sergeants, inspectors and chief inspectors can belong.

3　Martis, Royston, 'In figures, the forgotten police suicides', *Police Oracle*, November 8, 2012, available from www.policeoracle.com/news/Comment/2012/Nov/08/Comment-In-Figures,-The-Forgotten-Police-Suicides_57812.html; accessed November 17, 2012.

4　Verkaik, Robert, 'Half of senior police say they are stressed and depressed', *Independent*, September 4, 2009, available from www.independent.co.uk/news/uk/home-news/half-of-senior-police-say-they-are-stressed-and-depressed-1781473.html?origin=internalSearch; accessed December 12, 2011.

5　Barron, Stephen W. (2007) *Police Officer Suicide: A Review and Examination Using a Psychological Autopsy*, October 2007, available from www.barronpsych.com.au/research/Police%20suicide%20in%20NSW.doc; accessed February 12, 2017 (p. 9).

6　A UK occupational health (OH) manager explained that following the selection process, successful applicants are required to undertake a full medical examination, which includes their psychological well-being. This includes enquiries into the history of suicide within the applicant's family (see Chapter 4, section entitled 'History of Suicide within the Family'). If there is concern regarding any health issue, further advice will be sought from the applicant's general practitioner or an appropriate specialist. The results of the health check are collated to ensure the health of all applicants conforms to standards set by the Police Regulations. The OH manager commented that psychological screening is controversial; for example, applicants (and serving officers) who have a diagnosed history of depression will be more aware of potential emotional vulnerability than those whose vulnerability has not been recognised or identified.

7　Barron, *Police Officer Suicide*, p. 16.

8　Ibid., p. 18.

9　McDermott, Jasmin, 'Force health units cannot cope with stressed staff', *Police Oracle*, October 14, 2013, www.policeoracle.com/news/Police+Staff/2013/Oct/11/Force-health-units-cannot-cope-with-stressed-staff_72300.html; accessed October 21, 2013.

10　HMIC (2012) *Lessons Learned Review: Wiltshire Police*, available from www.justiceinspectorates.gov.uk/hmic/media/lessons-learned-review-wiltshire-20120926.pdf; accessed September 26, 2012.

11　Barron, *Police Officer Suicide*, p. 21.

12　University of Maryland Medical Center, 'Traumatic events', n.d., available from http://umm.edu/health/medical/ency/articles/traumatic-events; accessed 9 February 2017.

13　Suffolk Police, 'TriM trauma risk management, our response to trauma', available from www.suffolk.police.uk/sites/suffolk/files/002936-16_data_-_leaflet_temp_0.pdf; accessed February 9, 2017.

14　Verkaik, 'Half of senior police say they are stressed and depressed'.

15　TRiM should not be confused with Critical Incident Stress Debriefing, which is a controversial process that is criticised by some for re-traumatising witnesses and traumatising those who were not directly involved with the incident. The NICE guidelines state that 'for individuals who have experienced a traumatic event, the systematic provision to that individual alone of brief, single-session interventions (often referred to as debriefing) that focus on the traumatic incident should not be routine practice when delivering services': NICE (2005) 'Do not do recommendations', available from www.nice.org.uk/donotdo/for-individuals-who-have-experienced-a-traumatic-event-the-systematic-provision-to-that-individual-alone-of-brief-singlesession-interventions-often-referred-to-as-debriefing-that-focus-on-the; accessed February 7, 2017.

16　Suffolk Police, 'TriM trauma risk management'.

17 In April 2007, Audrey Fagan – the second most senior female police officer in Australia, and the chief of the Australian Capital Territory (ACT) police force – took her own life, at the age of 44.

18 Barron, *Police Officer Suicide*, p. 21.

19 McDermott, Jasmin, 'Officers face "double jeopardy" in professional standards probes', *Police Oracle*, May 8, 2014, available from www.policeoracle.com/news/Uniformed+Operations/2014/May/08/Officers-face-double-jeopardy-in-professional-standards-probes_81920.html?utm_source=weekly; accessed May 10, 2014.

20 Metropolitan Police, Directorate of Professional Standards (April 2013), *Guidance for Welfare Support Officers – DPS Formal Misconduct Proceedings*.

21 Ibid.

22 HMIC, *Lessons Learned Review: Wiltshire Police*.

23 Barron, *Police Officer Suicide*, p. 21.

24 Ibid., p. 16.

25 Ibid., p. 8.

26 Ibid., p. 21.

27 Verkaik, 'Half of senior police say they are stressed and depressed'.

28 Brunetti, Nic, 'Officers and staff being bullied in forces', *Police Oracle*, September 18, 2013, available from www.policeoracle.com/news/HR%2C+Personnel+and+Staff+Development/2013/Sep/17/Officers-and-staff-being-bullied-in-forces_70903.html; accessed September 22, 2013.

29 Somers, Jack, 'Force loses "bullying" appeal', *Police Oracle*, May 21, 2013, available from www.policeoracle.com/news/Race+and+Diversity/2013/May/21/Force-loses-bullying-appeal_65442.html; accessed May 29, 2013.

30 Ibid.

31 Martis, Royston, 'One in two PCs want to leave service', *Police Oracle*, August 19, 2013, available from www.policeoracle.com/news/HR%2C+Personnel+and+Staff+-Development/2013/Aug/16/One-in-two-PCs-want-to-leave-service_69589.html; accessed September 3, 2013.

32 Caswell, Cliff, 'Custody shift pattern "risks officers burning out"', *Police Oracle*, May 27, 2014, available from www.policeoracle.com/news/Uniformed+Operations/2014/May/23/TUES-1-Custody-shift-pattern-risks-officers-burning-out_82721.html?utm_source=weeklyNewsletter&utm_medium=email&utm_campaign=140515; accessed June 4, 2014.

33 Ibid.

34 Barron, *Police Officer Suicide*, p. 17.

35 Ibid., p. 21.

36 *State of New South Wales v. Seedsman* (2000) NSWCA 119 and *State of New South Wales v. Williamson* (2005) NSWCA 352.

37 Barron, *Police Officer Suicide*, p. 20.

Bibliography

Barron, Stephen W. (2007) Police Officer Suicide: A Review and Examination Using a Psychological Autopsy, October 2007, available from www.barronpsych.com.au/research/Police%20 suicide%20in%20NSW.doc; accessed February 12, 2017, p. 9.

Beehr, Terry A., Johnson, Leanor B. and Nieva, Ronie (1995) Occupational Stress: Coping of Police and Their Spouses, *Journal of Organizational Behaviour*, Vol. 16, No. 1, 3–25.

Chae, Mark H. and Boyle, Douglas J. (2013) Police Suicide: Prevalence, Risk, and Protective Factors, *Policing: An International Journal of Police Strategies & Management*, Vol. 36, No. 1, 91–118.

Chappell, Duncan (2010) From Sorcery to Stun Guns and Suicide: The Eclectic and Global Challenges of Policing and the Mentally Ill, *Police Practice and Research*, Vol. 11, No. 4, 289–300.

Ivanoff, A. (1994) *The New York City Police Suicide Training Project.* New York: Police Foundation.

Kirschman, Ellen (1997) *I Love a Cop.* New York: Guilford Press.

Larned, Jean G. (2010) Understanding Police Suicide, *Forensic Examiner,* Vol. 19, No. 3, 64–71.

Lesse, Stanley (Ed.) (1998) *What We Know about Suicidal Behavior and How to Treat It.* Northvale: Jason Aronson.

Martinez, Louis Enrique (2010) *The Secret Deaths: Police Officer's Testimonial Views on Police Suicides and Why Suicides Continue to be Hidden in Police Departments.* Denver: Outskirts Press.

Miller, Laurence (2006) *Practical Police Psychology: Stress Management and Crisis Intervention for Law Enforcement.* Springfield: Charles C. Thomas.

Murphy, George (1998) The Prediction of Suicide. In Lesse, Stanley (Ed.) *What We Know About Suicidal Behavior and How to Treat It.* Northvale: Jason Aronson, pp. 47–58.

Ramos, Orlando (2007) *A Leadership Perspective for Understanding Police Suicide: An Analysis Based on the Suicide Attitude Questionnaire.* Boca Raton: Dissertation.com.

Reintzell, John F. (1990) *The Police Officer's Guide to Survival, Health and Fitness.* Springfield: Charles C. Thomas.

Reiser, Martin (1982) *Police Psychology: Collected Papers.* Los Angeles: LEHI.

Rostow, Cary D. and Davis, Robert D. (2004) *A Handbook for Psychological Fitness-for-Duty Evaluations in Law Enforcement.* New York: Haworth Clinical Practice Press/Haworth Reference Press.

Violanti, John M. (2007) *Police Suicide: Epidemic in Blue* (2nd edition). Springfield: Charles C. Thomas.

Waters, Judith A. and Ussery, William (2007) Police Stress: History, Contributing Factors, Symptoms and Interventions, *Policing: An International Journal of Police Strategies & Management,* Vol. 30, No. 2, 169–87.

9   Personal Initiatives

Introductory Comments

Reporting on a survey of more than 1,000 superintendents and chief superintendents, *Police Oracle* highlighted that some 'senior operational officers are suffering from unmanageable working hours, high stress levels and anxiety'. In the article, Jasmin McDermott reported that, because of forces' different approaches to those suffering from stress and anxiety, 'senior officers must take some individual responsibility for their own welfare and workloads'.

The article gave details of an interview between *Police Oracle* and a senior officer, Chief Superintendent Richards, and reported his view that 'while forces must ensure they support their personnel, officers must also take responsibility'. Chief Superintendent Richards was cited as saying:

> To forces, we are saying don't work people into the ground. To individuals we are saying they should take some responsibility and manage their time as best they can and try and work reasonable hours to balance their work and home life.[1]

With an analysis of suicide precipitators having been offered in the earlier chapters, Chapter 8 set out preventative measures that police forces might implement to give greater support to officers experiencing suicidal ideation. As Chief Superintendent Richards commented, the implementation of welfare measures is the responsibility of the police organisation but, as he likewise suggests, some responsibility lies with officers also. Officers must accept a level of responsibility for their own emotional welfare and survival, whether in relation to the hours they work and time-management or with regard to other potential stress factors in their lives.

This chapter therefore focuses on measures which officers themselves might adopt to ensure their own emotional survival and welfare. The chapter first examines the importance of officers acknowledging and understanding their potential vulnerability to the pressures of working in the service. It continues by identifying some of the major potential stressors that officers may encounter; analysis suggests that as well as acknowledging their vulnerability, officers must also be aware of the stress precipitators and the signs of stress which they may be experiencing. Finally, the chapter draws attention to the decisive actions that officers might take to engage with a range of preventative measures to ensure their emotional survival.

Acknowledging and Understanding the Vulnerability

Analysis offered earlier in this book identified key groups of officers that may be vulnerable to suicidal ideation. As noted in Chapter 4 (section entitled 'Officer and Staff Ratio'), the case-studies within the primary research showed that it was predominantly officers who had taken their own lives, rather than those who worked as staff members. (Further reference to this was also made in Chapter 7, section entitled 'The Ratio of Officers to Staff'.) It was also stated that the majority of these suicides were male (Chapter 4, section entitled 'Data Related to the Different Sexes'), that their deaths occurred at key ages (Table 4.2) and that the greater the male officer's length of service, the greater was the risk of suicidal ideation (Chapter 4, section entitled 'Length of Service').

With reference to female suicides, the analysis of the case-studies revealed that the suicides had generally occurred at a younger age and after less service than their male counterparts. However, as noted in Chapter 7 (section entitled 'Ratio of Male to Female'), the report *Occupational Mortality in England and Wales* (Coggon et al. 2009) indicated that female police officers, rather than their male counterparts, were in an occupation that entailed a higher risk of suicide than many others.

The primary research of the case-studies identified that many of the officers who had completed suicide had been highly regarded by their respective families, colleagues and the communities in which they had worked (Chapter 4, section entitled 'The Acknowledged Calibre of Officers'). Reference was equally made to the high standards that the officers in question had set for themselves (Chapters 6 and 7, sections entitled 'High Standards').

It is the suggestion of this research that certain important trends with regard to sex, age and length of service may be identified. Nevertheless, it is the further suggestion of this research, as demonstrated in earlier chapters, that the contextual stress of working within the police service, which can lead to suicide, is not restricted to the sex, age or length of service of the officers concerned.

In spite of officers being held in high esteem and conforming to the high standards which those experiencing suicidal ideation may place on themselves, this research has drawn attention to the way in which many regard themselves as being invulnerable to stress and its potential impact (Chapter 6, section entitled 'Invulnerability'; Chapter 7, section entitled 'Invulnerability, Peer Pressure, Shift Work and Training'). The causes of this notion of invulnerability may be many. As demonstrated, the desperation involved in having failed to maintain high expectations and a sense of 'rugged individualism' (Chapter 6) are key precipitators, among many others. 'Macho-man' syndrome can lead officers to regard suffering from stress as a sign of weakness that affects only others. As Kevin Gilmartin explains, this opinion can mean that when officer-colleagues take their own lives, officers 'tell themselves that the suicide must have been the result of some flaw in the individual psychological makeup of the dead officer'. He refers to this thought process as 'keeping psychological distance' (Gilmartin 2002: 12–13) so that officers can create within themselves a false sense of psychological security. Chappell offers an example of this 'psychological distance' when he refers to 'police executives who remain extremely reluctant to admit even to themselves that they need help' (Chappell 2010: 296).

It is the basic precept of this chapter that all officers are vulnerable to stress and its potential impacts. Furthermore, it is the suggestion of this chapter that an acknowledgement of personal vulnerability is the first step for officers to take in ensuring their emotional survival. As Larned comments, when officers encounter stressful periods in their lives, 'it is important to understand what is happening to the body mentally and physically, and to then adjust accordingly' (Larned 2010: 71).

Officers' Acceptance and Identification of the Potential Stressors and Their Effects

The analysis of the case-studies offered in Chapter 4 and the references to the causes of suicidal ideation identified by the research analysis suggest a broad range of stress factors with the potential to become suicide precipitators. In addition to acknowledging their vulnerability, it is the suggestion of this book that officers should, as Larned suggests, also understand the specific stressors they may face. The stresses that officers may encounter may be the same as those encountered by any other member of the wider community, or may be police-specific. As demonstrated in the analysis of the case-studies, precipitators that are common both to officers and to those in the general community include:

- bereavement
- issues around partner relationships
- estrangement from the family
- financial difficulties
- physical illness
- PTSD
- significant loss: an actual loss or a threatened loss.

Other stresses identified within the case-studies which are either police-specific or directly related to the work of an officer include:

- alleged bullying, harassment or victimisation in the workplace
- criminal investigation
- fear of damaging the reputation of the force

- fear of unemployment following disciplinary hearings
- bureaucratic and authoritarian processes leading to feelings of:
  - disillusionment
  - having been betrayed by management
  - being trapped by the job
  - being victimised
  - the unfair re-assignment of the working role
- internal investigations for professional misconduct
- organisational structures, procedures and culture
- shift work and disturbed biological rhythms.

Whether the stressful pressures are directly or indirectly work-related, it would appear that the issues are compounded by a police-specific context and may include:

- shift work
- self-imposed macho-man image
- denial of vulnerability
- feelings that there is a lack of:
  - communication
  - welfare support
  - colleague support
- feelings of isolation
- lack of control
- dichotomised decision-making
- community contagion.

One might hope that officers have been trained to understand the emotional issues they encounter, and have the workplace resources to enable them to respond creatively to these issues. However, as Chopko et al. comment, 'many officers, especially those employed by small police agencies, receive inadequate or no training on stress management and police suicide' (Chopko et al. 2013: 7). Further references to this lack of training are made in Chapter 8 (section entitled 'Training').

Stress behind the Badge, an International Association of Chiefs of Police (IAPC) presentation aimed at ensuring officers are sufficiently resourced to respond to the many pressures they encounter, comments that as a consequence of this lack of training, 'after working a 12 hour shift and dealing with the negative things on the job, you're supposed to turn off the switch and go home and be normal'.[2] Unfortunately, there are officers who go home and are unable to be 'normal'. Larned describes how, in their everyday lives, stressed officers can experience 'a sense of bewilderment; loss of interest in everyday events; and even physiological effects like loss of appetite, sleep, and concentration and increased illness through a weakened immune system' (Larned 2010: 71). The case-studies examined in Chapter 4 revealed other effects of stress: depression; anger, which may be expressed through domestic cruelty, alcohol abuse and negative self-perceptions; feelings of victimisation and isolation from friends and colleagues; an inability to make personal decisions; and a loss of control – all of which may be compounded by denial that support is required.

Officers' emotional survival will be enhanced by acknowledging and understanding their vulnerability, as suggested earlier in this chapter, and by recognising the potential stressors and the consequences of those stressors, as suggested in this section. Once this vulnerability is acknowledged, identified and accepted by the officers concerned, these officers may apply a number of preventative measures that contribute to ensuring their emotional survival.

As Violanti (2007) states, stress cannot be necessarily avoided, but officers can be provided with an understanding of suicide and of the preventative measures that can be implemented. So resourced, the measures will reduce the risk of suicide and the officer's vulnerability to that risk.

Larned writes: 'There are a surprising number of simple mechanisms officers can use to address stress … if you follow only these simple coping techniques and nothing else, you will still greatly increase your chances of becoming a survivor' (Larned 2010: 70). Chae and Boyle offer similar comments and suggest that officers should be proactive in adopting positive coping mechanisms to confront their everyday stress and the trauma of their work. They suggest that research clearly indicates the positive impact that a proactive approach to coping mechanisms can have for officers (Chae and Boyle 2013: 109).

Reference to these measures is made in the sections that follow, including to measures that may be adopted by those experiencing significant stress. These are also measures which all officers might adopt so as to manage everyday stressors before the impact of stress causes significant damage.

Adopting Preventative Measures

Taking Control

Referring to the training that newly recruited officers might receive, Gilmartin suggests that 'the first step clearly is to teach officers to maintain control of their personal lives' (Gilmartin 2002: 112). He explains: 'The greater the degree of control or autonomy an individual has in her or his life, the greater the degree of empowerment, stability, and autonomy she or he will experience emotionally' (ibid.: 78), and reaffirms this requirement when he comments that newly recruited officers should be trained 'in what it takes to maintain a sense of control in their personal lives' (ibid.: 112).

Police officers may be successfully trained to take control of the situations they encounter on the streets and in their working lives. However, like many in the community, they may not be trained in the philosophy that one is in control of one's own life, especially when that life becomes particularly stressful. The

IAPC presentation on emotional survival, *Stress behind the Badge*, refers to personal responsibility:

- You are in control of you and only you.
- Establish priorities in your life.
- Learn to say NO![3]

The presentation encourages officers, having control over their personal decisions, to live by those decisions and have the courage to deny requests that do not accord with the priorities they have chosen.

In the current climate, when financial pressures are making increasing demands on officers and their workloads, taking control over a work–life balance is increasingly difficult. However, a knowledge that they are in control is the baseline by which officers can be empowered to make the important choices and decisions that will impact on their emotional survival. This chapter continues with regard to some of these choices.

Time-Management

Gilmartin writes at length concerning personal time-management. Because, as he suggests, 'police work requires an on duty reactive orientation' (Gilmartin 2002: 113), it is more difficult for officers to be proactive when off-duty. He comments that officers can fail to apply the time-management discipline they adopt in the workplace to their non-police roles.

He comments that a fundamental survivor route will be gained 'by controlling personal time' (ibid.: 118) and further states that 'survivors learn to be disciplined in their personal time orientation' (ibid.: 119). Consequently, he suggests that officers 'need to *make the time* to do what they want to do' (ibid.: 119). To this end, he recommends that officers ensure they 'maintain a preplanned, written personal calendar or agenda that lists goals, requirements, and choices in their personal time that they will implement' (ibid.: 117–18).

Offering a similar approach to time-management, Larned comments that officers must ensure that they 'take time to enjoy life' (Larned 2010: 71), while the IACP presentation urges officers to use their personal time to 'schedule time out ... do something good for yourself'.[4] The same presentation slide also suggests that those officers who are anxious about a particular situation might 'schedule "worry time"', so that the anxiety does not permeate into the times when the officer is engaged in other activities. With reference to time-management, Waters and Ussery suggest that officers must ensure that they make arrangements to have 'regular vacations' (Waters and Ussery 2007: 184).

Positive time-management, like taking control, is a basic principle on which many other factors depend, whether the time-management relates to day-to-day events or long-term planning. Time-management is to be highly commended.

Relationships

Gilmartin comments on the effects of potential isolation on officers as they become increasingly detached from the non-police world. He describes how personal relationships with partners and children can be destroyed as a consequence of the way in which officers focus on their careers. He suggests that the human cost paid for an officer's career journey can 'be tabulated personally in failed marriages, children in trouble, and life views dominated by negativity, social isolation, and alienation from fellow human beings' (Gilmartin 2002: 5).

In identifying how officers may overcome this sense of negativity and isolation, Chae and Boyle refer to research which reveals the importance of a 'healthy and supportive social context' (Chae and Boyle 2013: 109). They explain research has demonstrated that officers in stable partner relationships suffer less from psychological difficulties, including suicidal ideation, than those who may be without the support of a partner (Chae and Boyle 2013: 109). Emphasising the need to improve relationships, Larned writes that 'developing social support from friends, family and colleagues both in and outside of law enforcement is crucial' (Larned 2010: 71).

In the analysis of the case-studies, reference was made to those experiencing difficulties in family relationships (Chapter 4, section entitled 'Difficulties within the Home and Family Context'). A significant number of the case-studies were experiencing such difficulties at the time they took their own lives. A commitment to developing strong relationships and an understanding of the importance of those relationships will enhance the emotional strength of those working in stressful situations. Two slides in the IAPC presentation affirm this importance: one comments that 'Relationships are very important to the law enforcement officer … On and Off the job … It's that need to be needed', and the second urges officers to 'Maintain supportive relationships … manage your relationships'.[5] Larned offers similar comments with specific reference to family relationships when encouraging officers to 'engage in emotionally fulfilling activities that enhance the quality of life and the lives of loved ones' (Larned 2010: 71).

Analysis of the case-studies offered examples of the importance of positive personal relationships, especially when officers are involved in disciplinary matters and have no contact with their work colleagues (Chapter 4, sections entitled 'Criminal Investigations' and 'Internal Investigations for Professional Misconduct'). The importance of working to create confident relationships (and managing the breakdown of failing relationships) is not to be underestimated. In part, these will only be achieved by officers taking control of their personal lives, dedicating time to building those relationships and knowing how to communicate both in domestic relationships and in a social context.

Having considered the issues of taking control and dedicating time, focus is now given to the importance of communication.

Communication

Larned stresses the significance of officers being able to communicate success-fully with those to whom they are emotionally close. Discussing available sup-port, he refers to the importance of 'good communication with a significant other and extended family' (Larned 2010: 71). Waters and Ussery refer to the need for enhanced knowledge of how to communicate effectively in order to strengthen officers' emotional well-being (Waters and Ussery 2007: 183).

Good communication is a two-way process. Officers need to be able to express their feelings and also to be able to listen with empathy to others. On the one hand, 'the more an officer talks about his or her feelings, the better they are going to be' (Larned 2010: 71). Equally, however, as the IAPC presentation states, referring to the importance of good communication, 'it's what every relationship needs ... Listen ... Take the cotton out of your ears and put it in your mouth!' (Slide 25). Because of the dichotomised thought process with which some officers work and respond (Chapter 6, section entitled 'Dichotomised Decision-Making'), empathetic listening may not always be a natural skill. Nevertheless, it is a skill which, if learned, will be to officers' emotional benefit.

Two-way communication skills give officers a way in which to express their feelings freely (Waters and Ussery 2007: 183). As Gilmartin explains – referring to both the officer and the officer's family – if the family are unaware of the offi-cer's stress, 'they can't be expected to take the appropriate corrective action and avoid the devastating effect'. Good communication skills offer officers the ability to avoid 'irritability, frustration, and emotional volatility' (Gilmartin 2002: 126). Examples of anger are demonstrated in the case-studies offered in Chapter 4 (sec-tion entitled 'Anger'). Reference to officers' feeling of anger and frustration is made later in this chapter.

Officers should remember that communication with managers is also a two-way process. Not only do officers need to ensure that they communicate with their families, but they also need to ensure that they communicate with managers and other force members.

With good communication, it is possible to lessen feelings of anger, frustra-tion and emotional volatility. Good communication skills are essential to the officer.

Physical Exercise

A regular routine of physical exercise is strongly encouraged by those who advise on the emotional welfare of officers. Larned comments:

> Exercise is a tremendous stress reliever as well as a factor in good health. Officers spend a significant amount of time at work in vehicles and may be fatigued from stress and long hours. Exercise actually helps to even out hor-monal processes and reduce stress. Exercise should be frequent. Be fit!
>
> (Larned 2010: 71)

Waters and Ussery suggest 'muscle relaxation exercises' (Waters and Ussery 2007: 184), 'a regular exercise program with a minimal time expenditure of 30 minutes a session' (ibid.: 183) and the 'use of biofeedback' (ibid.: 184). Gilmartin suggests that officers should undertake 'approximately thirty to forty minutes of aerobic activity, four to five times per week' (Gilmartin 2002: 125) and writes at length concerning the benefits of physical exercise, including how 'moderate physical exercise is also an essential element in any program of anger reduction' (ibid.: 126). Physical exercise, he suggests, can be emotionally beneficial and have a profound effect on improved personal relationships. Regular physical exercise is not only healthy for the body; it is healthy for the mind as well, and contributes significantly to the emotional well-being of the officer.

Relaxation

The benefits of relaxation may be so self-evident as to be overlooked by officers. However, as Larned writes, 'rest, relaxation, and recreation are easy ways to reduce stress' (Larned 2010: 71). He further advocates that officers should 'develop hobbies' (ibid.: 71), and Waters and Ussery offer similar advice, suggesting lifestyle changes that encourage recreational pastimes (Waters and Ussery 2007: 184). As Gilmartin comments, a commitment to recreational pastimes, as well as offering a means of relaxation, can offer a counterbalance to the heavy demands of the police schedule – a consequence of which can be that 'it's very easy for an officer to start developing the victim orientation' (Gilmartin 2002: 112). An IACP slide promotes the benefits of recreation, suggesting that officers should 'Laugh … Have fun … Enjoy life … You only get one!'[6]

Officers must give themselves time to relax and enjoy letting go of work and other pressures, either with or without other activities to fill the non-active time.

Food and Drink

Whereas the hitherto referenced preventative measures encourage adopting positive coping mechanisms, in references to alcohol, particularly alcohol abuse, it is strongly advised that its use as a coping mechanism should be avoided. As the analysis of the case-studies in Chapter 4 (section entitled 'Alcohol Abuse') revealed, eight of those who took their own lives were or had been dealing with alcohol-abuse problems.

Even though the analysis of the case-studies did not concur with Larned's assertion that alcohol 'is present in 95% of police suicides' (Larned 2010: 70), it is nevertheless important to note his comment that 'While alcohol may provide a temporary feeling of wellness, it is a fact that alcohol affects the brain in areas that promote depression, impair judgment, and remove inhibitions' (Larned 2010: 70–1).

The IACP recommends that officers should:

- Eat a balanced diet with high fiber, low salt, and low cholesterol
- Be aware of poisons: Caffeine, fats, nicotine, processed foods
- Drink water instead of soda.[7]

Awareness of a nutritious diet and an appropriate response to that awareness are further preventative measures that officers might adopt to ensure their emotional survival.

Careful medical advice and supervision should also be sought when considering the use of antidepressants. It is reported that 'medication-induced suicide has taken the life of both younger and older patients. Without proper warning of risks from doctors and manufacturers, people take antidepressants in hopes of curing their depression. The outcomes can be devastating'.[8] Hence the *BMJ*'s warning that 'patients taking antidepressant drugs should be carefully monitored, especially during early treatment with antidepressants and when stopping treatment'.[9] As careful attention should be paid to the use of prescribed drugs, clearly all illegal drugs should be totally avoided.

Financial Control

The issue of financial instability was raised in Chapter 4 (section entitled 'Financial Concerns'), where it was reported that four of those featured in the case-studies were experiencing financial difficulties at the time of their death. Gilmartin writes at length about the financial astuteness of officers. His general premise is that many officers, despite being in a profession that offers financial stability, appear to lack financial astuteness. This, he suggests, consequently inhibits their emotional constancy. Gilmartin draws a connection between physical activity and attentiveness towards financial matters and describes this link by stating: 'One surprising aspect of physical fitness appears to be that officers who aggressively practice physical fitness and pursue physical activities in their personal lives appear to be somewhat more stable financially' (Gilmartin 2002: 128).

Gilmartin comments that male officers' spending extravaganzas are similar to the spending pattern of the male in the general community. He suggests that male officers will tend to buy large, expensive items, unlike their female counterparts, who generally enjoy retail therapy within a manageable budget. The male officer instead, Gilmartin comments, tends to purchase large items which are outside his budget. Gilmartin suggests that 'This spending pattern can represent a vicious cycle that affects many officers and families who have not been trained in emotional survival. These families often fall prey to stress-related consumerism' (Gilmartin 2002: 129).

Gilmartin concludes that those who are able to manage their financial affairs successfully will be 'in a position to free themselves of anger and frustration at their employers' (Gilmartin 2002: 131). Not only will these officers be released from frustration and anger at their employers (who have been traditionally wary of officers in debt because of the implications of financial vulnerability), but they will be released from the negative emotions they may hold towards others generally.

Spirituality

Gilmartin refers to 'spirituality' as one of the ways of 'viewing the world' which may assist officers in reducing a one-dimensional view of life (Gilmartin 2002: 73). Barron similarly refers to research which suggests the importance of a 'strong spiritual or religious faith' or officers having 'a sense of meaning and purpose to life'.[10] Using the term 'religiosity', Beehr et al. refer to the research of others and suggest, however, that religiosity is an indication of 'a stable personality dimension' which seems 'to have no effect, one way or the other, on the police officers' strains'. They comment further that 'while turning to religion was clearly a coping technique reported by some officers, it appears unlikely to be either particularly helpful or harmful in coping with police stress' (Beehr et al. 1995: 19).

Nevertheless, officers are encouraged by many researchers to engage with the spiritual dimension, whether God-linked or otherwise. Larned advises that officers might 'express spirituality' (Larned 2010: 71) and Waters and Ussery suggest the practice of 'meditation' (Waters and Ussery 2007: 184), which might for some be undertaken according to a systemised approach, or might simply take the form of 'thinking time'. The IAPC presentation advises that officers participate in 'thinking time' or 'Reflection' so as to:

- Know your stress triggers
- Be aware of stress symptoms
- Check your balance in life
- Improve your relationship with yourself.[11]

It is the suggestion of this research that when officers achieve self-understanding, they may also learn how to forgive. Larned draws attention to this requirement in reference to Dr Lyubomirsky of the University of California, who lists this aptitude as one way of achieving 'a more satisfying and happier life' (Larned 2010: 70). The need for forgiveness was identified within the case-studies, whether this is self-forgiveness or forgiveness of others.

Knowing, acknowledging and identifying stress triggers and symptoms is where this chapter began, and where the cycle to ensure emotional survival was first examined. However, there is one more important preventative measure on which to focus – the importance of those officers under stress accessing support by asking for help.

Asking for Help

Accessing support is not only important for those who may be experiencing suicidal ideation; the wise officer asks for support before difficult issues become intricately compounded. Referring to officers' reluctance to seek support in potential stressful situations, Kirschman comments: 'If there is a common thread linking these elements, it is the doomed officer's inability to ask for or find confidential help before small problems snowball into a tidal wave of torment' (Kirschman 1997: 169). Accordingly, Larned encourages officers to 'embrace support systems' (Larned 2010: 71), while Waters and Ussery suggest that reliable support systems should be developed (Waters and Ussery 2007: 183) and that officers might attend self-help groups (ibid.: 184).

The IAPC presentation offers two key slides encouraging officers to ask for help:

- For a law enforcement officer, it's one of the toughest things to do
- Everyone else has problems ... It takes courage to be a cop
- And it takes courage to ask for help!
- Don't Go It Alone.[12]

Even when officers are aware that support is required, they may feel powerless to seek the help available to them. Martinez offers an officer's comment that 'Troubled officers want to be rescued, but do not want to ask for assistance or [know] what specific help to request' (Martinez 2010: 80).

Those who are part of support systems and experienced in offering assistance will know how to respond as soon as an officer makes a request for help. The first essential requirement is for the officer to make a phone call or send an email or text message. The question of to whom the initial approach is made will matter little. Those who are experienced in offering support will direct the officer to those more qualified to respond to their particular need.

The IAPC presentation lists a number of groups to which an approach may be made. The slide is entitled 'Getting Help ... What's Available?' and includes:

- Counseling
- Life Coaching
- EAP Program (Employee Assistance Program)
- Internal or External Program
- Peer Support Program
- Chaplains.[13]

As the examination of preventative measures has demonstrated, there are many other possible avenues which might be explored. Counselling, for example, is a very broad area and may include psychological support, but also embraces debt and relationship issues, including how to successfully manage a breakdown in partner and family relationships.

A wide range of different support mechanisms are available to the officer; however, as the case-studies illustrate, they are support mechanisms which some officers either cannot engage with or may have chosen to ignore.

Concluding Comments

Many references have been made in this chapter to Gilmartin, who writes at length describing the psychological dynamics of the officer's life and the effects of a demanding police schedule. He refers to the constant state of alertness that officers must be in when they are at work and comments that this need for alertness is often explained in terms of the officer's physical safety. However, he suggests, this sense of alertness or hypervigilance has much broader emotional implications.[14] The constant awareness of potential threats to safety and the state of readiness to respond to harrowing incidents that an officer is required to be in, placed alongside the stressful or traumatic situations officers may experience in their personal lives, place a tremendous emotional strain on officers.

This emotional strain must be acknowledged and understood by the officers themselves. As was stated earlier in this chapter, an acknowledgement of personal vulnerability is the first step that officers can take in ensuring their emotional survival. Understanding their vulnerability to stress will assist officers in appreciating the specific stressors and the possible effects of occupational stress. It will also assist officers in their understanding that suffering from stress is not a sign of weakness but a symptom of the context in which they work and in which they must survive, if not flourish.

As referenced earlier in this chapter and in Chapter 8, the training in stress survival that officers receive is minimal. As Gilmartin comments, '[Officers] are trained in how to handle the streets, they just aren't trained in how to handle the job and its effects on their personal lives' (Gilmartin 2002: 72). Seldom are 'the changes in a new officer's personal life seen as anything but inevitable' (Gilmartin 2002: 4). The nature of police work may adversely affect the psychological bearing of the officer, and change may be inevitable, but officers are 'hardly ever told or shown how to minimize the negative effects of the journey through the police career' (Gilmartin 2002: 4). However, as this chapter has demonstrated, there are some simple mechanisms that officers can adopt to ensure their emotional survival.

The first is that officers must accept that they have control over the choices they make. Each of these choices will have practical implications which need to be balanced one against the other, but officers should recognise that they have this control and must ensure that they remain in control, particularly with regard to their personal lives. One of the first decisions officers must make, conscious of this sense of control, is to manage their time, especially with regard to their work–life balance.

Time-management is essential. As Gilmartin asserts, 'the development and use of a specific personal-time-management technique is extremely important for police work' (Gilmartin 2002: 113). As this chapter has demonstrated, much depends on positive time-management, including good relationships with those to whom the officer is emotionally bound, time for physical exercise and the opportunity to relax.

As also indicated in this chapter, an officer's philosophy that career and work take priority over personal issues of relationships with family and friends can be to the detriment of that officer. Relationships with one's partner, family and non-police friends can so easily be destroyed by a consuming identification with the police role, and thereby place the officer at emotional risk.

Positive time-management will allocate time for regular physical exercise. Such exercise is important to ensure the physical fitness necessary to carry out the police role, but it is also crucial to ensure emotional stability. As was shown earlier in this chapter, physical exercise reduces stress and anger. This anger may be directed inwardly towards the self or towards those in the home environment, with consequences which can cause irreparable damage, both physical and emotional.

Time-management ensures that time can be allocated to simple relaxation. This may entail involvement in interests or relaxing socially with family and friends, enabling the officer to become less one-dimensional and more socially integrated.

Other measures of which officers need to be aware relate to their lifestyle and include diet and financial awareness. Once again, taking control is the key phrase for both of these concerns.

Officers need to be in control of what they consume. A rigid dietary discipline is not required, but as Violanti comments, with reference to poor diet, alcohol abuse and smoking, 'some mortality studies show that officers tended to die at a greater ratio than the general population for heart disease, liver problems (alcohol), suicides, and homicides' (Violanti 2007: 103).

Within this chapter, control of a realistic financial budget has also been shown to be important. Focus has been drawn to Gilmartin's comments on the importance of financial awareness. He suggests that some officers, mature in service, appear to have learned little about financial acumen as the years have gone by, and yet financial astuteness is crucial to the emotional stability of officers, whose budgets can go beyond their control.

Other factors suggested in this chapter that are of importance to officers wishing to ensure their emotional survival may be placed under the heading of relationships; that is, the relationships which officers develop with their family, with their friends and with themselves. Gilmartin comments on the ease with which the 'non-police dimensions of officers' lives, such as spirituality, cultural and ethnic identification, core values, family, friends, hobbies, and other perceptual sets or ways of viewing the world, reduce if not disappear' (Gilmartin 2002: 73).

As has been shown within this chapter, officers need to ensure that they develop their skills of communication, for the following reasons:

- When officers fail to see the importance of communication in the workplace with colleagues and line-managers, their ability to ask for support will not be forthcoming.
- When they fail to communicate with those on whose love there is a mutual dependency, the relationships will eventually fail.

- When officers fail to communicate with themselves, either through 'thinking time' or a more formal system of meditation/spirituality, their self-understanding will be considerably limited.

The officers on whom this research has focused are typical of the majority of those who work within the police service in that they offer commitment, reliability and dedication to their chosen career. Many will be emotionally strong and respond to the challenges of their working and personal lives but some, for various reasons, will not. Some will achieve all they desire in their careers and some will not. However, whatever the officer's role and whatever the officer's workplace achievements, Gilmartin offers the observation:

> On occasion, even though they [the officers] are deserving of it, they are not promoted or they are not chosen for the assignment they would like to have received, but they are still the most successful officers. Emotional survivors may appear to finish in last place, but that is because they are usually running a different race.

> (Gilmartin 2002: 138)

It is essential for officers to ensure they are in control of the race they decide to run.

Notes

1 McDermott, Jasmin, 'Police workload and welfare: officers must take responsibility', *Police Oracle*, September 4, 2014, available from www.policeoracle.com/news/Police-workload-and-welfare:-Officers-must-take-responsibility_85329.html; accessed September 10, 2014.
2 International Association of Chiefs of Police, *Stress behind the Badge: Understanding the Law Enforcement Culture and How It Affects the Officer and Family … Plus Tools and Skills to Overcome the Challenges*, available from www.theiacp.org/-Sample-Presentations; accessed August 26, 2014 (slide 13).
3 Ibid., slide 40.
4 Ibid., slide 45.
5 Ibid., slides 24 and 43.
6 Ibid., slide 45.
7 Ibid., slide 44.
8 *Drugwatch*, 'Suicide & Antidepressants', n.d., available from www.drugwatch.com/ssri/suicide/; accessed June 2, 2016.
9 BMJ, 'Antidepressant use and risk of suicide and attempted suicide or self-harm in people aged 20 to 64: cohort study using a primary care database', February 18, 2015, http://dx.doi.org/10.1136/bmj.h517; accessed June 12, 2015.
10 Barron, Stephen W. (2007) *Police Officer Suicide: A Review and Examination Using a Psychological Autopsy*, October 2007, available from www.barronpsych.com.au/research/Police%20suicide%20in%20NSW.doc; accessed February 12, 2017 (p. 6).
11 IACP, *Stress behind the Badge*, slides 41 and 43.
12 Ibid., slides 29–30.
13 Ibid., slide 31. Reference is made to chaplains in Chapter 12, section entitled 'Identified Weaknesses and Omissions'.
14 Gilmartin defines hypervigilance as 'the necessary manner of viewing the world from a threat-based perspective, having the mind-set to see the events unfolding as potentially hazardous' (Gilmartin 2002: 35).

Bibliography

Beehr, Terry A., Johnson, Leanor B. and Nieva, Ronie (1995) Occupational Stress: Coping of Police and Their Spouses, *Journal of Organizational Behaviour*, Vol. 16, No. 1, 3–25.

Chae, Mark H. and Boyle, Douglas J. (2013) Police Suicide: Prevalence, Risk, and Protective Factors, *Policing: An International Journal of Police Strategies & Management*, Vol. 36, No. 1, 91–118.

Chappell, Duncan (2010) From Sorcery to Stun Guns and Suicide: The Eclectic and Global Challenges of Policing and the Mentally Ill, *Police Practice and Research*, Vol. 11, No. 4, 289–300.

Chopko, Brian A., Palmieri, Patrick A. and Facemire, Vanessa C. (2013) Prevalence and Predictors of Suicidal Ideation among US Law Enforcement Officers, *Journal of Police and Criminal Psychology*, Vol. 29, No. 1, 1–9.

Coggon, David, Harris, E. Clare, Brown, T., Rice, Simon and Palmer, Keith T. (2009) *Occupational Mortality in England and Wales*. Luton: Office for National Statistics.

Gilmartin, Kevin M. (2002) *Emotional Survival for Law Enforcement Officers*. Tucson: E-S Press.

Kirschman, Ellen (1997) *I Love a Cop*. New York: Guilford Press.

Larned, Jean G. (2010) Understanding Police Suicide, *Forensic Examiner*, Vol. 19, No. 3, 64–71.

Martinez, Louis Enrique (2010) *The Secret Deaths: Police Officer's Testimonial Views on Police Suicides and Why Suicides Continue to be Hidden in Police Departments*. Denver: Outskirts Press.

Violanti, John M. (2007) *Police Suicide: Epidemic in Blue* (2nd edition). Springfield: Charles C. Thomas.

Waters, Judith A. and Ussery, William (2007) Police Stress: History, Contributing Factors, Symptoms and Interventions, *Policing: An International Journal of Police Strategies & Management*, Vol. 30, No. 2, 169–87.

10 Support Initiatives by Family and Friends

Introductory Comments

In the preceding two chapters, an examination was offered of preventative measures that could be initiated by the police service as the employer and by officers themselves. This chapter examines the potential for family and close friends to intervene and support officers at risk of suicidal ideation.

Violanti (2007) warns that officers, who can find it difficult to accept their own depression, may find it is more difficult to express their feelings to partners. However, in a positive sense, he also comments that the officer's partner may be the perfect choice for such expression and a key person to whom the officer can turn. Martinez makes similar observations affirming the importance of family and friends and reports one officer's observation:

> I feel that I would not like to discuss my problems with a stranger. It would be a little uncomfortable for me, especially discussing personal problems. I would rather speak to a family member or a close friend, because I don't like to discuss my personal life with someone I do not know.
>
> (Martinez 2010: 67)

Jorm and Kitchener use the term 'gatekeeper' when referring to those who may offer intervention, and comment:

> Most gatekeeper training is aimed at health professionals or others involved in human services such as teachers, police, or clergy. However, it has been suggested that family and friends may make better gatekeepers because they have the greatest contact with the suicidal.
>
> (Jorm and Kitchener 2011: 803)

Family, friends and colleagues have a significant contribution to make in responding to officers experiencing suicidal ideation. It is therefore to these people that this chapter is particularly addressed.

To enable family and friends to support an officer to whom they may be emotionally close, this chapter first identifies and examines the warning signs and indicators which the officer contemplating suicide may reveal to them. Having identified these indicators, the chapter offers an analysis of the misunderstandings relating to parasuicide and suicide, which family and friends should first and foremost reject. These misconceptions, sometimes commonly held, must be disregarded by family and friends if they are to have a greater understanding of the matter, through which they can offer their proactive support.

Having listed and offered the reasonings behind the misconceptions, the chapter goes on to examine family and friends' appropriate responses to the suicidal officer. The analysis first describes actions that should *not* be undertaken by those wishing to support, before recommending paths that should be followed.

Identifying Risk Factors, Warning Signs and Precipitators

Although some of those featured in the case-studies spoke clearly of their intention to complete suicide, other deaths were less foreseeable. In one of the case-studies, the coroner stated: 'by no means does everybody make it abundantly clear what they're about to do.' The media reports in other case-studies indicated that some officers, while having experienced difficulties in their lives prior to suicide, had given no clear cause for concern regarding their suicidal ideation. The reports included comments such as:

> The officer had 'looked a bit down', but a friend had not thought he was 'on the verge of something'.

> The officer 'seemed positive and we arranged to meet friends the next day'.

> The officer 'seemed fine. There were no signs at all'.

In other case-studies, the media reports suggested that the officer possibly had not been functioning as usual, but had offered no indication that suicide was imminent. The reports included such comments as:

> The officer had been 'slightly different' when engaged in a social activity before leaving to take his own life.

> The officer 'became withdrawn and quiet'.

> It appears while the officer's low moods had been improving, the officer may have 'harboured dark thoughts that he didn't discuss with anybody'.

The analysis of the case-studies offers evidence that family and friends can be confused when trying to recognise the signs of suicidal ideation. However, on the occasions when signs *had* been recognised, it would further appear that family and friends were unsure as to how they might respond.

This confusion is not limited to the family and close friends of officers; it is shared by others who have been close to those who have taken their own lives. It is as result of such confusion that Jorm and Kitchener, in common with others, suggest the community at large requires a greater understanding of the signs that someone may be suicidal. At the same time, they offer the overriding message that 'all thoughts of suicide need to be taken seriously' (Jorm and Kitchener 2011: 803).

With specific reference to family and friends, Owens et al. comment that an awareness of the signs of suicide, combined with an appropriate response, may be additionally complicated by the family and friends' 'proximity to the suicidal person and emotional investment in the relationship' (Owens et al. 2011: 834). This closeness, they suggest, may hinder family and friends' awareness of warning signs, impede their ability to speak openly and, if they are aware, inhibit family and friends from seeking assistance from those outside the family circle. Taking all these issues into account, Owens concludes that 'relatives and friends experience great difficulty in deciphering and heeding warning signs and taking appropriate action' (ibid.).

Referring to possible further difficulties involved in identifying the warning signs, Violanti comments on how some officers in the home environment 'tend to shut down emotions towards the family, leading to a process of detachment and the seeking of outside relationships' (Violanti 2007: 55). This detachment will further compound the family's inability to recognise the warning signs.

Specifying particular obstacles and referring to the research undertaken by Owens et al. (2011), Jorm and Kitchener suggest that there are 'three main barriers to recognition of suicidal distress and intervention to help the person'. These are:

(i) That the person who had completed suicide had difficulties in communicating distress, either by not expressing their distress or giving ambiguous signals.
(ii) Difficulties in interpreting and heeding distress signals.
(iii) Difficulties in taking action. Such difficulties include a reluctance to raise the topic of suicide, to involve others in the social network, or to encourage seeking professional help.

(Jorm and Kitchener 2011: 803)

In spite of the many difficulties involved in identifying warning signs, Jorm and Kitchener are nevertheless among those who affirm the key value of family and friends in their role as 'gatekeepers' (discussed earlier in this chapter). To enable these and other would-be members of a support network to identify and understand the prime warning signs, non-clinicians and clinicians alike have written at length, and it is on some of these warning signs that this chapter now focuses.

As will be seen from the indicators listed below, some indicators (or warning signs) – for example, alcohol abuse, depression, anxiety and a sense of isolation from family, friends and colleagues – may also be precipitators in their own right. These were identified as precipitators earlier in this book; as considerable reference to them has already been made, it is unnecessary to reiterate this information, but they should be known and understood by those offering support.

The National Negotiators Group (NNG) document *Crisis Intervention and Potential Suicide Avoidance* offers a list of what the NNG refers to as 'warning signs'. The leaflet lists:

- A previous suicide attempt or act of self-harm
- Drug abuse
- Expressing suicidal thoughts
- Sudden changes in mood or behaviour
- Preoccupation with death
- Becoming isolated
- Impulsiveness, recklessness and risk-taking behaviour
- Making 'final' arrangements, e.g. giving away possessions (such as books, CDs, DVDs)
- Depression
- Alcohol abuse.[1]

Offering examples of the various warning signs, Kirschman also refers to 'giving away possessions' and explains that those planning suicide may 'give things away happily because they have made a decision that looks like a solution to their problems and because, in their distorted thinking, others will benefit more from their death than their life' (Kirschman 1997: 173).

Miller comments that not all suicidal officers will offer indications, but suggests that 'a supervisor [should] take action' when 'a few' of the following warning signs are revealed. He lists these under the two categories of verbal and behavioural clues:

> *Verbal clues:*
> - Threatening self
> - Threatening others
> - Surrendering control
> - Throwing it all away
> - Out of control
> - Hostile, blaming and insubordinate
> - Defeated
> - Morbid attraction to suicide or homicide
> - Overwhelmed
> - Out of options
>
> *Behavioural clues:*
> - Gestures
> - Weapon surrender

- Weapon overkill
- Excessive risk-taking
- Boundary violations
- Procedural violations
- Final plans
- Surrendering control.

(Miller 2006: 189–90)

Miller's reference to surrendering control relates to the way in which those who are ambivalent about suicide may surrender certain aspects of control of their life to others. Karolynn Siegel, however, discusses the suicidal person's control mechanism from two different perspectives. Describing those who undertake what she terms 'rational suicide', she explains, 'these individuals often seem conditionally attached to life and willing to continue living only if their conditions are met' (Siegel 1998: 98). She also refers to the way in which the suicidal person can 'derive a feeling of comfort from the knowledge that they will determine the time and circumstances of their death'. She comments that 'a sense of controlling exactly how and when they will die appeals to the omnipotent strivings of these individuals' (Siegel 1998: 97).

Fremouw et al. offer two lists of what they refer to as 'indicators' of suicide: 'historical-situational indicators' and 'psychological indicators':

Historical-Situational Indicators

- Daily functioning
- Life-style
- Coping ability
- Significant others … social isolation and loneliness
- Psychiatric history
- Medical history
- Family history of suicide
- Previous suicide attempts

Psychological Indicators

- Recent losses
- Depression – Anxiety
- Isolation – Withdrawal
- Hostility
- Hopelessness
- Disorientation – Disorganization
- Alcohol and drug abuse
- Change in clinical features
- Suicide plan
- Final arrangements.

(Fremouw et al. 1990: 37ff.)

Dalton and Noble also offer warning signs. They write specifically for those in medical training and their approach may be somewhat clinical for the layperson. However, their references may be helpful to the non-clinician in appreciating the risk factors and warning signs. They include:

- Act carried out in isolation
- Act timed so that intervention unlikely
- Precautions taken to avoid discovery
- Preparations made in anticipation of death (e.g. making will, organising insurance)
- Preparations made for the act (e.g. purchasing means, saving up tablets)
- Communicating intent to others beforehand
- Leaving a note
- Not alerting potential helpers after the act.

(Dalton and Noble 2006: 172)

As stated, the warning signs listed above are all indicators that someone may be experiencing suicidal ideation. However, both the NNG leaflet and Dalton and Noble offer a note of caution. The NNG leaflet, for example, comments that some of these warning signs 'can be associated with everyday behaviour and should be looked at in context with the overall picture of the person you are concerned about. However, the more warning signs and risk factors, the higher the possible risk'.

Dalton and Noble also warn of the dangers of misinterpreting parasuicidal actions and comment that what appears to be a simple overdose should not be dismissed as a 'low-intention attempt'. The overriding concern should be whether the person in question thought that the overdose would result in death. They offer the example that 'a bag of peanuts doesn't sound suicidal until you discover he has a peanut allergy!' (Dalton and Noble 2006: 171). Warning signs must be seen and understood in the context of the person for whom concern is raised.

Each of the different case-studies analysed in Chapter 4 featured one or more of the indicators referenced in this section, with two exceptions (a morbid attraction to suicide or homicide and a preoccupation with death). However, it is not possible to say with any certainty which of the deaths within the case-studies could have been averted had the risk factors and the warning signs been more clearly identified. In one case-study, suicide was completed when in custody and on suicide watch; the risk factor had been successfully identified and precautions had been taken, but death still occurred. Nevertheless, it is the suggestion of this research that when precipitators, risk factors and warning signs are identified, there is a greater likelihood that suicide may be averted.

Understanding the Misconceptions around Suicide

If a greater understanding of suicidal ideation is to be gained by family members and friends, it is important to dispel any misconceptions about suicide that they may hold. The misconceptions offered in the following examination may not be specific to police officers, but may have contributed to some of the case-study deaths.

Misconceptions around suicide – both those held by professionals and those held at a wider level – are many. The National Negotiators Group (NNG), Fremouw et al. (1990), Miller (2006) and the Samaritans are among those who refer at length to some of these misconceptions. The NNG document *Crisis Intervention and Potential Suicide Avoidance*, for example, provides a list of general misconceptions, while Fremouw et al. offer two lists: one of popular misconceptions and one of misconceptions held by professionals.

This chapter now identifies some of the major misconceptions and offers responses which may be helpful to those wishing to offer their support.

Misconception (a):

One should not try to discuss suicide with depressed people; it might give them the idea or upset them enough 'to push them over the edge'.

(Fremouw et al. 1990: 15)

Talking about suicide is a bad idea as it may give someone the idea to try it.[2]

Misconception (a) was experienced within this research project. As reported in Chapter 1, an article relating to the suicide research was rejected for publication partly because an editorial team felt it could encourage some readers to take their lives.

Misconception (a) is strongly refuted by the Samaritans and the NNG leaflet, using almost identical wording. The two documents comment on how suicide can be regarded as a forbidden topic, and yet those who feel suicidal can find conversations on the subject a welcome release from the pressures they are experiencing.

The documents suggest that those who feel suicidal may not wish to 'worry or burden' or to 'frighten' others, and consequently do not talk about their feelings. Therefore, the documents suggest, raising the subject of suicide can give those who feel suicidal 'permission to talk'. The NNG leaflet explains that 'once someone starts talking they have a greater chance of discovering other options to suicide',[3] so that their initial intention is averted.

Fremouw et al. (1990) also comment that raising the subject of suicide can give those who feel suicidal permission to talk, and that discussing the subject can bring them a sense of relief. Miller (2006) offers very similar comments and suggests that even some clinicians hold the same misconception concerning conversations about suicide. He comments that initiating a discussion of suicide with a non-suicidal person will not suggest that suicide is a realistic possibility. Open discussion is to be encouraged so that any notion of suicide can be appropriately rejected.

Misconception (b):

Once a person has made a serious suicide attempt, that person is unlikely to make another.[4]

Once the suicidal crisis has passed or the person's mood has improved, the danger is over.

(Miller 2006: 185)

As the case-studies demonstrated (Chapter 4, section entitled 'Premeditated or Impulsive'), many of those who completed suicide had previously sought to end their lives.

The Samaritans comment that those who have previously sought to kill themselves are 'significantly more likely to eventually die by suicide than the rest of the population'.[5]

Miller's comment above regarding the perceived improvement following a suicidal crisis is a misconception which Fremouw et al. suggest professionals may hold. They comment that for some people, suicidal ideation can recur when stress returns or becomes more intense.

Misconception (c):

> People who really want to die will find a way; it won't help to try to stop them.
>
> (Fremouw et al. 1990: 15)

> If a person is serious about killing themselves then there is nothing you can do.[6]

> Once suicidal, always suicidal.
>
> (Miller 2006: 185)

As reported in Chapter 6 (section entitled 'Contextual Factors Leading to Suicidal Ideation in the General Population'), and as explained throughout this chapter, intervention by family members and friends can be crucial. Even though the case-studies primarily referred to those who had completed suicide, analysis of the research indicates a group of people who had engaged in parasuicidal actions, but suicide had not occurred because of successful intervention.

The Samaritans and the NNG leaflet both comment on the temporary nature of suicidal ideation, regardless of the length of time for which the person has been experiencing depression. Both documents explain why, because of this temporary nature, intervention and support can be essential if suicide is to be avoided.

As Miller and Fremouw et al. both explain, intervention can reduce suicidal ideation. Fremouw et al. note that many of the symptoms are treatable and that once these symptoms have been relieved, the desire to complete suicide may also be resolved. Appropriate psychological support can give those suffering from suicidal ideation the coping mechanisms to overcome times of crisis and be consciously aware of alternative responses.

Misconception (d):

> People who threaten suicide are just attention seeking and shouldn't be taken seriously.[7]

The case-studies in Chapter 4 (section entitled 'Premeditated or Impulsive') offer examples of those who had previously spoken of completing suicide before their deaths. Analysis of the case-studies demonstrated that the voices of some of those who died were heard, but equally that the voices of others were either ignored or disregarded.

The NNG and the Samaritans both affirm that those who threaten suicide should be taken seriously, as seeking attention is a way of calling out for support and 'giving them this attention may save their life'.[8] As Miller states, 'many people express suicidal intentions or make suicidal gestures because they're really hoping to be rescued' (Miller 2006: 184). As is further explained in later this chapter, attention should always be paid to suicidal gestures or discussions of suicide.

Misconception (e):

> People often commit suicide without warning.
>
> (Fremouw et al. 1990: 13)

> Suicide is always an impulsive act.
>
> (Miller 2006: 184)

As shown in the case-studies in Chapter 4 (section entitled 'Premeditated or Impulsive') and as referenced above (misconception (d)), many of those who took their own lives had intimated their wish to do so before the suicide occurred.

Fremouw et al. strongly refute misconception (e) (Fremouw et al. 1990: 13); Miller agrees that sometimes suicide may be impulsive but comments that generally the suicidal person is ambivalent, and will have previously expressed their intention while leaving 'room for intervention' (Miller 2006: 184).

Misconception (f):

> People who threaten suicide don't do it.
>
> (Fremouw et al. 1990: 15)

> Those who threaten suicide don't really do it.
>
> (Miller 2006: 183)

> People who talk about suicide aren't serious and won't go through with it.[9]

As the case-studies demonstrate, and as referenced above, many of those who took their own lives had intimated their wish to do so before suicide occurred. Fremouw et al. appear to support this conclusion and note that, according to research, the majority of those who complete suicide have previously spoken of their intent.

Similarly to the comment made with reference to misconception (d) above, the Samaritans highlight that 'while it's possible that someone might talk about suicide as a way of getting the attention they need, it's vitally important to take anybody who talks about feeling suicidal seriously'.[10] Miller suggests that the response to the suicidal person both demonstrates the supporter's concern for the suicidal person and raises awareness of the consequences that could potentially follow; 'therefore, all suicidal threats should be taken seriously' (Miller 2006: 184).

Misconception (g):

> People who are suicidal want to die.[11]

An analysis of the majority of the case-studies would seem to suggest that most of the officers sought death; however, both the NNG and the Samaritans offer identical comment, and state:

> The majority of people who feel suicidal do not actually want to die; they do not want to live the life they have. The distinction may seem small but is in fact very important and is why talking through other options at the right time is so vital.[12]

Harry Olin also rejects misconception (g) and explains what he defines as 'the third wish' (as previously noted, Olin writes that suicide may become 'a means of dying without terminal death': Olin 1998: 78).

Misconception (h):

> Sometimes a minor event ... can push an otherwise normal person to commit suicide.
>
> (Fremouw et al. 1990: 14)

As the case-studies demonstrate (Chapter 4; Chapter 7, section entitled 'Accumulated Factors'), the majority of the officers who took their own lives did so following an accumulation of long-standing precipitators. Rarely was there a single precipitator, and where a single precipitator was apparently the main 'cause' in a case-study, this was not a 'minor event'.

Fremouw et al. refute misconception (h), suggesting that poor coping/self-management skills, in combination with a need to adapt to changed circumstances and possible psychological difficulties, can result in suicidal ideation. Their observations resonate with comments made in Chapter 6 (section entitled 'Dichotomised Decision-Making'), where reference is made to the suicidal officer's decision-making process.

Misconception (i):

> Only crazy people commit suicide.
>
> (Fremouw et al. 1990: 14)

> You have to be mentally ill to think about suicide.[13]

> Individuals who commit suicide are mentally ill.
>
> (Miller 2006: 184)

The analysis of the case-studies in Chapter 4 demonstrates that many of those featured were depressed at the time of their suicidal ideation, but this characteristic does not imply that they were 'crazy' or 'mentally ill'.

Fremouw et al. note that the majority of those who experience suicidal ideation are not suffering with psychological illnesses. The Samaritans suggest that
'most people have thought of suicide from time to time'[14] and that not all those
who complete suicide do so while experiencing health problems of a psychological nature. However, Miller suggests that many of those who take their own lives
may have been 'mentally ill' previously and suggests that a knowledge of their
medical history will be important to the process of 'formulating an intervention
strategy that realistically takes this variable into account' (Miller 2006: 184).

Misconception (j):

> Suicide is always an irrational act.
>
> > (Miller 2006: 184)

Miller comments that 'sometimes it is and sometimes it isn't' (ibid.), but that a
severely depressed person will have a different perspective on situations. Different people respond differently to stress in different situations.

The case-studies all revealed that those who had taken their lives were experiencing a heightened level of pain; what may have been an irrational act to their
family and friends was not necessarily irrational to those who completed suicide.

Misconception (k):

> If a person committed suicide, his or her situation was probably so bad that
> death was the best solution.
>
> > (Fremouw et al. 1990: 14)

Fremouw et al. respond to this misconception by suggesting that it presumes 'to
know the value of human life' (Fremouw et al. 1990: 14). It is not possible to
comment on the value those featured in the case-studies placed on their lives.
However, examination of the reports of those case-studies in which individuals
engaged in parasuicidal actions, and interviews with individuals who spoke of
taking their own lives, suggest that the value they (and others) placed on their
lives finally outweighed their reasons for completing suicide.

The suicidal will be best supported by the intervener assisting those talking of
suicide to gain an understanding of their choices (this chapter, section entitled
'Identifying Options'). If, to quote the aphorism, suicide is a permanent solution
to a temporary problem, then the person considering suicide should be helped to
identify other options that respond to their 'temporary' problem, through which
they can regain their self-esteem.

Misconception (l):

> The tendency towards suicide is inherited and passed from generation to
> generation.
>
> > (Fremouw et al. 1990: 15)

> Suicide runs in families.
>
> > (Miller 2006: 184)

In certain of the case-studies there had been a history of suicide within the family (Chapter 4, section entitled 'History of Suicide within the Family'). Other references have been made to this theory (for example, sections entitled 'Family History' in Chapters 6 and 7). Fremouw et al. reject misconception (l) but accept that those who come from families where suicide has been unknown are at the lowest risk, indicating that there may be some degree of truth in that misconception. Nevertheless, they comment that a family history of suicide does not suggest that the value of support can be negated.

Miller offers similar comments and states that for those who come from families with a history of suicide, the risk may be greater; however, with appropriate intervention, any propensity to suicidal ideation can be overcome.

Misconception (m):

> The great majority of suicides are among minority groups from lower sociological classes; the age group at highest risk these days is young people.
>
> (Fremouw et al. 1990: 16)

The case-studies in Chapter 4 generally concur with the researchers' rejection of this misconception. There was no indication that they came from 'lower sociological classes'. With regard to age, Fremouw et al. refer to statistical evidence to suggest that suicide is more prevalent in older males. This concurs with the majority of the case-studies. However, statistics with regard to the age at which officers complete suicide will need to be reassessed in light of changes in recruitment age, and considering future research.

Misconception (n):

> Suicides occur in greatest numbers around Christmas and Thanksgiving.
>
> (Fremouw et al. 1990: 16).

> Most suicides happen in the winter months.[15]

The Samaritans state that in the UK, suicide 'is more common in the spring and summer months'.[16] Similarly, Fremouw et al. comment that in the USA the number of suicides is higher in the spring than in the other seasons, although it is 'relatively consistent throughout the year' (Fremouw et al. 1990: 16).

The analysis of the case-studies did not suggest that there was any seasonal variation in the suicides that were examined.

Fremouw et al. suggest the misconceptions in the following list may be held by some medical professionals; they are of equal interest to those who are not medically trained.

Misconception (o):

> If a person survives a suicide attempt, he or she must have been doing it as a manipulation.
>
> (Fremouw et al. 1990: 17)

Fremouw et al.'s response to this misconception is that parasuicidal actions may have many different underlying causes, and those who wish to offer support should not assume knowledge of the relevant issues. Simple judgements concerning potential manipulation cannot be made.

Analysis of the case-studies revealed no suicidal or parasuicidal action that sought to be manipulative. The analysis supports a rejection of misconception (o) and, similarly, misconception (p) which follows. The evidence of the case-study analysis suggests that in each of the case-studies, the individuals were serious in their intent.

Misconception (p):

> There are two groups of suicidal patients: those who are serious about dying and those who are trying to manipulate somebody.
>
> (Fremouw et al. 1990: 19)

Fremouw et al. warn against this oversimplification. They comment that those experiencing suicidal ideation may have conflicting feelings about their intended actions; even though they may no longer wish to live, they may still hope that someone will intervene. It is essential, the researchers state, that these two parallel thoughts are fully acknowledged.

Misconception (q):

> Improvement following a suicidal crisis means the suicide risk is over.
>
> (Fremouw et al. 1990: 16)

Fremouw et al. comment that a noticeable improvement in the person's depression may indicate that the person's psychological welfare is improving. However, they offer a warning that the improvement may result from the person finding release – the choice to complete suicide has been made and life will be concluded. Case-study 17 in Chapter 4 (section entitled 'Premeditated or Impulsive') offers a possible example by which to reject this misconception, whereby the officer 'had hinted at suicide months before his death but not in the immediate days or weeks before he was found hanged ... he had seemed normal on the day he died'.

Misconception (r):

> Most people who parasuicide once can be expected to make multiple attempts; most people who kill themselves usually have made previous non-lethal attempts.
>
> (Fremouw et al. 1990: 17)

Fremouw et al. comment that as the first attempt is successful for many, further attempts are unnecessary – one is sufficient. The case-studies in Chapter 4 (section entitled 'Premeditated or Impulsive') offer numerous examples supporting Fremouw et al.'s rejection of this misconception.

Misconception (s):

> One should not reinforce pathological behavior by attending to vague references to suicide.
>
> (Fremouw et al. 1990: 17)

Fremouw et al. suggest that even if a potentially suicidal person might be hinting at suicide to gain attention, the clinician should be prepared to respond fully each and every time the issue is raised.

Misconception (t):

> If a person is talking to a therapist about suicide, he or she probably is not going to do it. A person truly intent on suicide is likely to hide it from people who might stop him or her.
>
> (Fremouw et al. 1990: 17–18)

According to Fremouw et al., 80 per cent of those who have completed suicide have previously expressed their intention to do so. The researchers say that expressing thoughts of suicide can indicate a serious intention to end one's life and that such conversations should not be dismissed. Case-study 18 in Chapter 4 (section entitled 'Premeditated or Impulsive') offers an example of an officer who took his own life after attending counselling with a psychologist.

Misconception (u):

> Suicide is to be expected in cases of severe hardship, especially in persons with terminal illness.
>
> (Fremouw et al. 1990: 18)

Fremouw et al. discuss the extent to which this may or not be a misconception and offer some evidence which suggests that suicide among terminal cancer patients is extremely rare. However, as indicated in Chapter 4 (section entitled 'Health Concerns of a Physical Nature'), illness and perceived illness were contributory factors in the suicides in four of the case-studies.

Misconception (v):

> The main factor in suicide is psychopathology; suicidal people have about the same level of life stress as nonsuicidal people.
>
> (Fremouw et al. 1990: 18)

Different people have different abilities to cope with stress, and Fremouw et al. suggest that stressors can be more intense and numerous for those who become suicidal than they are for the average person. Regardless of its intensity, stress, combined with insufficient coping mechanisms, may result in suicidal ideation.

Misconception (w):

> A person who makes a non-life-endangering attempt or who makes an attempt with a high chance of rescue must not have been serious about dying and is not at high risk for suicide.
>
> (Fremouw et al. 1990: 19)

Fremouw et al. comment that the passion of those who wish to end their lives cannot be measured against the harm that those people inflict upon themselves. Minimal self-harm cannot equate to insignificant intent. Those involved in clinical support should not draw conclusions which may be flawed. Due consideration should be given to all who engage in parasuicidal actions; as Fremouw et al. suggest, underlying reasons and actions can be elusive and multi-faceted.

All of the misconceptions set out above are strongly refuted by psychologists and counsellors. They are equally refuted by the analysis of the case-studies – especially those misconceptions that focus on officers who have spoken about suicide prior to their deaths. Furthermore, the misconceptions are likewise rejected as a result of examination of the importance of the preventative measures presented in the preceding chapters, and those which are suggested later in this chapter.

A stark fact on which to conclude this section is that raised by the NNG leaflet: 'people who have attempted to kill themselves are significantly more likely to eventually die by suicide than the rest of the population'.[17] Those who talk of ending their lives must be heard and an appropriate response must be given. This chapter therefore now focuses on appropriate responses.

Responding to the Warning Signs

Having rejected the misconceptions, and realising that suicide is a real possibility, a significant number of essential responses are required of the supporter. This chapter continues by looking at these responses. Before identification and examination of positive responses, it must be noted that there are a number of ways in which the one supporting should *not* respond. An examination of these negative actions now follows.

Negative Actions

Kirschman (1997) addresses herself to family, friends and colleagues of suicidal officers and offers a number of suggestions. She comments that the supporter should *not*:

- Attempt to cheer someone up
- Argue, threaten or deliver an ultimatum

- Give lectures or 'sermons'
- Tell people:
  - that others are in a worse predicament
  - that suicide is sinful
  - how they should feel

- Threaten, deliver an ultimatum or take control away from the person unless that person's life is in immediate danger.

Expanding on what not to do, Kirschman explains that in seeking to 'cheer up' someone who is suicidal, that person may infer that 'you simply don't understand the depth of his or her despair' (Kirschman 1997: 176). If this impression is given, the person offering support will be ignored and consequently the suicidal officer may feel more alone and isolated. Kirschman explains that arguing, lecturing, sermonising and commenting that others are worse off and that the suicidal shouldn't feel the way they do 'may only make the suicidal more defensive and make you less helpful' (Kirschman 1997: 177).

With regard to taking control from someone who is contemplating suicide, it should be noted that the suicidal may already feel that they are unable to exercise control over their lives and 'may believe suicide is the only way to get back into control' (Kirschman 1997: 177). The supporter should encourage the person contemplating suicide to be aware that they have control over the problems confronting them.

Larned's advice to colleagues of a suicidal officer is that they shouldn't take their colleague 'out for the proverbial drink when they are feeling down [as this] can exacerbate the situation' (Larned 2010: 70). He explains that 'while alcohol may provide a temporary feeling of wellness, it is a fact that alcohol affects the brain in areas that promote depression, impair judgment, and remove inhibitions' (ibid.).

The National Negotiators Group also offers a list of what should not be said or done to the suicidal person. The NNG leaflet is primarily written for officers who may be the first person to respond to a call from someone who is suicidal (first responders). Nevertheless, the suggestions made in the leaflet may be helpful in that they offer advice to friends and family members, who could equally be first responders or could become involved in a situation which they had not envisaged. Some of the advice offered is also appropriate to those who may be emotionally close to the suicidal person. The NNG leaflet instructs:

a) Do not grab the individual; this is placing yourself in severe danger.
b) Do not go along with *last wishes*, final demands or *verbal wills* – it's better to keep open some *unfinished business*.
c) Do not lie. Be honest with them at all times. They need to trust you before progress can be made.
d) Do not judge or criticise the subject or their situation.
e) Do not create a theatre of stress and tension. Keep it quiet and keep onlookers as far back as possible.

f) Do not use a friend, family member or a third party until they can be properly assessed by a trained negotiator. They may be part of the problem and the subject may wish to commit suicide in their presence.

g) Discourage them from continual alcohol or drug abuse.

h) Avoid the phrase *I understand what you are going through.*[18]

Suggestion (f) above brings into focus the relationship between the first responder and the suicidal person. Those who are supporting the suicidal person should remember that they themselves may be a catalyst for what is taking place. In such a scenario, it will be essential for them to withdraw as soon as is realistically expedient and for someone more objective (and possibly more qualified) to attend. Further reference to including others in a support role is made later in this chapter (section entitled 'Acquiring Assistance').

An article in the periodical *BMJ* also offers advice to supporters of the suicidal person:

- 'Watchful waiting' is not an appropriate strategy
- It is never appropriate to promise to keep a person's suicidal plans a secret.

(Jorm and Kitchener 2011: 803)

Taking positive action is always more appropriate than 'watchful waiting'. The next section discusses the actions that should be initiated.

Positive Actions

Stress-Awareness Training and Information

Before the suggested positive actions that follow within this section (which is concerned with how the supporter may intervene in a suicidal crisis), this first section refers to the family's understanding of a serving officer's potential stress.

As was stated in Chapter 8, considerable benefit can be gained from forces involving and addressing families on the subject of officers' stress whenever the opportunity allows. As suggested in Chapter 8 (section entitled 'Family Participation'), it will be beneficial to families if they are invited to share in relevant in-service training. Equally, information on potential officer-stress may be shared at formal police gatherings, for example when officers' families attend attestation ceremonies.

With reference to educating both officers and their family members about the stress factors in an officer's work, Gilmartin (2002) comments on how families might be brought into relevant training sessions at different points throughout an officer's career. He suggests that this could be done with parents, partners and children depending on the officer's stage in life.

Family support is crucial to officers experiencing suicidal ideation. It is therefore the suggestion of this research that family members should avail themselves at all times of the police programmes, events and information leaflets available to them that may offer this resource knowledge. So resourced, and with an informed understanding of stress and its possible implications, families will be in an influential position to respond to the emotional needs of the officer.

Affirming Intervention

As previously indicated, family and friends may feel unable to intervene with someone who has spoken of suicide or who has indicated that suicide is something they have been considering. However, as Kirschman comments, 'Intervention is the key to preventing suicide. The consequences of getting help to someone are never as permanent as the consequences of suicide' (Kirschman 1997: 176). As was demonstrated earlier in this chapter, family, friends and close colleagues must 'take the threat [of suicide] seriously'.[19] Those who are close to a suicidal officer should do this in the knowledge that 'most people who feel suicidal don't necessarily want to die; they just want an end to their pain'.[20] This is a worthy starting point from which those wishing to support may feel confident in their desire to intervene.

When referring to appropriate intervention, Miller (2006) addresses himself to work associates and medical professionals; however, his comments can be equally addressed to family and friends. He suggests that if proactive support is given to the seriously depressed officer, even when there is no immediate or present cause for crucial concern, a future crisis may be averted.

There are different processes which the supporter might adopt in their intervention, but the supporter's mere presence enables a stressed officer to know that they are not alone. As Miller comments: 'Just helping the person feel like he or she is not all alone in the world can have a powerful effect. Reducing isolation can occur in two main, sometimes overlapping, ways: commiseration and support' (Miller 2006: 191).

Preparing and Taking Precautions

Once the supporter has acknowledged that intervention will be helpful, Kirschman suggests that that supporter should be prepared 'for a lot of angry denial. Remember, cops think they should solve problems, not have them' (Kirschman 1997: 176). She lists a number of possibilities for the supporter to consider in anticipation of the initial intervention:

- plan [the meeting] in advance
- have phone numbers available [should assistance be required]
- have someone standing by a telephone
- take a friend along
- pick an appropriate time and place to raise your concerns – one that is private, comfortable, and unhurried.

(Kirschman 1997: 175)

Kirschman (writing for American readers, but with UK parallels) and the National Negotiators Group both also suggest that the supporter should take certain precautions:

- 'assess the level of danger – the more specific the plan the more imminent and deadly. You need to know if you should call 911 right away or if you have time to do something else.' (Kirschman 1997: 175)
- 'take sufficient precautions. Remember, there are guns around.' (Kirschman 1997: 177)
- 'think personal safety.'[21]
- 'ask the subject to remove or reduce any immediate danger.'[22]

Asking Questions

Jorm and Kitchener report that 'evidence from community surveys … supports the finding that members of the public are reluctant to ask about suicidal feelings' (Jorm and Kitchener 2011: 803). Asking questions is essential if the supporter is to elicit information regarding the immediacy of the suicidal intent. Acknowledging the difference between thinking about suicide and suicidal intent, Dalton and Noble suggest that 'if a patient mentions that they feel suicidal or have thought about killing themselves, it is worth asking if they are planning to act on these thoughts' (Dalton and Noble 2006: 172).[23]

In similar vein, the National Negotiators Group suggests that 'if it is unclear to you whether the person is suicidal or not, ask them'. Elaborating further, the NNG suggest that by asking questions, the supporter will first be able to 'find the focus of the problem' and consequently can 'find the hook – reason to live'.[24]

Miller refers to the process of asking questions of the suicidal person as 'defining the problem'. The object of asking questions is, he writes, 'to help the subject clarify in his or her own mind what exactly has led to the present crisis state' (Miller 2006: 192). The aim of these questions will be to focus attention on what is happening and to clarify the context.

Explaining that the purpose behind seeking to take one's own life is not one of self-destruction but of an endeavour 'to solve a current, intolerable, personal human problem of living', Ronald Mintz suggests that those who are close to the suicidal person should seek to understand the following:

- What is the problem in which this person feels so hopelessly caught?
- What is it that this person is so desperately trying to change?
- Why does he feel so hopeless about the possibility of being able to bring about any change?

(Mintz 1998: 245)

The prime way in which the supporter will discover answers to these questions is by asking questions of the person who is feeling suicidal.

Listening

Having asked the questions, the supporter must listen. The NNG leaflet states that the supporter should:

- Listen to what they are saying as it often contains the key issues
- Listen carefully to what they say and how they say it
- Seek to understand what the subject's loss is because if you do you will understand why the crisis has happened.[25]

David Wood emphasises the importance of active listening in an article concerning Army Reserve sergeant major Joe Saunders. Wood summarises Saunders' feelings after experiencing suicidal ideation: 'Looking back on these close brushes with death, Saunders concludes that the most effective suicide prevention tactic is simply to listen.'

Woods offers a number of quotations from Saunders, who states:

> No one can understand exactly how you feel ... But you just say, 'I don't need fixing, I just need you to listen'.

> [Listening] and then having people call and check up on you. That shows people really do care.[26]

Encouraging Dialogue

Positive and creative listening will lead to a two-way exchange. The supporter is advised by the NNG leaflet to do the following:

- If they admit to feeling suicidal, encourage them to talk about their thoughts and feelings, and the root causes
- Allow them to vent their anger, feelings and emotions
- Allow silences.[27]

Empathising

Larned suggests that supporters should employ their emotional intelligence in seeking to sustain the suicidal. He comments: 'Emotional intelligence centers on empathy and an understanding of others' feelings and perspectives and takes an active interest in their concerns ... while listening openly' (Larned 2010: 70). The NNG leaflet likewise suggests that the supporter should 'express personal concern and empathy but avoid the phrase *I understand what you are going through*'.[28] Miller also refers to empathy, commenting that 'a little empathy and commiseration can go a long way in establishing trust and encouraging a nonviolent resolution to the incident' (Miller 2006: 193).

Speaking Openly

Kirschman suggests that the supporter should, using empathy, 'be honest in describing your own experience with depression, hopelessness, or thinking about suicide' (Kirschman 1997: 176). The NNG encourages supporters to 'talk openly about the finality of death',[29] while Kirschman advises: 'don't hesitate to speak openly about suicide' (Kirschman 1997: 174). She also suggests that the supporter needs to 'be assertive' (ibid.: 175) and 'direct, yet tactful' (ibid.: 176).

Giving Hope

Miller, the National Negotiators Group and Kirschman all refer to the importance of offering the suicidal a sense of hope for the future.

Miller refers to the confused perceptions that a suicidal officer may experience when depressed. He comments that there will be 'feelings of helplessness and hopelessness' and suggests that 'interveners should try to create a more favorable balance by identifying and separating out areas of self-deprecation and despondency vs. self-worth and hope' (Miller 2006: 191). The National Negotiators Group leaflet suggests that supporters should:

Try and get them to think of ways forward focusing on positives

Explore what is meaningful to the subject and try to get them to tell you what *keeps them going*.[30]

Similarly, Kirschman suggests the supporter should 'Find out if this person has survived some past crisis. Sometimes remembering they have been through tough times before helps people to restore confidence and hope that they can do so again' (Kirschman 1997: 176). Miller also suggests that the dialogue between the officer and the person supporting should focus on working through the immediate situation, 'gently suggesting that the larger issues can be dealt with later – which of course implies that there will be a "later"' (Miller 2006: 193). Giving hope is important, for, as Kirschman states, 'hope is the awareness that one has options' (Kirschman 1997: 176).

The case-studies offer an example of how a supporter might seek to give hope to the suicidal person. At an inquest, a member of the force spoke of how 'I tried to talk to [the officer] at length about the positives in [the officer's] life, to deflect [the officer] away from the belief at that time that [the officer] shouldn't be alive'. In spite of this encouragement, however, in this case the officer completed suicide.

Identifying Options

Miller, the NNG leaflet and Kirschman all refer to the importance of enabling the suicidal person to see that they have options. Addressing himself to the intervener, Miller comments that 'your job is to gently expand the range of non-lethal options for resolving the crisis situation' (Miller 2006: 194). The NNG leaflet suggests that the supporter should 'stress that suicide is only one of many alternatives'. Kirschman suggests that the supporter should:

> Clearly say that pain can be managed and that there are other ways to solve these problems beside suicide. Let him know that getting help is a sign of strength, not weakness, and that it takes guts to face your problems and yourself.
>
> (Kirschman 1997: 175)

Making a Plan

Having discussed possible options, it is suggested by Miller that the supporter and the suicidal should agree a plan of future action. Miller refers to this as encouraging 'active problem solving' and explains that 'Sometimes, the best way for a person to break through a depressive, potentially suicidal, crisis is for them to take some corrective action, to achieve a measure of self-efficacy, competence, and confidence' (Miller 2006: 191).

Miller suggests that the plan should involve 'accessing practical supports and utilizing coping mechanisms' (Miller 2006: 194) and that both 'short and long term plans' may be included (Miller 2006: 195).

Obtaining Commitment

When a plan has been finally agreed, Miller states, it is important to 'make sure the subject understands the plan and is reasonably committed to following it' (Miller 2006: 195).

Without providing specific reference to a plan or a commitment to specific objectives, the National Negotiators Group leaflet informs the supporter that they should 'expect the person to have *ups and downs*'.[31] Any plan that is created and agreed may be as fragile as the person experiencing the suicidal ideation; however, if the person supporting is part of the agreed plan, that person must ensure that they do all that they have promised to undertake.

Acquiring Assistance

In addressing officer-colleagues and affirming the role of family and close friends, Miller suggests that if colleagues sense their support is unwelcome, they should urgently seek the support of others. Miller suggests that these might be 'friends, relatives and other people, e.g., clergy, that the officer trusts and has found a valuable source of support in the past' (Miller 2006: 190). Miller also includes supporters who may be 'co-workers, supervisors' and 'clinicians' (Miller 2006: 194).

Clearly, appropriate assistance, depending on the circumstances of the situation, will invariably be required. Few people, if any, will have all the necessary resources to respond to an officer experiencing suicidal ideation; as Kirschman highlights, the supporter must respect their own limitations (Kirschman 1997: 177). Kirschman further comments that the supporter must not, for whatever reason, offer support that cannot be delivered. In these circumstances, the supporter would be well advised to 'make a referral to a mental health professional' (Kirschman 1997: 177).

Within the UK setting, an initial referral to a health professional would usually involve a general practitioner (GP). However, the supporter may be reluctant to involve a GP because of both the bond of confidentiality and the supporter's emotional investment in the relationship (discussed earlier in this chapter). Because of this trust, if possible, permission to make a referral should be sought from the officer concerned. Jorm and Kitchener comment that 'mental health professionals and people who have been suicidal agree that telling others is appropriate if the suicidal person is involved in the decision' (Jorm and Kitchener 2011: 803). The success of medical intervention, and the reluctance of supporters to engage with the medical profession, lead Jorm and Kitchener to state that 'The benefits of asking a person if they are feeling suicidal and involving others who could help need to be widely promoted to the public' (ibid.).

The National Negotiators Group leaflet (which, as noted, was written primarily for first responders) states that at the most extreme point, where an emergency is imminent, the supporter should:

- Call 999 for police assistance
- Until the trained negotiator arrives, maintain contact with the person and keep encouraging their return to a safe location.[32]

Concluding Comments

Reference has been made in this chapter to the beneficial intervention of family members and close friends in their role as supporters, interveners and gatekeepers to officers experiencing suicidal ideation. The intervention of professional clinicians may also be essential; nonetheless, as is emphasised by those closely connected with the police service as well as by clinicians, the families and friends of officers have a unique contribution to make in their support for officers experiencing suicidal ideation. More than any other person, they may be able to detect the warning signs that the officer is in need of support.

Some warning signs may be obviously apparent: the suicidal may talk of their intentions. However, as noted earlier in this chapter, other indicators can be more difficult to recognise: in some cases reported on by Owens et al., 'signs and communications of distress were oblique, difficult to interpret, and easily outweighed by signs of "life as usual"' (Owens et al. 2011: 834).

When warning signs are detected, families and friends will face the challenge of rejecting the misconceptions of suicide as encouraged by popular myths. This chapter examined some of these misconceptions and demonstrated the fundamental and beneficial impact of intervention. As the rejection of the misconceptions reveals, family and friends should not be reserved in initiating discussions on the subject of suicide when concerned for someone to whom they are emotionally close; while they may be 'reluctant to say anything to the distressed person' (Owens et al. 2011: 834); they must overcome this.

As the rejection of the misconceptions also reveals, parasuicide and talk of taking one's life should not be regarded by family and friends as a means of manipulation. Without reservation, 'the message that needs to be promoted to the public is that all thoughts of suicide need to be taken seriously' (Jorm and Kitchener 2011: 803).

For the potential supporter, 'watchful waiting' is not satisfactory. Some other responses are equally inappropriate and unhelpful to the suicidal officer. Many of these relate to ways in which a lack of empathy can be demonstrated, causing the supported to lose confidence in the supporter. Avoiding negative methods of engagement will be as important as actions that are positive and proactive – which, as demonstrated in this chapter, are numerous. To illustrate the contrasting consequences of adopting negative or positive actions, Figure 10.1 uses examples of different actions which the supporter may choose to adopt.

Most of the positive actions which the family or friend-supporter might carry out do not require professional expertise. As previously stated, professional clinical support may, and probably will, also be required, but there are many interventions which the non-clinical family member or friend can also offer. The majority of the interventions that have been introduced within this chapter refer to creating a context in which active listening can occur between the supporter and the supported. Asking questions of the suicidal to determine the core issues of the suicidal ideation; empathy; plain speaking; suggesting and developing other options – all of these will assist the suicidal officer to work through the suicidal ideation, which may be only temporary. First and foremost, active listening is paramount.

However, as has been stated, family members and friends must recognise the limitations of their skills and should ensure the involvement of others who may have additional clinical and pastoral skills. There will be many resources on which to call. Ideally, a team of supporters should emerge, all of whom have an important support role to offer. As a *BMJ* editorial notes, relatives and friends seeking assistance from others 'may need to be reassured that to act on their concerns may save life and that this may mean having to disregard customary codes of respect that usually limit intrusion into another person's emotional life' (*BMJ* Editorial Comment, 2011: 833).

In spite of what has been discussed herein, it must be finally stated and emphasised that there will be occasions when 'people at risk may not necessarily express suicidal feelings or actions, hopelessness, or distress' (Jorm and Kitchener 2011: 803). There may be no warning signs or indicators. Consequently, as Kirschman comments, 'sometimes there is no way to stop people from killing themselves or to have read their mind beforehand' (Kirschman 1997: 177). Offering important reassurance to those who have been close to an officer who has completed suicide,

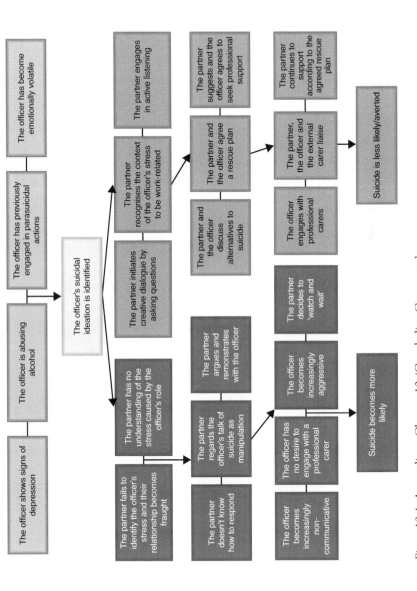

Figure 10.1 Appendix to Chapter 10, 'Concluding Comments'.

Kirschman also states that 'one person cannot drive another to suicide except under the most extreme circumstances' (ibid.) and, crucially, adds that 'people who kill themselves are responsible for their choices' (ibid.).

This and the preceding two chapters offered suggestions as to intervention measures that could be implemented. The next, penultimate, chapter offers recommendations which, if adopted, could successfully lessen officers' vulnerability to suicidal ideation.

Notes

1 National Negotiators Group (NNG) (2013) *Crisis Intervention and Potential Suicide Avoidance.*
2 NNG, *Crisis Intervention*; Samaritans, 'Myths about suicide', available from www. samaritans.org/how-we-can-help-you/myths-about-suicide; accessed October 21, 2014. The material published by the Samaritans in 2014 relating to myths and misconceptions was first accessed from the Samaritans website in 2010. The text is almost identical to that of the National Negotiators Group publication from 2013. It would seem probable that the NNG relied on text first published by the Samaritans.
3 NNG, *Crisis Intervention.*
4 NNG, *Crisis Intervention*; Samaritans, 'Myths about suicide'.
5 Samaritans, 'Myths about suicide'.
6 NNG, *Crisis Intervention*; Samaritans, 'Myths about suicide'.
7 NNG, *Crisis Intervention*; Samaritans, 'Myths about suicide'.
8 Samaritans, 'Myths about suicide'.
9 Ibid.
10 Ibid.
11 NNG, *Crisis Intervention*; Samaritans, 'Myths about suicide'.
12 NNG, *Crisis Intervention*; Samaritans, 'Myths about suicide'.
13 Samaritans, 'Myths about suicide'.
14 Ibid.
15 Ibid.
16 Ibid.
17 NNG, *Crisis Intervention.*
18 Ibid.
19 Ibid.
20 Ibid.
21 Ibid.
22 Ibid.
23 Dalton and Noble comment that 'a person making active plans is much more of a worry than someone talking about it' (Dalton and Noble 2006: 172).
24 NNG, *Crisis Intervention.*
25 Ibid.
26 Wood, David, 'Vet who attempted suicide asks to be heard, not fixed', *Huff Post Impact*, September 9, 2013, available from www.huffingtonpost.com/2013/09/09/ vet-suicide_n_3859738.html; accessed September 10, 2013.
27 NNG, *Crisis Intervention.*
28 Ibid.
29 Ibid.
30 Ibid.
31 Ibid.
32 Ibid.

Bibliography

BMJ Editorial Comment (2011) Suicidal Behaviour from a Lay Perspective, *BMJ*, Vol. 343, No. 7828 (October 22), 833.

Dalton, H.R. and Noble, S.I.R. (2006) *Communication Skills for Final MB*. London: Elsevier.

Fremouw, William J., de Perczel, Maria and Ellis, Thomas E. (1990) *Suicide Risk: Assessment and Response Guidelines*. New York: Pergamon Press.

Gilmartin, Kevin M. (2002) *Emotional Survival for Law Enforcement Officers*. Tucson: E-S Press.

Jorm, Anthony F. and Kitchener, Betty A. (2011) Giving Support to a Suicidal Person, *BMJ*, Vol. 343, No. 7828 (October 22), 803–4.

Kirschman, Ellen (1997) *I Love a Cop*. New York: Guilford Press.

Larned, Jean G. (2010) Understanding Police Suicide, *Forensic Examiner*, Vol. 19, No. 3, 64–71.

Lesse, Stanley (Ed.) (1998) *What We Know about Suicidal Behavior and How to Treat It*. Northvale: Jason Aronson.

Martinez, Louis Enrique (2010) *The Secret Deaths: Police Officer's Testimonial Views on Police Suicides and Why Suicides Continue to be Hidden in Police Departments*. Denver: Outskirts Press.

Miller, Laurence (2006) *Practical Police Psychology: Stress Management and Crisis Intervention for Law Enforcement*. Springfield: Charles C. Thomas.

Mintz, Ronald (1998) Psychotherapy of the Depressed Suicidal Patient. In Lesse, Stanley (Ed.) *What We Know about Suicidal Behavior and How to Treat It*. Northvale: Jason Aronson, pp. 241–64.

Olin, Harry (1998) The Third Wish. In Lesse, Stanley (Ed.) *What We Know about Suicidal Behavior and How to Treat It*. Northvale: Jason Aronson, pp. 77–84.

Owens, Cristabel, Owen, Gareth, Belan, Judith, Lloyd, Keith, Rapport, Frances and Donovan, Jenny (2011) Recognising and Responding to Suicidal Crisis within Family and Social Networks: Qualitative Study, *BMJ*, Vol. 343, No. 7828 (October 22), 834.

Siegel, Karolynn (1998) Rational Suicide. In Lesse, Stanley (Ed.) *What We Know about Suicidal Behavior and How to Treat It*. Northvale: Jason Aronson, pp. 85–102.

Violanti, John M. (2007) *Police Suicide: Epidemic in Blue* (2nd edition). Springfield: Charles C. Thomas.

11 Recommendations

Acknowledging that good practice exists, the recommendations that follow have all been drawn from comment and suggestions in the previous chapters.[1] The recommendations specifically relate to the analysis of the case-studies and primary research from other sources that discusses the implementation of intervention mechanisms.

The recommendations are offered in six sections according to the different categories that were identified by analysis and examination and that reflect issues of significance and importance that became evident during the research. They are as follows:

- research, acquisition of data and analysis
- working practices
- training
- welfare
- personal initiatives of officers and staff
- the initiatives of family and friends.

Following the recommendations, two tables are presented. The first refers to the potential costs of adopting the recommendations and the second to the effort that would be required of those embracing the lower-cost recommendations.

Research, Acquisition of Data and Analysis

As explained in the earlier chapters of this study, research relating to the deaths of UK officers and staff that were recorded as suicides or with open and narrative verdicts is extremely limited. The analytical research presented in this study has opened up an area of concern which appears to have been previously under-researched. Sufficient case-studies were selected to make this research viable. However, there remains a need for further in-depth research that examines details of suicidal ideation that were unavailable to this research project.

To ensure consistency and thoroughness, this future research should be undertaken initially at force level, with the identified information collated and analysed at national level. From such research, guidelines for the implementation of preventative measures will be further established.

Valuable insight can be gained by researching the most recent deaths, but as this study has indicated, further on-going research should be undertaken which takes into account the changing patterns in recruitment and deployment of officers and staff. The recommendations that follow within this section consequently refer to:

- the recording of statistical data
- the analysis of recorded data
- future research and analysis.

The Recording of Statistical Data

Recommendation 1.1.1

Each UK force should record the statistical data relating to in-service deaths of their officers/staff which were classified as suicide or which were recorded with narrative or open verdicts.

This recorded data would differentiate between:

- Officers and staff
- Rank/management grade
- Male and female.

The recorded data would show:

- The age at which the death occurred
- The length of service before death occurred
- The sexual orientation, race and religion of the officer/staff member.

Any reasons identified by the coroner indicating cause of death should be recorded.

Recommendation 1.1.2

There may be practical difficulties in gathering data,[2] but where possible each UK force should record the statistical data relating to deaths of their former officers/staff. The reason for an officer's/staff member's exit from the service should be recorded, for example following dismissal, resignation or retirement. Data should also be gathered stating the interval of time between leaving the police service and the death.

When the death of an officer/staff member has occurred in a force area different from that in which the officer/staff member had worked, the employing force should be the one that records the relevant data, having received the necessary information from the force in which the death had occurred; so if, for example, the death occurred in West Mercia but the member had worked in Lancashire, the death would be recorded by Lancashire Police.

As with *Recommendation 1.1.1*, this recorded data would differentiate between:

- Officers and staff
- Rank/management grade
- Male and female.

The recorded data would show:

- The age at which the death occurred
- The length of service before death occurred
- The sexual orientation, race and religion of the officer/staff member.

Any reasons identified by the coroner indicating cause of death should be recorded.

Recommendation 1.1.3

Each UK force should record the statistical data relating to serving officers/ staff who have engaged in a parasuicidal incident which was considered to be life-threatening at the time of the incident.

As with *Recommendation 1.1.1*, this recorded data would differentiate between:

- Officers and staff
- Male and female
- Rank/management grade.

The recorded data would show:

- The age at which the death occurred
- The length of service before death occurred
- The sexual orientation, race and religion of the officer/staff member.

Anything identified by the force to indicate underlying reasons for the parasuicidal intent should also be recorded.

Recommendation 1.1.4

The data discussed in *Recommendations 1.1.1* to *1.1.3* should initially be collected at force level and then submitted for analysis at a national level by the Group, as agreed in *Recommendation 1.2.1*.

The Analysis of Recorded Data

Recommendation 1.2.1

In accordance with *Recommendation 1.1.3*, the UK Home Office/NPCC (National Police Chiefs' Council) should appoint a Group to be responsible for analysis of the statistics acquired in relation to *Recommendations 1.1.1* to *1.1.4*.

Recommendation 1.2.2

Analysis of the data should be undertaken to identify the underlying causes of the suicides and parasuicidal incidents. This analysis would include determining:

- Emerging patterns of suicidal ideation
- The potential impact of the 'Werther effect' at both national and force levels.

Future Research and Analysis

Recommendation 1.3.1

The recording of statistical data and its analysis, at national level, should be both long-term and on-going, including both qualitative and quantitative methods where appropriate. This recording of data should take into account evolutionary changes in:

- the ages at which officers/staff are recruited;
- male/female recruitment ratio;
- the roles undertaken by staff, which had previously been undertaken by officers;
- any other identified evolutionary changes; for example, with regard to race, sexual orientation, redeployments or disciplinary procedures.

Recommendation 1.3.2

Qualitative research, undertaken at a national level, will include psychological autopsies to tease out the multi-dimensional causes and context of each of the examined suicides. There would need to be a sample of case-studies drawn from a broad cross-section of police/staff suicides from across the UK forces.

Recommendations 1.3.3 to *1.3.7* which follow are offered as a result of the analysis of the case-studies within this primary research. Other writers suggest similar recommendations. However, as the number of case-studies within the primary research may be considered relatively low, further research at a national level would seem desirable to substantiate the research findings and to gain further insight, which will impact on appropriate intervention measures.

Recommendation 1.3.3

Qualitative research should be undertaken considering officers/staff at different stages throughout their careers, to determine the effects of stress in relation to their work.

Recommendation 1.3.4

Analysis should be undertaken to determine the extent to which stress leading to suicidal ideation is caused by increased workloads.

Recommendation 1.3.5

Using an appropriate sample of serving officers and staff, qualitative research should be undertaken to determine the impact of PTSD experienced by officers/staff before entering the police service.

Recommendation 1.3.6

Using an appropriate sample of serving officers, research should be undertaken to determine the causes of 'rugged individualism'/false personalisation and whether these begin before or after recruitment. If it is found that they begin after recruitment, research should determine whether this is a consequence of social acquisition due to the police sub-culture.

Recommendation 1.3.7

Research should specifically examine the relationship between alcohol abuse, difficulties in partner relationships, stress and suicide.

Recommendation 1.3.8

In Chapter 10, important references were made to Jorm and Kitchener's observations regarding the importance of intervention measures that families might employ. Commenting on the research work of Owens et al. (2011), they suggest that research should be undertaken to determine the extent to which the family's awareness of suicidal ideation is helpful in averting suicides (Jorm and Kitchener 2011: 803). In keeping with their suggestion, it is recommended that research should be undertaken to assess whether greater family knowledge of how to support suicidal officers/staff has a positive effect on that person's suicidal behaviours.

Recommendation 1.3.9

A complementary study to that described in *Recommendation 1.3.8* should be undertaken to determine whether actions by family and friends have a positive influence on the suicidal officer/staff member. The findings of this recommendation and *Recommendation 1.3.8* would inform training programmes and presentations given when family members are present.

Recommendation 1.3.10

As opposed to 'chilling' (see Chapter 2, section entitled 'Research Difficulties'), forces and departments should be required to support studies into police suicide by assisting researchers to meet the challenge of practical difficulties, such as working in accordance with data protection requirements.

Recommendation 1.3.11

As opposed to 'chilling', forces and departments should actively encourage interested members of their force to discuss stress (in spoken and written discussion) and its implications in relation to suicidal ideation.

Working Practices

It was evident that working in the context of the police service was a key precipitator of suicidal ideation in many of the case-studies. In other case-studies where the working context may not have been central to suicidal ideation, it was nevertheless significant as one of a number of accumulated precipitators. The recommendations offered within this section relate to a broad range of issues, such as responsibility, awareness, financial resources, policy and processes, and relate to:

- chief officers
- shift patterns
- bullying, harassment and victimisation
- communication
- selection of officers/staff
- investigation – complaints and discipline.

Chief Officers

Recommendation 2.1.1

Chief officers should acknowledge that suicides of officers/staff are of organisational concern (Chapter 2) and thereby commit their force to suicide-prevention training programmes.[3]

Recommendation 2.1.2

Chief officers should be further aware of the risk of community contagion so as to be able to commit extra human and financial resources should a suicide occur.

Recommendation 2.1.3

Chief officers should consider the cost benefits of the psychological welfare of all officers/staff and recognise that limiting relevant financial resources may be to the detriment of the force's overall performance, financial liability and moral responsibility.

Shift Patterns

Recommendation 2.2.1

Based on the premise that shift work lowers physiological resistance to stress, forces should be advised on and adopt operational shift patterns that cause the least disruptive psychological damage to officers/staff. The reasoning behind the pattern that is adopted should be explained to the workforce and the force should demonstrate that the pattern has the confidence of its workforce. The adopted pattern should be evaluated periodically.

Recommendation 2.2.2

Forces should acknowledge the additional stress to officers/staff of changing shift patterns at short notice because of staff shortages. Consequently, shifts should only be changed at short notice in extreme operational circumstances.

Bullying, Harassment and Victimisation

Recommendation 2.3.1

The force should demonstrate that the implementation of policy guidelines concerning allegations of bullying, harassment and victimisation has the confidence of the workforce.

Communication

Good communication skills can ensure that officers and staff receive information that is timely and accurate. The primary research indicated that the knowledge which officers and staff held in relation to the following three recommendations was at times incorrect.

Recommendation 2.4.1

Forces should ensure that, through training, supervisors recognise the importance of good communication skills, with particular reference to organisational management.

Recommendation 2.4.2

Forces should improve their methods of communication in relation to the perceptions officers/staff may have regarding the process of misconduct hearings.

Recommendation 2.4.3

Forces should improve their methods of communicating information relating to redeployment, particularly when this is caused by a departmental reorganisation or personal need.

Selection

The following recommendations relating to selection appreciate the difficulty that may exist in obtaining the medical history of both the applicant and the applicant's immediate family. With regard to the applicant's medical history, the recommendations envisage that the applicant will be required to give permission for that history to be released. Information regarding the applicant's family history will rely on the applicant's honesty in the application process.

Recommendation 2.5.1

The selection process should be guided by the results of *Recommendation 1.3.5* with regard to applicants who have previously suffered from PTSD.

Recommendation 2.5.2

The selection process should ascertain whether there is a history of suicide in the applicant's family. If such a history exists this should be recorded, guided by medical advice, to indicate that the successful applicant may have an increased vulnerability to suicide during their working career.

Recommendation 2.5.3

Selection should be influenced by the previously discussed research into the causes of coping mechanisms that result in 'rugged individualism' (see *Recommendation 1.3.6*).

Investigations, Complaints and Discipline

Recommendation 2.6.1

All information on process, and any other relevant information, should be given verbally to the officer/staff member in person and supported in writing for the officer/staff member's later consideration.

Recommendation 2.6.2

The time span between the officer/staff member's initial notification of a pending investigation and the hearing should be shortened considerably.

Recommendation 2.6.3

When officers/staff are suspended for a potentially criminal offence, they should have immediate and on-going access to free and informed legal advice through their professional bodies.

Recommendation 2.6.4

Investigations should be conducted to a prescribed timetable that is made known to the officer/staff member. This timetable must be stringently followed by those involved in the investigation. The date by which the intended investigation and hearing will be completed should be made known to the officer/staff member. There may be exceptional circumstances which may cause a delay. If this should occur, the officer/staff member should be told the reasons for the delay and given a revised timetable.

Recommendation 2.6.5

Communication with the officer/staff member should be in accordance with an agreed timetable. This timetable should be made available in writing to the officer/staff member by all concerned with the investigation, including those responsible for the officer/staff member's welfare.

Recommendation 2.6.6

The officer/staff member should be given clear guidelines as to how the misconduct investigation will proceed.

Recommendation 2.6.7

Only those officers/staff members directly involved with the primary cause of the investigation should be barred from contacting the officer/staff member. Colleague-officers and line-managers should make every effort to maintain contact with the person under investigation. There may be exceptional circumstances in which, because of potential legal implications, it may not be possible for this recommendation to be implemented; for example, if colleagues of the person under investigation could be accused of collusion or impropriety. If such circumstances should occur, the situation will be explained to the officer/staff member under investigation and extra support mechanisms should be put in place.

Recommendation 2.6.8

The role of the appointed welfare officer should be made clear to those under investigation, especially with regard to the extent to which the appointed welfare officer offers those under investigation an assurance of confidentiality.

Training

The research undertaken in this study suggests that enhanced training programmes could make a significant contribution to suicide-preventative measures. The programmes that are envisaged and recommended will embrace all members of the police service at different levels and in different roles.

The recommended training programmes are extensive and will need to compete within the overall demands of an already full training schedule. The programmes will also need to be cost-effective and compete within budget constraints. Bearing in mind these practical difficulties, the training programmes could be implemented through a range of methods. Some programmes may need to be classroom-based but others could be offered, for example, through online internet training, such as that provided by the National Centre for Applied Learning Technologies (NCALT). Advantage should also be taken of the availability of resources external to the police service, such as those of the Advisory, Conciliation and Arbitration Service (Acas), the Samaritans and Cruse Bereavement Care. The introduction of extra training programmes may be challenging, but the psychological safety of officers and staff must be paramount, and training to support this should equal all programmes that support the physical safety of those employed within a force.

In addition to programmes for officers and staff, it is recommended that aware-ness training should be made available for close family members. Unlike officers and staff, family members cannot be required to attend, but their involvement in the opportunities presented can be encouraged.

The training recommendations are offered under the following sub-headings:

- initial training
- in-service training
- supervisory and line-management training
- training opportunities for the family.

Initial Training

Recommendation 3.1.1

Opportunities for any considerable amount of input relating to emotional strength will be limited when placed alongside the other training that will be required. However, it is recommended that initial training might specifically include *intro-ductions* to the following areas:

- The importance of developing strong family relationships and how these might be maintained when working according to a shift system.
- The importance of developing and maintaining strong social networks and activities outside the police service and culture.
- The importance of basic intervention techniques to relieve stress.
- The warning signs of depression and psychological illnesses.
- Suicide and the myths of suicide.
- Available support groups, both those within the force and those external.
- The importance of communicating with family, work colleagues and line-managers.
- The dangers of 'rugged individualism'.
- The importance of sharing emotional feelings in a confidential context.

In-Service Training

Recommendation 3.2.1

Alongside officer (physical) safety training, psychological safety training should be offered to enable officers/staff members to identify and respond to stress in themselves and their peers. These programmes would be mandatory and occur at regular intervals throughout the officer/staff member's career. The programmes should encourage and allow officers/staff members to take ownership of difficulties, to discuss the challenges they face and to seek support where necessary.

The programmes would include:

- An introduction to a basic understanding of psychological illness.
- How to identify and recognise risk factors.
- How to identify and recognise the warning signs of depression within themselves and in colleagues.
- An understanding of vulnerability to stress leading to suicidal ideation.
- Stress management, including an identification of coping mechanisms, stress-reduction techniques and problem-solving and decision-making strategies.
- An understanding of a community-policing philosophy to minimise officer isolationism.
- The importance of developing emotional intelligence.
- The dangers of 'rugged individualism' and dichotomised decision-making.
- Partner, family and social relationships; parenting skills; marital conflict; addiction; and management of finances.

Recommendation 3.2.2

The case-study research revealed that it is possible for an officer/staff member, particularly one taking on new responsibilities, to feel ill-equipped for the role. Realistic job-related training in police functions should be provided to prevent officers/ staff losing confidence in their ability to fulfil line-management expectations.

Recommendation 3.2.3

As discussed in Chapter 8 (section entitled 'Peer Support'), peer supporters appointed by the force should receive periodic training in support techniques. This training should be on-going and include:

- Pastoral and self-awareness skills, including how to develop and employ emotional intelligence, empathy and listening skills.
- An exploration of potential stress factors and how to recognise risk factors in policing.
- An identification of the warning signs of stress, depression, anger and psychological illnesses.
- An introduction to self-harming behaviours, addiction and alcohol abuse.
- An understanding of the vulnerability to stress leading to suicidal ideation and how to identify officers/staff vulnerable to suicidal ideation.
- An introduction to suicide and common misconceptions of suicide held by the general public.
- An introduction to stress management, including an identification of coping mechanisms, stress-reduction techniques, problem-solving and decision-making strategies.

- Available support groups, both within the force and external.
- The importance of communicating with family, work colleagues and line-managers.
- Techniques of crisis intervention and referral.
- How peer supporters can be supported.

Supervisory and Line-Manager Training

Recommendation 3.3.1

Mid-level management training should build on recruitment and in-service training. This training would be designed to assist supervisors in line-management techniques. Training should:

- Introduce general stress factors in police work.
- Emphasise the importance of communication and how to communicate.
- Enable the line-manager to apply basic psychological principles to field situations so as to act as a resource to the line-managed officer/staff member in relation to potential stresses.
- Demonstrate how to recognise the symptoms of stress and identify early warning signs of emotional distress in others, including self-harming behaviours, addiction/alcohol abuse, anger and depression.
- Describe the danger of dichotomised decision-making and 'rugged individualism'.
- Establish how to identify officers/staff vulnerable to suicidal ideation.
- Introduce suicide-prevention programmes.
- Offer an explanation of how to develop and employ emotional intelligence.
- Offer an understanding of how officers/staff can develop active coping styles.
- Demonstrate how to supervise high-risk officers/staff.
- Make known the resources that are available, including in-house welfare support, mental health services, community-based services and social support systems.
- Explain techniques of crisis intervention and referral.
- Describe the risk of community contagion.

Training for the Family

Recommendation 3.4.1

Each force should offer appropriate training sessions and encourage partners or immediate family members to participate. These programmes would describe:

- The stress of police work, to enable families to identify, understand and encourage officers/staff through the difficulties that officers/staff may encounter in the work context.
- How police work may affect partner and family relationships.

Other gatherings (such as attestation ceremonies) will also offer opportunities for the police service to assist families in their understanding of the pressures that officers/staff may face.

Welfare

The primary health-care responsibility for officers and police staff lies within the general community and not within the police service. Nevertheless, as the employer, the police service has considerable responsibility for all its members. All who work in the service should make a commitment to accept this responsibility and ensure that measures are in place to offer appropriate support.

Furthermore, through its occupational health and welfare units, the police service plays a pivotal role in the lives of officers and staff. Such support services have invaluable resource knowledge with regard to the demands of the police role and the culture in which officers and staff work. As invaluable as this support may be, it is recommended that the occupational health and welfare facilities that are available should be supplemented by a complementary range of additional support mechanisms. These provisions are reflected in the recommendations offered below.

Recommendation 4.1

Welfare provision should include peer support on a structured basis.

Recommendation 4.2

Those who offer psychological and emotional support should be invited to attend briefings and introduced so as to become known to officers/staff and thereby be integrated into mainstream policing, to diminish mistrust and suspicion.

Recommendation 4.3

Records should be kept (possibly by occupational health and welfare units) so that support can be offered on the anniversary of key traumatic events and contact can be made by occupational health/welfare units or line-managers to reassure vulnerable officers/staff that support is available.

Recommendation 4.4

A mandatory system to identify post-incident vulnerability should be in place and special attention/support should be given to officers/staff working in identified high-stress/high-risk areas, for example trauma risk management (see Chapter 8, section entitled 'A Process to Identify Risk').

Recommendation 4.5

A process should be in place by which colleagues and supervisors are able to make confidential referrals of officers and staff whom they have identified as suffering from undue stress or depression.

Recommendation 4.6

Support mechanisms should be regularly monitored and evaluated.

Recommendation 4.7

Financial resources should be made available to offer psychological support. If they are unavailable, the force should appoint a named person to make every effort to identify financial resources from such in-service organisations as staff associations or the Police Mutual Foundation, and wherever possible from external charitable agencies.

Recommendation 4.8

Officers/staff should have access to confidential psychological and emotional support without going through the force's internal procedures. This could be provided by, for example, access to a 24-hour telephone crisis-support line. This support line would be staffed by trained counsellors.

Recommendation 4.9

Officers/staff should be assured of client confidentiality. However, they should be encouraged to permit key people to share confidential information in order to ensure support is coordinated.

Recommendation 4.10

A 24-hour telephone crisis-support line resourced solely by current and former retired officers/staff should be introduced. This could be initiated as a joint venture between the NPCC, staff associations and NARPO (the National Association of Retired Police Officers). This support would complement *Recommendation 4.8*, which refers to a telephone support line resourced by trained counsellors, and would assist in the method of support suggested by that recommendation.

Personal Initiatives of Officers and Staff

The recommendations that follow underline general principles which officers and staff should be encouraged to accept as being necessary for their general welfare and well-being.

If these preventative recommendations are to have a significant impact on the officers'/staff members' continued well-being, the principles will be recognised when officers/staff members are emotionally strong. It will be difficult, if not impossible – and beyond their emotional ability – for the officer/staff member to implement some of the recommendations when experiencing suicidal ideation. At such times they will need to rely on the support of others.

Recommendation 5.1

Officers/staff should give due consideration to their lifestyle and its impact on their health. They should think about such issues as physical fitness, diet, relaxation, engaging in social activities outside the police circle and taking time for personal reflection.

Recommendation 5.2

Officers/staff should acknowledge the importance of initiating contact with those in caring professions if they identify signs of undue stress. They should also acknowledge the importance of accepting support.

Recommendation 5.3

Officers/staff should acknowledge the importance of willingness to initiate and respond, as appropriate, to communication/contact with their partner/family, friends/colleagues, welfare supporters and line-managers/supervisors.

Recommendation 5.4

Officers/staff should encourage their families to participate in police training programmes which enhance familial understanding of the difficulties and challenges involved in the officer/staff role.

Recommendation 5.5

Officers/staff should accept a level of personal responsibility for and control over such issues as their financial budgets and time-management of their life/work balance, for example with regard to the time committed to family and recreational pursuits.

Recommendation 5.6

Officers/staff should accept a level of responsibility for their own emotional welfare, acknowledge their vulnerability to emotional stress and identify stressors which may be specific to them.

Recommendation 5.7

Officers/staff should recognise the emotional investment of proactively creating stable relationships with family and close friends.

Recommendation 5.8

Officers/staff should recognise the dangers of 'rugged individualism'/false personalisation and dichotomised decision-making. These may prevent the development of a mature and realistic self-appreciation, which may contribute to such emotional issues as an inability to forgive oneself.

The Initiatives of Family and Friends

As indicated in Chapter 10, the family and close friends of those who work within the police service have a unique role in supporting an officer/staff member experiencing suicidal ideation. Yet theirs may also be the most difficult role. Family and friends will be closer emotionally than any others, and therefore more able to identify the warning signs of stress and depression. However, as previously referenced, this emotional closeness may be a barrier in offering support. Family and friends may also have the least knowledge of the stress factors of working in the police service. Nevertheless, they should be confident in the contribution they can make. To enable family (and close friends) to be confident in offering their support, the following recommendations are made.

Recommendation 6.1

Family members of officers/staff should be encouraged to participate in any opportunities provided by the police service that discuss the police role and its potential stressors. There are clear links between this recommendation and *Recommendations 3.4.1* and *5.4*.

Recommendation 6.2

Family and friends should recognise their important role in acting as supporters and gatekeepers to officers/staff experiencing excessive stress.[4]

Recommendation 6.3

Family members should be confident in referring the officer/staff member to professional carers with responsibility for the officer's/staff member's primary health care, and not allow misplaced loyalty or 'emotional investment' (Owens et al. 2011: 834) to prevent them from intervening.

Recommendation 6.4

Family and friends of an officer/staff member experiencing depression should seek to understand the possible root causes of that depression and respond in a proactive manner.

Recommendation 6.5

Family and friends of an officer/staff member experiencing depression should consider the possibility that the officer/staff member may be considering suicide. They should seek to identify warning signs, dismiss popular misconceptions and enter into a proactive dialogue with the officer/staff member.

The Required Cost and Effort in Adopting the Recommendations

No matter how important the recommendations set out in this chapter may be, they will only be adopted if they are perceived to fall within budget limitations and can be adopted with relative ease. A costing exercise is therefore shown in Table 11.1.[5] For each recommendation, it tabulates the relative financial costs, ranging from 'none' to 'high', and indicates those responsible for adopting the particular recommendations. Following this, Table 11.2 demonstrates the relative effort with which the recommendations could be adopted.

The estimated costing shown in Table 11.1 is relative and subject to different contexts. Some of the recommendations, for example, may already be in operation, and there would therefore be no additional cost. Equally, some of the 'none' or 'low-cost' recommendations may have future cost implications if those to whom they refer accept the principle of the recommendations. Therefore, the costing exercise is carried out according to a broad estimate of costs and cannot be definitive; it offers an approximation of potential costs that are relative. The categories used in the costing exercise referenced in Table 11.1 are defined as follows:

None:

- Some of the recommendations are unlikely to incur costs. These would require a change of attitude by individuals, the development of current force procedures and processes, the communication of current force procedures and a force response to research.

None to low:

- Other recommendations will require no or only minor expenditure. These relate to a change in individuals' understanding and the development of current force procedures and processes.

Low:

- For some recommendations, a small cost would be incurred as extra time would need to be allocated, although this extra time would be minimal.

Low–medium:

- Some recommendations would require the extension of current resources, requiring extra time and therefore having cost implications.

Medium:

- For some recommendations, extra external resources would be required. These would need a moderate increase in budget allocation.

Table 11.1 Cost implications above the current financial budget

Recommendations	None	Low	Medium	High	Action by
1.3.10; 1.3.11; 2.2.1; 2.2.2; 2.3.1; 2.4.1; 2.4.2; 2.4.3; 2.5.3; 2.6.5; 2.6.6; 2.6.7; 2.6.8	*				Force
2.1.1; 2.1.2; 2.1.3; 2.6.1; 4.1; 4.4	*				Force
1.1.1; 1.1.2; 1.1.3; 1.1.4; 2.5.1; 2.5.2; 2.6.2; 2.6.4; 3.1.1; 3.2.1; 3.2.2; 3.2.3; 3.3.1; 4.3; 4.5		*			Force
3.4.1; 4.2; 4.6			*		Force
4.8			*		Force
4.7				*	Force/professional associations or other identified support groups
4.9; 5.1; 5.2; 5.3; 5.4; 5.5; 5.6; 5.7; 5.8	*				Officer/staff member
6.1; 6.2; 6.3; 6.4; 6.5	*				Partner/close friend
1.3.1; 1.3.2; 1.3.3; 1.3.4; 1.3.5; 1.3.6; 1.3.7; 1.3.8; 1.3.9				*	National
1.2.1; 1.2.2			*		National
2.6.3				*	Professional associations
4.10				*	NPCC/staff association/NARPO

High:

- For some recommendations, professional support and resources would be required, with potentially high budget costs.

Table 11.2, taking into account all the recommendations, shows the effort needed to put them into practice. The categories of effort required set out in Table 11.2 are defined as follows:

Minimum effort with no financial cost or no to low financial cost:

- The attitude of individuals
- Processes in the workplace
- Improved communication skills.

Table 11.2 The effort required at local and national levels to implement the recommendations

Recommendation	Minimum effort	Moderate effort	Maximum effort
Recommendations with no financial cost			
1.3.10; 1.3.11; 2.2.1; 2.2.2; 2.3.1; 2.4.1; 2.4.2; 2.4.3; 2.5.3; 2.6.5; 2.6.6; 2.6.7; 2.6.8; 5.1; 5.2; 5.3; 5.4; 5.5; 5.6; 5.7; 5.8; 6.1; 6.2; 6.3; 6.4; 6.5	*		
Recommendations with no to low financial cost			
2.1.1; 2.1.2; 2.1.3; 2.6.1; 4.4	*		
4.1		*	
Low financial cost			
1.1.4; 2.5.1; 2.5.2; 2.6.4; 3.2.2; 4.3; 4.5; 4.9	*		
1.1.1; 1.1.2; 1.1.3; 3.2.3		*	
2.6.2; 3.1.1; 3.2.1; 3.3.1		*	
Low to medium financial cost			
3.4.1; 4.6		*	
4.2			*
Medium financial cost			
1.2.1; 4.8	*		
1.2.2		*	
High financial cost			
2.6.3	*		
4.7		*	
1.3.1; 1.3.2; 1.3.3; 1.3.4; 1.3.5; 1.3.6; 1.3.7; 1.3.8; 1.3.9; 4.10			*

Minimum effort with low financial cost:

- Processes in the workplace.

Minimum effort with high financial cost:

- Access to professional support.

Minimum effort with medium financial cost:

- Access to general professional support
- Processes at national level.

Minimum to moderate effort with low financial cost:

- Processes in the workplace.

Minimum to moderate effort with low to medium financial cost:

- Processes in the workplace
- Training processes.

Minimum to moderate effort with high financial cost:

- Access to professional support.

Moderate effort with no to low financial cost:

- Processes in the workplace.

Moderate effort with low financial cost:

- Training processes
- General processes.

Moderate effort with medium financial cost:

- Processes at national level.

Maximum effort with low to medium financial cost:

- Processes in the workplace.

Maximum effort with high financial cost:

- Processes at national level.

Table 11.1 demonstrates that the majority of recommendations in this chapter would necessitate minimal extra costs to a force's overall budget, while Table 11.2 further shows that the majority of all the recommendations could be adopted with minimum to moderate effort.

Furthermore, many of the recommendations that could be adopted with minimum/moderate effort would have either no or low financial cost implications.

Other than professional psychological support provided by the forces, the higher-cost recommendations are those for which responsibility would be taken at the national level. These recommendations are also, in the main, the ones that require the greatest effort. Financial responsibility for some of these recommendations could be shared by different bodies in joint projects. As referenced earlier, for example, *Recommendation 4.10* could be a shared project between NARPO and staff associations, supported by the NPCC or the Home Office.

Concluding Comments

Following the research undertaken for this study and as a result of the analysis offered in the earlier chapters, it became evident that recommendations could and should be made to lessen the vulnerability to suicide of those who work within the police service. Therefore, within this chapter, some recommendations have been made that embrace a wide range of support provision and support mechanisms. This provision should be guided by further research and analysis. These particular recommendations are primarily those that will have the greatest financial implications for resource budgets, but they will be achievable if resolve and commitment exist on the part of those with relevant policy and budget responsibilities at national level.

Other recommendations which have been offered, as this chapter indicates, refer to the introduction of procedures which are not dependent upon future research and which have either no or low cost implications. These are procedures that relate to processes – processes in the workplace, such as the practice around disciplinary action; training, which can be enhanced; and welfare provision, which can be broadened. Other recommendations with no or low cost implications refer to initiatives which officers and staff might embrace and employ.

It is the conclusion of this chapter that, as well as being desirable, the majority of the recommendations are financially possible and could be implemented without undue effort on the part of individuals and local forces. The higher-cost recommendations will depend on policy makers' resolve to invest in the commitment of those in the workplace.

A final chapter now follows, in which some concluding reflections are offered.

Appendix 11.1: Research, Acquisition of Data and Analysis

The Recording of Statistical Data

Recommendation 1.1.1

Each UK force should record the statistical data relating to in-service deaths of their officers/staff which were classified as suicide or which were recorded with narrative or open verdicts.

This recorded data would differentiate between:

- Officers and staff
- Rank/management grade
- Male and female.

The recorded data would show:

- The age at which the death occurred
- The length of service before death occurred
- The sexual orientation, race and religion of the officer/staff member.

Any reasons identified by the coroner indicating the cause of the death should be recorded.

Recommendation 1.1.2

There may be practical difficulties in gathering data, but where possible each UK force should record the statistical data relating to deaths of their former officers/staff. The reason for an officer's/staff member's exit from the service should be recorded, for example following dismissal, resignation or retirement. Data should also be gathered stating the interval of time between leaving the police service and the death.

When the death of an officer/staff member has occurred in a force area different from that in which the officer/staff member had worked, the employing force should be the one that records the relevant data, having received the necessary information from the force in which the death had occurred; so if, for example, the death occurred in West Mercia but the member had worked in Lancashire, the death would be recorded by Lancashire Police.

As with *Recommendation 1.1.1*, this recorded data would differentiate between:

- Officers and staff
- Rank/management grade
- Male and female.

The recorded data would show:

- The age at which the death occurred
- The length of service before death occurred
- The sexual orientation, race and religion of the officer/staff member.

Any reasons identified by the coroner indicating the cause of the death should be recorded.

Recommendation 1.1.3

Each UK force should record the statistical data relating to serving officers/ staff who have engaged in a parasuicidal incident which was considered to be life-threatening at the time of the incident.

As with *Recommendation 1.1.1*, this recorded data would differentiate between:

- Officers and staff
- Male and female
- Rank/management grade.

The recorded data would show:

- The age at which the death occurred
- The length of service before death occurred
- The sexual orientation, race and religion of the officer/staff member.

Anything identified by the force to indicate the underlying reasons for the para-suicidal intent should also be recorded.

Recommendation 1.1.4

The data discussed in *Recommendations 1.1.1* to *1.1.3* should initially be collected at force level and then submitted for analysis at a national level by the Group, as agreed in *Recommendation 1.2.1*.

The Analysis of Recorded Data

Recommendation 1.2.1

The Home Office/NPCC should appoint a Group to be responsible for an analysis of the statistics acquired in relation to *Recommendations 1.1.1* to *1.1. 4*.

Recommendation 1.2.2

Analysis of the data should be undertaken to identify the underlying causes of the suicides and parasuicidal incidents. This analysis would include determining:

- Emerging patterns of suicidal ideation
- The potential impact of the 'Werther effect' at both national and force levels.

Future Research and Analysis

Recommendation 1.3.1

The recording of statistical data and its analysis, at national level, should be on-going and include both qualitative and quantitative methods where appropriate.
    This recording of data should take into account evolutionary changes in:

- the ages at which officers/staff are recruited;
- male/female recruitment ratio;
- roles undertaken by staff that had previously been undertaken by officers;
- any other identified evolutionary changes; for example, with regard to race, sexual orientation, redeployments, disciplinary procedures.

Recommendation 1.3.2

Qualitative research, undertaken at a national level, will include psychological autopsies to tease out the multi-dimensional causes and context of each of the examined suicides. There would need to be a sample of case-studies drawn from a broad cross-section of police/staff suicides from across the UK forces.

Recommendation 1.3.3

Qualitative research should be undertaken considering officers/staff at different stages throughout their careers, to determine the effects of stress in relation to their work.

Recommendation 1.3.4

Analysis should be undertaken to determine the extent to which stress leading to suicidal ideation is caused by increased workloads.

Recommendation 1.3.5

Using an appropriate sample of serving officers and staff, qualitative research should be undertaken to determine the impact of PTSD experienced by officers/ staff before entering the police service.

Recommendation 1.3.6

Using an appropriate sample of serving officers, research should be undertaken to determine the causes of 'rugged individualism'/false personalisation and whether these begin before or after recruitment. If it is found that they begin after recruitment, research should determine whether this is a consequence of social acquisition due to the police sub-culture.

Recommendation 1.3.7

Research should specifically examine the relationship between alcohol abuse, difficulties in partner relationships, stress and suicide.

Recommendation 1.3.8

Research should be undertaken to assess whether greater family knowledge of how to support suicidal officers/staff has a positive effect on that person's suicidal behaviours.

Recommendation 1.3.9

A complementary study to that described in *Recommendation 1.3.8* should be undertaken to determine whether actions by family and friends have a positive influence on the suicidal officer/staff member. The findings of this recommendation and *Recommendation 1.3.8* would inform training programmes and presentations given when family members are present.

Recommendation 1.3.10

As opposed to 'chilling', forces and departments should be required to support studies into police suicides by assisting researchers to meet the challenge of practical difficulties, such as working in accordance with data protection requirements.

Recommendation 1.3.11

As opposed to 'chilling', forces and departments should actively encourage interested members of their force to discuss stress (in spoken and written discussion) and its implications in relation to suicidal ideation.

Working practices

Chief Officers

Recommendation 2.1.1

Chief officers should acknowledge that suicides of officers/staff are of organisational concern and thereby commit their force to suicide-prevention training programmes.

Recommendation 2.1.2

Chief officers should be further aware of the risk of community contagion so as to be able to commit extra human and financial resources should a suicide occur.

Recommendation 2.1.3

Chief officers should consider the cost benefits of the psychological welfare of all officers/staff and recognise that limiting relevant financial resources may be to the detriment of the force's overall performance, financial liability and moral responsibility.

Shift Patterns

Recommendation 2.2.1

Based on the premise that shift work lowers physiological resistance to stress, forces should be advised on and adopt operational shift patterns that cause the least disruptive psychological damage to officers/staff. The reasoning behind the pattern that is adopted should be explained to the workforce and the force should demonstrate that the pattern has the confidence of its workforce. The adopted pattern should be evaluated periodically.

Recommendation 2.2.2

Forces should acknowledge the additional stress to officers/staff of changing shift patterns at short notice because of staff shortages. Consequently, shifts should only be changed at short notice in extreme operational circumstances.

Bullying, Harassment and Victimisation

Recommendation 2.3.1

The force should demonstrate that the implementation of policy guidelines concerning allegations of bullying, harassment and victimisation has the confidence of the workforce.

Recommendation 2.4.1

Forces should ensure that, through training, supervisors recognise the importance of good communication skills, with particular reference to organisational management.

Recommendation 2.4.2

Forces should improve their methods of communication in relation to the perceptions officers/staff may have regarding the process of misconduct hearings.

Recommendation 2.4.3

Forces should improve their methods of communicating information relating to redeployment.

Selection

Recommendation 2.5.1

The selection process should be guided by the results of *Recommendation 1.3.5* with regard to applicants who have previously suffered from PTSD.

Recommendation 2.5.2

Guided by medical advice, the selection process should determine the suicide risk of officers/staff where there is a medical history of suicide within the immediate family.

Recommendation 2.5.3

Selection should be influenced by the previously discussed research into the causes of coping mechanisms that result in 'rugged individualism' (see *Recommendation 1.3.6*).

Investigations, Complaints and Discipline

Recommendation 2.6.1

All information should be given verbally to the officer/staff member in person and supported in writing for the officer/staff member's later consideration.

Recommendation 2.6.2

The time span between the officer/staff member's initial notification of a pending investigation and the hearing should be shortened considerably.

Recommendation 2.6.3

When officers/staff are suspended for a potentially criminal offence, they should have immediate and on-going access to free and informed legal advice through their professional bodies.

Recommendation 2.6.4

Investigations should be conducted to a prescribed timetable that is made known to the officer/staff member. This timetable must be stringently followed by those involved in the investigation. The date by which the intended investigation and hearing will be completed should be made known to the officer/staff member. There may be exceptional circumstances which may cause a delay. If this should occur, the officer/staff member should be told the reasons for the delay and given a revised timetable.

Recommendation 2.6.5

Communication with the officer/staff member should be in accordance with an agreed timetable. This timetable should be made available in writing to the officer/staff member by all concerned with the investigation, including those responsible for the officer/staff member's welfare.

Recommendation 2.6.6

The officer/staff member should be given clear guidelines as to how the misconduct investigation will proceed.

Recommendation 2.6.7

Only those officers/staff members directly involved with the primary cause of the investigation should be barred from contacting the officer/staff member. Colleague-officers and line-managers should make every effort to maintain contact with the person under investigation. There may be exceptional circumstances in which, because of potential legal implications, it may not be possible for this recommendation to be implemented; for example, if colleagues of the person under investigation could be accused of collusion or impropriety. If such circumstances should occur, the situation will be explained to the officer/staff member under investigation and extra support mechanisms should be put in place.

Recommendation 2.6.8

The role of the appointed welfare officer should be made clear to those under investigation, especially with regard to the extent to which the appointed welfare officer offers those under investigation an assurance of confidentiality.

Training

Initial Training

Recommendation 3.1.1

Opportunities for any considerable amount of input relating to emotional strength will be limited when placed alongside the other training that will be required. However, it is recommended that initial training might specifically include *introductions* to the following areas:

- The importance of developing strong family relationships and how these might be maintained when working according to a shift system.
- The importance of developing and maintaining strong social networks and activities outside the police service and culture.
- The importance of basic intervention techniques to relieve stress.
- The warning signs of depression and psychological illnesses.
- Suicide and the myths of suicide.
- Available support groups, both those within the force and those external.
- The importance of communicating with family, work colleagues and line-managers.
- The dangers of 'rugged individualism'.
- The importance of sharing emotional feelings in a confidential context.

In-Service Training

Recommendation 3.2.1

Alongside officer (physical) safety training, psychological safety training should be offered to enable officers/staff members to identify and respond to stress in themselves and their peers. These programmes would be mandatory and occur at regular intervals throughout the officer/staff member's career. The programmes should encourage and allow officers/staff members to take ownership of difficulties, to discuss the challenges they face and to seek support where necessary.

The programmes would include:

- An introduction to a basic understanding of psychological illness.
- How to identify and recognise risk factors.
- How to identify and recognise the warning signs of depression within themselves and in colleagues.
- An understanding of vulnerability to stress leading to suicidal ideation.
- Stress management, including an identification of coping mechanisms, stress-reduction techniques and problem-solving and decision-making strategies.
- An understanding of a community-policing philosophy to minimise officer isolationism.
- The importance of developing emotional intelligence.
- The dangers of 'rugged individualism' and dichotomised decision-making.
- Partner, family and social relationships; parenting skills; marital conflict; addiction; and management of finances.

Recommendation 3.2.2

Realistic job-related training in police functions should be provided to prevent officers/staff from losing confidence in their ability to fulfil line-management expectations.

Recommendation 3.2.3

Peer supporters appointed by the force should receive training. This training should be on-going and embrace:

- Pastoral and self-awareness skills, including how to develop and employ emotional intelligence, empathy and listening skills.
- An exploration of potential stress factors and how to recognise risk factors in policing.
- An identification of the warning signs of stress, depression, anger and psychological illnesses.
- An introduction to self-harming behaviours, addiction and alcohol abuse.
- An understanding of the vulnerability to stress leading to suicide ideation and how to identify officers/staff vulnerable to suicide ideation.
- An introduction to suicide and common misconceptions of suicide held by the general public.
- An introduction to stress management, including an identification of coping mechanisms, stress-reduction techniques, problem-solving and decision-making strategies.
- Available support groups, both within the force and external.

- The importance of communicating with family, work colleagues and line-managers.
- Techniques of crisis intervention and referral.
- How peer supporters can be supported.

Supervisory and Line-Manager Training

Recommendation 3.3.1

Mid-level management training should build on recruitment and in-service training. This training would be designed to assist supervisors in line-management techniques. Training should:

- Introduce general stress factors in police work.
- Emphasise the importance of communication and how to communicate.
- Enable the line-manger to apply basic psychological principles to field situations so as to act as a resource to the line-managed officer/staff member in relation to potential stresses.
- Demonstrate how to recognise the symptoms of stress and identify early warning signs of emotional distress in others, including self-harming behaviours, addiction/alcohol abuse, anger and depression.
- Describe the danger of dichotomised decision-making and 'rugged individualism'.
- Establish how to identify officers/staff vulnerable to suicidal ideation.
- Introduce suicide-prevention programmes.
- Offer an explanation of how to develop and employ emotional intelligence.
- Offer an understanding of how officers/staff can develop active coping styles.
- Demonstrate how to supervise high-risk officers/staff.
- Make known the resources that are available, including in-house welfare support, mental health services, community-based services and social support systems.
- Explain techniques of crisis intervention and referral.
- Describe the risk of community contagion.

Training for the Family

Recommendation 3.4.1

Each force should offer appropriate training sessions and encourage partners or immediate family members to participate. These programmes would describe:

- The stress of police work, to enable families to identify, understand and encourage officers/staff through the difficulties that officers/staff may encounter in the work context.
- How police work may affect partner and family relationships.

Other gatherings (such as attestation ceremonies) will also offer opportunities for the police service to assist families in their understanding of the pressures that officers/staff may face.

Welfare

Recommendation 4.1

It is recommended that the occupational health and welfare facilities that are available should be supplemented by a complementary range of additional support mechanisms. In addition to the provision of welfare support in the recommendations that follow, welfare provision should include peer support on a structured basis.

Recommendation 4.2

Those who offer psychological and emotional support should be invited to attend briefings and introduced so as to become known to officers/staff and thereby be integrated into mainstream policing, to diminish mistrust and suspicion.

Recommendation 4.3

Records should be kept (possibly by occupational health and welfare units) so that support can be offered on the anniversary of key traumatic events and contact can be made by occupational health/welfare units or line-managers to reassure vulnerable officers/staff that support is available.

Recommendation 4.4

A mandatory system to identify post-incident vulnerability should be in place and special attention/support should be given to officers/staff working in identified high-stress/high-risk areas, for example trauma risk management.

Recommendation 4.5

A process should be in place by which colleagues and supervisors are able to make confidential referrals of officers and staff whom they have identified as suffering from undue stress or depression.

Recommendation 4.6

Support mechanisms should be regularly monitored and evaluated.

Recommendation 4.7

Financial resources should be made available to offer psychological support. If they are unavailable, the force should appoint a named person to make every effort to identify financial resources from such in-service organisations as staff associations or the Police Mutual Foundation, and wherever possible from external charitable agencies.

Recommendation 4.8

Officers/staff should have access to confidential psychological and emotional support without going through the force's internal procedures. This could be provided by, for example, access to a 24-hour telephone crisis-support line. This support line would be staffed by trained counsellors.

Recommendation 4.9

Officers/staff should be assured of client confidentiality. However, they should be encouraged to permit key people to share confidential information in order to ensure support is coordinated.

Recommendation 4.10

A 24-hour telephone crisis-support line resourced solely by current and former retired officers/staff should be introduced. This could be initiated as a joint venture between the NPCC, staff associations and NARPO (the National Association of Retired Police Officers). This support would complement *Recommendation 4.8*, which refers to a telephone support line resourced by trained counsellors, and would assist in the method of support suggested by that recommendation.

Personal Initiatives of Officers and Staff

Recommendation 5.1

Officers/staff should give due consideration to their lifestyle and its impact on their health. They should think about such issues as physical fitness, diet, relaxation, engaging in social activities outside the police circle and taking time for personal reflection.

Recommendation 5.2

Officers/staff should acknowledge the importance of initiating contact with those in caring professions if they identify signs of undue stress. They should also acknowledge the importance of accepting support.

Recommendation 5.3

Officers/staff should acknowledge the importance of willingness to initiate and respond, as appropriate, to communication/contact with their partner/family, friends/colleagues, welfare supporters and line-managers/supervisors.

Recommendation 5.4

Officers/staff should encourage their families to participate in police training programmes which enhance familial understanding of the difficulties and challenges involved in the officer/staff role.

Recommendation 5.5

Officers/staff should accept a level of personal responsibility for and control over such issues as their financial budgets and time-management of their life/work balance, for example with regard to the time committed to family and recreational pursuits.

Recommendation 5.6

Officers/staff should accept a level of responsibility for their own emotional welfare, acknowledge their vulnerability to emotional stress and identify stressors which may be specific to them.

Recommendation 5.7

Officers/staff should recognise the emotional investment of proactively creating stable relationships with family and close friends.

Recommendation 5.8

Officers/staff should recognise the dangers of 'rugged individualism'/false personalisation and dichotomised decision-making. These may prevent the development of a mature and realistic self-appreciation, which may contribute to such emotional issues as an inability to forgive oneself.

The Initiatives of Family and Friends

Recommendation 6.1

Family members of officers/staff should be encouraged to participate in any opportunities provided by the police service that discuss the police role and its potential stressors.

Recommendation 6.2

Family and friends should recognise their important role in acting as supporters and gatekeepers to officers/staff experiencing excessive stress.

Recommendation 6.3

Family members should be confident in referring the officer/staff member to professional carers and not allow misplaced loyalty or 'emotional investment' to prevent them from intervening.

Recommendation 6.4

Family and friends of an officer/staff member experiencing depression should seek to understand the possible root causes of that depression and respond in a proactive manner.

Recommendation 6.5

Family and friends of an officer/staff member experiencing depression should consider the possibility that the officer/staff member may be considering suicide. They should seek to identify warning signs, dismiss popular misconceptions and enter into a proactive dialogue with the officer/staff member.

Notes

1 The Recommendations are also provided in Appendix 11.1, where they are offered without any explanatory notes.
2 It may be difficult to identify those who have left their force and have taken their own lives, but this is not an impossible task. Those who work within a force will have anecdotal knowledge, while others will be called to investigate when a sudden death has occurred.
3 Reference to the breadth of possible training programmes is made in the introductory comments to the section of this chapter entitled 'Training'.
4 'Gatekeeper' is a term used in Chapter 10. It refers to those who are particularly close to officers/staff, who can identify signs of stress and assist by suggesting creative options for their family member.
5 Both Tables 11.1 and 11.2 use categories which have been purposely created as part of this research and for this exercise.

Bibliography

Jorm, Anthony F. and Kitchener, Betty A. (2011) Giving Support to a Suicidal Person, *BMJ*, Vol. 343, No. 7828 (October 22), 803–4.
Owens, Cristabel, Owen, Gareth, Belan, Judith, Lloyd, Keith, Rapport, Frances and Donovan, Jenny (2011) Recognising and Responding to Suicidal Crisis within Family and Social Networks: Qualitative Study, *BMJ*, Vol. 343, No. 7828 (October 22), 834.

12 Concluding Reflections and Implications

Satisfactions and Frustrations

The most moving and memorable of occasions, over the course of the research, were the meetings with the families of those who had taken their own lives. Much gratitude is owed to them. It was also significantly reassuring to meet those people who were proactively concerned with the emotional welfare of the individual within the police service; they and other officers and staff revealed a similar concern for the families, colleagues and friends of those who had taken their own lives.

However, there were equally corresponding frustrations. These frustrations included meeting:

- those who showed little interest in officers' and staff members' experiences of stress and depression that might lead to suicidal ideation;
- those for whom the seemingly bureaucratic processes hindered research enquiries;
- the well-informed and well-meaning individuals whose understanding of suicide nevertheless limited their willingness to support the aims of the research;
- those who were complacent and suggested that everything necessary was currently being undertaken to offer appropriate welfare to officers and staff.

At the very beginning of this research study, and as referenced in Chapter 1 (section entitled 'Initial Difficulties and Successes'), a chief officer indicated that in his opinion, the proposed research would be difficult to pursue. On meeting with him, he related how his own initial inquiries into undertaking similar research had been thwarted by his inability to identify people who would proactively support his proposed research. His comments were to reflect some of the difficulties experienced in the encounters as this research progressed.

In addition to these frustrations, it was disappointing to identify a dearth of UK research on the suicidal ideation of officers and police staff. One force in particular was identified which had investigated its vulnerability to suicidal ideation following a series of suicides; others may have done likewise but, other than one unpublished paper, comprehensive nationwide research was found to be wanting. This lack of earlier UK research was disappointing as it meant no information was available for analysis. Subsequently, considerable reference had to be made to research undertaken outside the UK, which may have reduced the depth of this research study.

Identified Weaknesses and Omissions

Even though privileged personal information was made available by one particular force, this was limited to specific situations and, for reasons of confidentiality, it was only possible to refer to this information in general terms in the earlier chapters of this research. Doing otherwise would have led to possible identification of those involved and broken the bounds of confidentiality. Again, more detailed information from a range of sources other than the details reported by the media and those in the public domain could have given greater depth to the research.

The research would have also been enhanced by detailed statistics on police suicides. As noted in Chapter 5, these statistics are not available. Such information would have enabled a comparative study of officer/staff suicides with those in the wider community and would have provided certain parameters on which to widen the breadth of the research and build additional analysis. Furthermore, data offering detailed information such as length of service, gender, sexual orientation and race of officers and staff who had experienced suicidal ideation and/or completed suicide would have been invaluable to this research. It is for all of these reasons that the recommendations in Chapter 11 regarding the acquisition of relevant data for further research and analysis were proposed.

Reflecting on the research undertaken, there were two particular areas that came to be of interest, but which were outside the remit of the research and were therefore omitted from the study. The first was the role of the medical practitioner and the police chaplain. This would have been an interesting avenue to investigate, particularly in terms of how these two different professions might work together to support officers and staff experiencing suicidal ideation. Limited resource material became available, but apart from this, an examination of these matters would have relied extensively on anecdotal comment rather than on specific evidential enquiry.

The second area of interest that was omitted, which would also have gone beyond the remit of this research, is a consideration of how the families of officers and staff who have taken their own lives might move forward. This research has sought to offer a genuine account of the context of the case-studies featured and the different theories concerning suicidal ideation. However, the families of those who have taken their own lives live with the harsh reality of their situation; they face a range of difficult emotions which they must work through. This research offers these families little support other than an endeavour to ensure that their anguish and pain is not shared by other families in the future. The two areas of research just identified (the approaches taken by medical practitioners working with religious leaders and how bereaved families of officers and staff might move forward) have the potential to offer a wealth of information which would be to the benefit of a broader understanding.

However, in spite of the frustrations involved – as detailed fully in Chapter 1 – and these identified omissions, this research project became a reality and positive results ensued, which are referenced in the following section.

The Goals that were Reached

As reported in the early chapters of this book, examination of UK research relating to the suicide of those employed in the UK police service revealed an absence of information of any substance. It was therefore apparent that the current research would contribute greatly to this important issue. Initial objectives were consequently formulated, as explained in Chapter 1.

The first objective of the research – to determine risk factors in the suicidal ideation of officers and staff – was identified by the analysis of the case-studies offered in Chapter 4. From these case-studies, it became possible to recognise key suicide precipitators. As explained fully in Chapter 3, this evidence was gained through interviews, verbal and written comment from different sources within forces and media reports on coronial enquiries. The case-studies offered hard facts, as revealed by the analysis of them in Chapter 4. Within the context of this pertinent information, it was possible to examine appropriate literature that referred to suicide by those in both the police and the general communities, as examined in Chapters 6 and 7.

By undertaking analysis of the case-study precipitators set against the theories of suicide to be found in different written resources, the second part of the research objectives became viable, in that the research was able to proceed to examine preventative intervention measures.

The examination of these measures concluded that there are three groups of people that might advantageously adopt preventative processes. As employer, the police service is the first body to which reference was made in Chapter 8. It became clear that much can be undertaken to develop and augment the preventative measures that the police service and individual forces might currently have in place.

However, it also became clear that, as well as the implementation of force initiatives, there are measures that those employed by the police service might themselves adopt, as referenced in Chapter 9. In addition to these personal measures, the research findings refer to support initiatives with which family members, close friends and colleagues might engage. Reference was made to these initiatives in Chapter 10.

The research made it possible to offer clear recommendations which, if implemented, should assist in reducing the number of suicides by those who work in the police service. As detailed in Chapter 11, these recommendations are comprehensive in terms of the areas to which they refer and those to whom they relate. The recommendations refer to research/analysis, force working practices, training, welfare, personal initiatives (Chapter 9) and initiatives on the part of family and friends (Chapter 10). A prime goal of this research was to make these recommendations from an informed position.

Implementation and Implications for Future Research

No matter what preventative measures are put in place, police officers and police staff will continue to experience suicidal ideation. No measures can or will eliminate the problem of suicide among those who work within the police service. However, the greater the understanding of officer/staff suicide and the greater the care for the individual officer and staff member, the fewer such suicides will occur. It is hoped, therefore, that this research will reach a sufficient audience to deepen this understanding of officer/staff suicidal ideation; hence the recommendations made in Chapter 11.

In the first place, it is hoped that this research might encourage the Home Office, chief officers and those who represent the forces on the relevant National Police Chiefs' Council (NPCC) committees and working groups to accept, initiate and implement further in-depth research. This commitment is essential, as the results of an analytical approach to suicidal ideation in a police context will bring many potential benefits to the police service.

Chapter 11 offered a large number of recommendations that refer to future research projects. In the first place, as Chapter 11 suggested, data must first be recoded and collated at both force and national levels. As far as is possible, this will be historical data on suicides and parasuicides. Thereafter, current data must be collated so that an accurate account of the dimensions of the situation can be formulated. This would enable a short-term response, but it would also give a base-line against which future and on-going research data can determine a long-term response, taking into account the constant changes taking place in the police service.

Chapter 11, and the recommendations as given in Appendix 11.1, offer a full account of the areas to be further researched. To recap briefly, these areas of research should refer to:

- selection and training
- workplace practices within the organisation
- welfare support and preventative measures offered by the organisation
- the responsibility of individuals within the organisation to ensure their own welfare and that of colleagues
- the support of families and friends outside the police service.

The results of analysis based on acquired data and future research will have profound implications for the police service and for staff and officers employed within the police service. This, however, will only be brought about by the commitment of the Home Office and the relevant NPCC committees assigned responsibility for the welfare of those employed by the service. With this commitment to future research, much can be achieved thereafter by those appointed to undertake the research, such as the College of Policing, NPCC working groups, staff associations and associated bodies. All within the police service have a responsibility to take research further, but this will only happen when there is recognition of the problem and a desire to bring change.

The Final Word

Table 11.1 includes all the recommendations made in Chapter 11 and, as it shows, the majority of these recommendations should be implemented by individual forces. Table 11.1 also shows that the majority of the recommendations would have either no or low financial implications for the forces concerned. Furthermore, as shown in Table 11.2, implementation of the majority of these recommendations (with either no or low financial implications) would require only minimum effort on the part of the individual forces.

Of the remaining recommendations which have either no or low cost implications, four recommendations require minimum to moderate effort to implement, while five would require moderate effort to implement. It would appear that these recommendations could be implemented without great difficulty.

Of the higher-cost recommendations, one refers to psychological support, one to legal support, one to peer support and others to future research. Whereas the potential high cost of the research would be financed at a national level by the Home Office or an appointed body, the expense of the other higher-cost recommendations would be met (and in some cases possibly shared) by a range of professional associations with the support of the NPCC, the College of Policing and the Home Office. As the results of this current research demonstrate, these cost implications may be challenging but they are justifiable.

Because the suicide of officers and staff is a consequence of many complex and interwoven precipitators faced by these officers and staff in the context of their work environment, so equally will the preventative measures need to be multi-faceted and interwoven. There can be no one single solution. All the primary constituent parts of the officer's/staff member's work and home lives must come together to ensure that the officer or staff member has the resilience to respond to the stress delivered by the work context. Exposure to work stressors cannot be avoided, but officers and staff can be resourced and supported to enable them to make appropriate responses. The aphorism is that suicide is a permanent solution to a temporary problem. If so, officers and staff must be given the resources and the support to discover that there is a more creative way forward than taking one's own life.

Index

Page numbers in bold, denote tables.
Page numbers in italic, denote figures.